D0206305

COMMUNITY ORGANIZATION FOR URBAN SOCIAL CHANGE

A Historical Perspective

COMMUNITY ORGANIZATION FOR URBAN SOCIAL CHANGE

A Historical Perspective

Edited by
Robert Fisher and Peter Romanofsky

GREENWOOD PRESS
Westport, Connecticut • London, England

Library of Congress Cataloging in Publication Data

Main entry under title:

Community organization for urban social change.

    Bibliography: p.
    Includes index.
    1. Community organization—History—Addresses,
essays, lectures. 2. Neighborhood—Addresses,
essays, lectures. 3. Community development—
United States—History—Addresses, essays, lectures.
I. Fisher, Robert, 1947-   II. Romanofsky,
Peter.
HN90.C6C663   307.7'6'0973   80-21498
ISBN 0-313-21427-1 (lib. bdg.)

Library of Congress Catalog Card Number: 80-21498
ISBN: 0-313-21427-1

First published in 1981

Greenwood Press
A division of Congressional Information Service, Inc.
88 Post Road West, Westport, Connecticut 06881

Printed in the United States of America

10 9 8 7 6 5 4 3 2 1

To the memory of
Peter Romanofsky
demanding scholar, loving friend

Contents

Acknowledgments

In coediting this collection, I have been helped by a number of people and institutions. The National Endowment for the Humanities awarded me a summer grant to attend a seminar on social history, where I tested many of my ideas on community organization; Clarke Chambers, the seminar director, and Ann Neel were especially helpful. Union College and the University of Houston Downtown College and my colleagues there, most notably Fred Jonas, Bob Wells, and Frank Abbott, assisted this project in countless ways. Steve Meacham and my other friends from Cambridgeport taught me about community organizing and were always there to tell me when I was straying or dragging my feet. Bayrd Still, my mentor at New York University, encouraged and supported my work far beyond the call of duty. Without Juliet Clarke, who shares my life and my work, none of this would have been possible or worthwhile. My utmost thanks go as well to my parents, Leo and Eve Fisher, who gave me the support and freedom to follow my inclinations. Lastly, Peter Romanofsky lived through all but the final stages of this volume. His vitality, editorial skills, demanding nature, and strength in the face of great adversity got me and this collection over many hurdles. He is deeply missed.

Introduction

The rebirth of interest in community organizing during the 1960s and 1970s is readily apparent from even a cursory tour through our nation's large cities. Signs on neighborhood buildings and storefronts announce food and bicycle cooperatives, day-care centers, community development corporations, little city halls, community action programs, antipoverty agencies, community health centers, tenant and homeowner organizations, community newspapers, and a host of other neighborhood-based social service and political action organizations. "Small is beautiful" seems to make increasing sense to a citizenry alienated from its economic and power centers.

Turning inward to community-based solutions is clearly a conservative act for many—a retreat from urban and national problems, a reaction against minority-group demands for social change, and a nostalgic longing for a simpler, mythical age. But neighborhood organizing can also be a progressive response by city dwellers who want to control the institutions that affect their lives. Neighborhood organizations committed in theory and practice to political and economic democracy reflect an emerging national opposition to corporate control of people's lives and to unresponsive government. Heirs of the civil rights, black power, and New Left movements, and stimulated by the Great Society programs of the 1960s, these urban residents have combined to fight real-estate speculation, absentee home ownership, red-lining, high rents and taxes, racism, sexism, and insufficient public services.

A vast literature on neighborhood organizing, emanating from two different sources, appeared almost simultaneously with this community movement. Urban planners, social workers, sociologists, and political scientists saw neighborhood-based organizations as a solution to the "urban crisis" of the 1960s. They wrote theoretical analyses on the nature of community organization and described, in countless case histories, the efforts of widely diverse community-based organizations. This professional literature, most apparent in a number of anthologies published in the late 1960s and early 1970s, asked how the strategies, level of citizen participation, and conditions in each neighborhood affected the success or failure of the organizing effort.

The other source of literature on community organization was non-professional community activists, who wrote for fellow organizers and who focused on how to organize a community. These activists saw community organizing as a democratic and cooperative alternative to the racist and militarist society that was brought to light by the civil rights movement and the Vietnam War. Their work is practical, describing, for example, how to print a community newspaper, confront city hall, or do investigative research. Together, the two strands of literature provide a rich, if incomplete, picture of the community organization movement of the last fifteen years.[1]

But these materials share an obvious failing: both are ahistorical. The description and evaluation of community organization efforts proceeds as if neighborhood-based solutions to problems in the United States are unprecedented, as if the attendant questions faced by organizers are unprecedented, as if historical roots offer little to our understanding of current and future efforts. This is not so. The absence of any substantial work on the history of a subject of such contemporary interest underlines the impetus for this volume.

The existing literature on the history of community organization provides no more than a scattered and rough outline of events. Historians who write about the history of social welfare discuss the topic only in passing. Sociologists and political scientists ignore the topic prior to the Federal Housing Act of 1949, except for some works on the history of the neighborhood as a political unit or on the organizing efforts of Saul Alinsky. Social work academicians have made the most substantial contribution, tracing the history of community organization for social welfare from the Charity Organization Societies of the late-nineteenth century through the Great Society programs of the 1960s. Sidney Dillick's *Community Organization for Neighborhood Development: Past and Present* (1953), the only book-length study of the history of community organization, provides only a sketch of developments through the 1940s.[2] Political activists have been even more presentist. Writing about their personal experiences, they focus almost entirely on "how to" and ignore the equally helpful question of how have others organized a community.

One of the problems facing a history of community organization is the ambiguous use of the term: it is difficult enough to agree on what a community organization is today, let alone what it was in 1900. Throughout this volume, community is defined in largely geographic terms; the focus is on organizing efforts based in and centered on urban neighborhoods, usually inner-city and working-class neighborhoods. A number of the essays describe community organizations that sought to organize larger geographic areas—the city, for example—and to organize neighborhood residents around issues that extended beyond neighborhood boundaries. To emphasize the diversity of organizing experiences, we included, in this collection, case studies of efforts in different cities, different regions, and different time periods that run the political gamut from reactionary to revolutionary. But all the community organizations included in this volume, irrespective of their politics and other differences, share a commitment to involve neighborhood residents in social issues based on neighborhood or, in the case of New Orleans, parish concerns and problems.

Community organizers in the past and the present often speak of a community organization movement. While this term tends to provide more coherence and structure than is truly justifiable, "movement" correctly implies the existence of connecting threads in the patterns of community organization. These patterns become clearer when viewed from a historical perspective.

Historically, there appear to be two dominant, distinctive, and relatively exclusive approaches to community organization, which we can label the social work tradition and the political activist tradition (see table 1). The social work tradition views the community essentially as a social organism; it focuses on social issues such as building a sense of community, gathering together social service organizations, or lobbying for and delivering social resources. It assumes that the community's basic problem is social disorganization. The organizer thus functions as an

Table 1

History of Community Organization: Two Dominant Traditions

	SOCIAL WORK TRADITION	*POLITICAL ACTIVIST TRADITION*
Concept of community	social organism	political unit
Problem condition	social dis-organization	powerlessness and exploitation
Role of organizer	professional social worker enabler and advocate coordinator and planner	political activist mobilizer agitator
Role of "client"	partner with professional recipient of benefits	fellow activists indigenous leaders mass support
Strategy	consensual gradualist work with power structure	conflict challenge power structure oppose mainstream institutions
Goals	group formation social integration and adjustment service delivery	obtain, maintain, or restructure power develop alternative institutions
Examples	Charity Organization Society Social Settlements Community Centers Cincinnati Social Unit Plan Community Chests Community development abroad	Unemployed Councils Alinsky programs Citizens' Councils Student Non-Violent Co-ordinating Committee Students for a Democratic Society

enabler to help the community gather itself together and achieve goals of social integration and adjustment. To a lesser extent, the organizer serves as an advocate seeking to secure additional services for the community. The strategy is gradualist and consensual, which means that organizers assume a unity of interest between the power structure and the community, and assume a willingness of at least some who are in power to meet community needs. The organizational structure in this tradition is usually characterized by professional leaders who are most often trained in schools of social work or trained by graduates of those institutions. Organizations in this tradition vary in the extent of indigenous participation and grass-roots leadership, but the professional community worker is almost always the core of the program. She or he provides at least the initial stimulus, program, and, quite often, the focus and personality of the organization. Most important, in the social work approach, the community organization sees itself as a social enterprise and functions as a subfield of social work and within the general orientation of that profession.

The political activist approach, on the other hand, sees the community as a political entity. The approach focuses on obtaining, maintaining, or restructuring power. Or, if it does not seek power, it is political in that its goal is to develop an alternative institution. The community problem, as defined by organizers, is the lack of power and the exploitation of the community. Their role is to educate, agitate, and mobilize the community to understand its problem and its power and to confront the enemy. Instead of directly challenging the enemy, organizers may seek to develop alternative organizations that indirectly oppose existing institutions. The strategy of the political activist ranges from consensual to confrontational, mostly closer to the latter, but in all cases, it is rooted in an understanding of the conflict of interest between the community and those in power. The organization usually has a less professional and less formal structure than groups in the social work tradition. Initiators and leaders often come from the indigenous population. Where the organizers focus on goals developed prior to entering the community and where they remain unresponsive to community needs and democratic participation, the political activist approach, like its social work counterpart, can take on an externally led and autocratic posture.[3]

For the most part, these traditions are isolated from each other.

Writers and practitioners of the social work approach prior to the mid-1960s would not have considered the Unemployed Council movement in the 1930s, tenant-organizing efforts in the 1930s and the 1940s, or the Citizens' Councils of the 1950s as community organization. They might briefly note the work of Saul Alinsky, primarily because Alinsky began his work within the social work tradition and because he continued to use much of his earlier-learned practices. The same isolation is true for the writers and practitioners of the political activist approach, which traces its roots back to political protest movements, not to the origins of social work practice. If political activist organizers have a sense of history, they refer back to efforts by socialists and communists if they are on the left; if they are on the right of the political spectrum, they refer to the Ku Klux Klan, other segregationist and reactionary organizations, or civic clubs organized to maintain exclusionary zoning. They do not recall efforts of social settlements, community centers, the Cincinnati Social Unit Plan, and neighborhood councils organized by professional community workers.

In the decades preceding World War I, the two traditions overlapped in the more progressive settlements like Hull House and Chicago Commons in Chicago and Henry Street Settlement in New York City. These settlements were pioneers in the social work tradition of community organization, but they also sought to mobilize neighborhood residents in political struggles against community power brokers—in this case, local political bosses. In the 1960s, the two approaches overlapped again as the decade's political ferment forced them together. Activist organizers and the organizations they were involved with—for instance, Student Non-Violent Coordinating Committee (SNCC), Students for a Democratic Society (SDS), and a host of other programs spawned by the black struggle and the New Left protest—forced those in the social work tradition to reexamine their reformist and social service approach to community organization. At the same time, the Great Society co-opted political activists into an approach to community organizing that straddled both traditions but that was ultimately much more similar to the social work approach. In these two periods of heightened community organization—1900-1920 and the 1960s—the two traditions often overlapped, and each was very much aware of the other.

Examples of both approaches belong in an introductory history of community organization. In this volume, the case studies on the community center movement and the Cincinnati Social Unit Plan reflect good, if early, examples of the social work tradition. The case studies of Communist organizing in Harlem, tenant organizing in New York City, Citizens' Councils in New Orleans, and the neighborhood organizing revolution of the 1970s illustrate the political activist tradition. The study on organizing in a Model Cities program in San Francisco is the only one that clearly overlaps both approaches and underlines the dilemma for organizations attempting to do so.

We have not sought, however, to mold the essays to fit our typology of community organization. That would have been rather restrictive. To provide intellectual unity to the volume, we asked contributors to address basic questions, where appropriate, about the origins, goals, structure, roles, and success of the organization and about the type of community within which the organization developed. The authors of the essays in this volume—historians, political scientists, and activists—differ in their methods of research and presentation and differ in their politics. They do not agree on the value of community organizing: some see it as a retreat from larger concerns; others, as a limited liberal palliative; and still others view community organizing as a progressive and radical force for social change. It is hoped that the variety of case studies approached and evaluated from different political perspectives and methodologies enhances the value of this introductory collection.

The essays in this collection, do, however, advance an overriding theme: that the success of local, community organizing efforts is often dependent on the extent to which the organizations align with or reflect social movements and the political-economic situation at the national level. This was true of liberal efforts in the Progressive era, more radical organizing strategies in the 1930s, reactionary programs in the 1950s, and progressive community action efforts in the Great Society era. This is not to conclude, of course, that community organization is simply a mirror image at the local level of national movements and developments, or that local social change efforts do not have a significant existence of their own. Rather it is to emphasize that the organizations addressed in this volume all developed in a political and economic context that transcended community boundaries, and that while conditions at the local level may have spawned and nurtured each effort, the larger political-economic context often determined the general tenor, success, and longevity of the community organization.

As an introduction to the subject, the volume necessarily has its limitations: many efforts and themes are not addressed. We have not felt it necessary, for example, to include case studies on the two most-written-about community organizing programs, the social settlement movement and the early Alinsky programs in Chicago, though both are referred to and described in case studies in the collection. Moreover, the articles in this volume are primarily organizational analyses that view community organizing from the perspective of the organizer rather than from the vantage point of the organized or unorganized. We need studies of community organization written from the receiver's perspective. What was it like to be a participant in these efforts? What were the social and cultural qualities, often equally important to the political and economic goals, that attracted people to these efforts and enabled organizers to get them to come to events, meetings, demonstrations, and the like? We need more material on organizing efforts led by women and racial minorities; most of the organizations discussed in this volume were led by white men. These limitations aside, we hope the collection serves the beginning needs of activists and scholars and encourages more discussion and systematic analysis of past and present efforts at community organizing.

NOTES

1. For examples of the professional-oriented literature of the last fifteen years, see George Frederickson, ed., *Neighborhood Control in the 1970s* (New York: Chandler Publishing, 1973); Hans Spiegel, ed., *Citizen Participation in Urban Development* (Washington, D.C.: National Training Laboratories Institute for Applied Behavioral Science, 1968); and Fred M. Cox et al., eds., *Strategies of Community Organization: A Book of Readings* (Itasca, Ill.: F. E. Peacock Publishers, 1974). On the activist-oriented literature, see David Morris and Karl Hess, *Neighborhood Power: The New Localism* (Boston: Beacon Press, 1975); The O. M. Collective, *The Organizer's Manual* (New York: Bantam Books, 1971).

2. For a listing of some representative examples of this literature, see the first four footnotes in the chapter by Robert Fisher in this volume.

3. The typology of community organization developed by Jack Rothman was most helpful. See Jack Rothman, "Three Models of Community Organization Practice," in *Strategies of Community Organization,* ed. Fred M. Cox et al., pp. 22-39.

COMMUNITY ORGANIZATION FOR URBAN SOCIAL CHANGE

A Historical Perspective

The Role and Concept of Neighborhood in American Cities

ZANE L. MILLER

TURNING INWARD

Two hallmarks of contemporary American civilization are the neighborhood organization revolution and the revival of white ethnic consciousness, both of which can be seen as symptomatic of a widespread tendency in American society to turn inward. The national media have been most intrigued by the psychological aspect of the tendency, reporting at length, if not in depth, on individuals turning inward to "personal" evangelical religion, or "est," or transcendental meditation. But a variety of social critics have not only noticed but also warned of the ways in which the drive for "self-fulfillment" or "self-actualization" diverts its practitioners and observers from considering and acting upon pressing issues of public policy stemming from severe social and economic problems.[1] Construed in this way, the neighborhood organization revolution and ethnic revival seem incompatible with the inward tendency, for both apparently thrive on a deep and serious preoccupation with social and economic problems confronting minority groups and local communities.

In fact, these movements also represent a turning inward—of urban neighborhoods turning away from citywide federation toward territorial autonomy; of minority groups moving away from cross-cultural and class coalitions toward the pursuit and defense of their separate heritages and destinies; and of suburbs moving away from cooperation, in the name of efficiency and good government, toward home rule and self-determination. Indeed, there are now even signs of big cities turning inward from the metropolis in an effort to fend off financial catastrophe brought on by what they view as the drain of metropolitan interdependence, and of interstate regions turning inward in a conflict pitting the Snowbelt against the Sunbelt.

But of all these varieties of turning inward on the urban scene, the neighborhood organization revolution is older, and its characteristic features and consequences are most clearly discernible. The movement draws its strength and vehemence from the widespread conviction that outside and malevolent forces stand ready to overwhelm the residents of particular locations unless these forces are confronted by an organized, vigilant, informed, and truculent grass-roots resistance. Moreover, the movement is distinguished by its pervasiveness: it runs as strong in the suburbs of metropolitan areas as in their core cities, and it is as common a feature of urban life in the dynamic Sunbelt as it is in the decaying Snowbelt. Even Cincinnati, seldom regarded as revolutionary terrain, has not escaped the revolution's broad sweep. Here and elsewhere, most observers misconstrue its essence, the way in which the appeal to neighborhoods veils a new mode of thought that, in fact, centers on autonomous individual actors as the basic units of society.

The neighborhood organization revolution rests on the contention that the neighborhood somehow comprises a basic unit in American cities, a relatively new idea, but one that possesses nonetheless a lively, if largely unwritten, history. It made its initial appearance in the latter nineteenth century, flourished through the first decade and a half of the twentieth, all but disappeared between 1920 and 1950, then revived during the 1950s, and gained momentum in the late 1960s and 1970s. Throughout those decades, its history has been inextricably entangled with shifting definitions of the city and the metropolis.

BEFORE THE NEIGHBORHOOD

Before the latter nineteenth century, varying conceptions of the city effectively barred the emergence of neighborhood as a critical component of city life. Until about 1840, Americans viewed cities as commercial communities: first, as corporations to regulate economic life in an era of scarcity; and then, after 1790, as collections of individuals and institutions gathered together under conditions of relative abundance for the pursuit of commerce and civilization. Though the functions of municipal governments and of beneficent organizations differed during those two epochs, during neither period did anyone regard the city as a social system made up of groups or units. After 1840, however, the urban gentry redefined the city, conceiving of it as a social system of amorphous groups of individuals and institutions whose interaction either fostered or jeopardized the welfare of the city and the groups that made up the whole.[2]

While a sense of intracity territoriality appeared in these mid-nineteenth-century years, it centered on nonresidential units, such as the identification of the central business district, of concentrations of noxious manufactures, and of the ward as an administrative unit and as a locus for organized political and civic activity, not merely as a division for political representation. To the extent that people in the mid-nineteenth century thought of areas of the city as the typical habitat of the poor, the wealthy, or immigrants and other newcomers, the perception emphasized the behavior of the individuals who formed the groups and drew no explicit connection between the neighborhood as such and the behavior of its inhabitants. In other words, the mid-nineteenth-century conception of the city did not posit the existence of distinct and differential residential neighborhoods that interacted as units within the urban social system, and therefore programs were not developed for the improvement of residential neighborhoods as a means of bettering the lot of "problem" groups. For example, housing appeared not as a neighborhood problem but as a tenement problem.[3]

THE CITY AND THE NEIGHBORHOOD, 1880-1920

That perception of the city persisted until about 1880, the appropriate date for the beginning of the first neighborhood organization revolution. That movement began in the late-nineteenth century, when innovations in mass rapid transit obliterated the historic walking city, initiating a more rigorous sorting out of land uses by function and of peoples by class, race, and ethnicity. Out of that process came the familiar sprawling configuration of the modern metropolis, which placed the poor at its heart in congested areas around the central business district and the blue- and white-collar classes in territory between the slums and the suburbs that were draped around the cool, green rim of the city. To those who knew this new urban form best, it seemed constituted of specialized, differentiated, and interdependent parts, which, like the turn-of-the-century concept of an organism, through coordination at the top, functioned together for the viability of the greater community. In this view, the city was a community of communities, all of which constantly expanded and changed, and each of which performed a function vital to the welfare of the whole.[4]

In the final analysis, the new view of the city rested upon a redefinition of American society generally in organic terms.[5] Adherents of this point of view tended to agree, for example, with Henry C. Adams, professor of political economy and finance at the University of Michigan. "Modern life," he wrote in 1893,

> has increased the dependence of men and classes to such a degree that interdependence is a thing which is felt, rather than an idea to be reasoned about. . . . Society is coming to be in fact organic, and the claim of a perfect organism that all parts should find harmony of life in the recognition of a common aim, shows itself in the attitude of which large numbers of persons are assuming before the vexed problems of the day.[6]

Given that point of view, adherents of the organic view looked for and sought to create a feeling of unity and order in society. As Josiah Strong put it in 1898, an organic society exhibited a structure

> whose life is one and whose interests are one. . . . [It] possesses different organs, having different functions, each of which exists, not for itself but to serve all the others. . . . If any organ refuses to perform its proper function, there is disease, perhaps death.[7]

But the appropriate nurture of each organ would bring about a "genuine inter-weaving where each individual [or group] had a full part in the whole-a-making. . . ."[8] The idea, as Edward T. Devine suggested, implied participating in the process of putting "into orderly arrangement that which had been disorganized or badly arranged."[9]

For many of those who approached American society from this angle, the city seemed the ideal seat of action. As Frederic C. Howe argued at the turn of the century, the city stood as the critical arena "where the social and political forces . . . coming to the fore would play" and presented not only the quintessential "problems . . . of civilization but . . . the hope of the future as well."[10] And for many of them, as Robert A. Woods reflected after roughly thirty years of urban neighborhood work, the city consisted of

> a cluster of interlacing communities, each having its own vital ways of expression and action, but all together creating the municipality which shall render the fullest service through the most spirited participation of all its citizens.[11]

The organic mode of thought about the city as a community fostered both centralization and decentralization. One consequence of this formulation, for example, was the notion that municipal boundaries ought to correspond with the "natural" social boundaries of the larger community, a conviction providing some of the impetus behind the great annexation movements between 1870 and 1920 that recaptured for municipalities across the country much of the commerce, industry, and population flowing outward on the tide of the new mobility. Another consequence of the organic approach to the city was the feeling that "natural" neighborhoods, not arbitrarily determined wards, ought to have a say in the making of public policy.

It was in that geographical and intellectual milieu that urban reformers sought to forge a cooperative relationship between the local and the citywide community, between the forces of centralization and of decentralization. In the 1890s, out of that context came the National Municipal League's program for municipal home rule and for centralized and departmentalized city governments geared to meet the special needs for coordination at the top of the differentiated urban environment. Out of it, too, Charles W. Dabney set up the Association of Urban Universities as a means of transforming municipal and city colleges into urban universities to function, as Dabney liked to put it, as the "brain" of the urban body politic. And it was in that context that Robert A. Woods and Wilbur Phillips, after the turn of the century, emerged as the principal Progressive era spokesmen for neighborhood organization as the salvation of

American democracy, and that the first neighborhood organization revolution took shape.[12]

Cincinnati's experience with local improvement associations, one of the most common but least studied aspects of the movement, provides a good symptomatic instance of how urban reformers in the late-nineteenth and early twentieth centuries reconciled centralization with parochialism. The process began in the late-nineteenth century with the founding, in outlying districts, of "improvement" associations devoted to looking after the service needs of particular places. These groups fought for local improvements, such as better sewers, lighting, schools, and fire and police protection, in part because the recently annexed territories felt underrepresented. From their perspective, ironically, the ward system discriminated against them. In a city council and a board of education chosen on the district system, the older, more numerous, and smaller wards of the inner city possessed the votes to control the balance of power in municipal and school affairs, a leverage the center used to place high-priority items from the periphery low on the agenda of urban public business. The improvement association proved useful, therefore, as a "representative" instrument for influencing the mayor, the superintendent of schools, department heads, and agency supervisors to adopt the policies favored by citizens of the periphery.

Still, the parochialism of the improvement association did not last. In 1907, the neighborhood groups formed a federation that, by 1913, claimed thirty-six affiliates, boasting a total of eight thousand members. The federation, moreover, concentrated, not on local, but on citywide issues in recognition of the notion that the city constituted a larger community made up of organically interdependent communities. According to the federation, not only did the health of the whole depend on the health of its parts, but also the health of the parts depended upon centralized, coordinated management to determine priorities, to distribute the public goods equitably for the maximum benefit of all, and to establish civic mores to which all citizens must adhere for the promotion of the public welfare.

Guided by this vision of urban polity, the Federated Improvement Association, after 1907, plunged enthusiastically into the mainstream of municipal progressivism. It agitated for the rational development of a citywide sewer and water system instead of the ad hoc construction of sewer and water lines. It joined the drive for a small school board elected at large, and supported progressive educational reforms in general. It pushed for smoke abatement; enlisted in the antidirty-dairy crusade; thumped for a gambling ban; backed the effort to enlarge and improve the city's park and playground facilities; and argued for the adoption of home rule, a small council elected at large, nonpartisan ballots, civil service, and the initiative, referendum, and reform. Some of its members even advocated municipal ownership of utilities and street railways, model tenements, and the establishment of a central planning department to map out a comprehensive blueprint for the development of the city.[13]

Though improvement associations appeared in cities of varying size across the country, settlement houses represent the best-known facet of the first neighborhood organization movement.[14] Invented in England, they came to the United States during the 1880s and 1890s, appearing first in New York and Chicago, and existed in virtually every major American city by 1910. Sponsored by churches, universities, or private philanthropists responding to the pleas of aggressive organizers working on their own, settlements comprised a distinctive type of community organization, combining preventive social work, "scientific" analyses of local conditions, and neighborhood reconstruction with a commitment to improve the city and society of which their neighborhoods formed a part. The earlier settlements, especially the Neighborhood Guild and the Hudson Guild in New York City, strove to ignite a civic renaissance by stimulating block-level grass-roots participation to monitor the delivery of municipal services and to raise money for the conduct of a variety of economic, educational, and recreational activities. Moreover, both self-consciously sought the betterment of the larger community as well as of the local neighborhood.

Most settlements, however, developed "institutional" programs, whose vitality stemmed from the voluntary efforts of outside and usually middle-class residents, and which failed either to organize the community effectively for social, political, or economic change or to elicit widespread and persistent participation in the settlements' programs by the neighborhoods' inhabitants. To be sure, settlement workers played a major role in various citywide, state, and national reform movements, but their status as outsiders, combined with the mobility of the populations they tried to serve, inhibited their effectiveness as agents of community organization.[15] In any case, and in one way or another, both the community organization and the institutional settlements recognized and acted upon larger community problems as well as neighborhood problems.

Regardless of their pervasiveness, neither settlement-house workers nor improvement-association workers monopolized the local organization field in the era of the organic city. Shortly after the turn of the century, for example, advocates of the social center idea entered the arena, differentiating themselves from the other two principally by their decision to select existing neighborhood institutions, such as a school, a playground, or a church, as organizational nodes for the local community. The public school proved the most popular choice as the setting for this movement, and those advocating the idea hoped to make each school a focus for education, recreation, social life, and the discussion of civic questions as a means of invigorating grass-roots democracy. Set up first in Rochester, New York, in 1907, the social center scheme spread rapidly to other cities, and, in 1916, its promoters established a National Community Center Association, which took as its charge encouraging more citizens to participate in local affairs and illustrating the relationship between the life of the neighborhood and that of the city as a whole. Though these organizations also fell short of their goals, serving more usually as centers of sociability than as dynamic factors leading local residents to assume the responsibility for their own affairs, they nonetheless exhibited the dual concern for locality and city that was characteristic of the late-nineteenth- and early twentieth-century neighborhood organization movement.[16]

The list of groups agitating for neighborhood organization during this period carries at least two more entries, Wilbur Phillips's social unit plan, discussed in detail elsewhere in this volume, and the Council of National Defense's community council idea, which fall in the same rubric because both began as national movements designed to plant local organizations in particular cities. Both tackled the familiar problem of fashioning organizations, not merely to provide service programs, but also to become a part of the fiber of the neighborhood itself. And both aimed specifically at bringing together democracy and expertise, first, in the neighborhood and, then, in the entire city. Neither got very far. The social unit movement collapsed after the Cincinnati experiment in the 1910s, and the drive for community councils, the last great effort at local action during the first neighborhood organization movement, expired shortly after the end of World War I, the event that had provided the occasion for its inception.

In the course of the war, the Council of National Defense (CND), a group composed of the Secretaries of War, the Navy, the Interior, Agriculture, Commerce, and Labor and seven civilians, worked with the U.S. Bureau of Education for the creation of local community (neighborhood) councils in cities across the country to speed community action on campaigns related to the war effort. Within six months, it reported an enrollment of approximately one and one-quarter million people in the endeavor. After the armistice, many of these local councils set up programs appropriate for peacetime conditions. New York City, for example, continued its support of the CND's community organizations, and, in December 1919, the National Social Unit Organization (NSUO) shifted its interest from the Cincinnati experiment to New York. The New York councils, organized to establish a close working relationship between citizens and specialists, mobilized the citizens of given neighborhoods into a voluntary organization. The local council met frequently to identify and discuss neighborhood problems, and possessed the power to appoint special committees to seek solutions to particular problems. At the same time, local councils sent representatives to a citywide organization, which, in turn, maintained a staff of specialists to supplement the experts from city agencies and other institutions responsible for handling local difficulties. Though the New York Council and NSUO cooperated in sponsoring a national Neighbors Day on June 14, 1920 to promote the idea of community organization, the New York operation floundered financially and voted itself out of existence in December 1920. In March of the following year, the NSUO itself went into receivership to satisfy its own outstanding debts.[17]

METROPOLIS AND THE COMMUNITY, 1920-1950

Though Phillips and others talked about neighborhood organization from their distinctive perspective for another twenty years, most Americans between 1920 and 1940 stopped thinking about neighborhoods as real and "natural" social entities and therefore as appropriate building blocks of community, which, if only correctly organized, would give coherence and unity to the city. But they did not give up on territory as a base for community. Throughout these years, many people talked and acted as if territorial community existed in America, and they defined it spatially as something larger than neighborhood, which nonetheless molded the desires, values, aspirations, and personalities of its inhabitants. And just as this mode of discourse made it possible to talk about and act upon the South and the West in new ways, it also became possible to talk about and act upon cities in new ways. The metropolis, or metropolitan region, now seemed a community with a distinctive culture. Louis Wirth, the prominent "Chicago-school" sociologist, laid out the principal characteristics tersely in his essay, "Urbanism as a Way of Life," the grimmer side of which raised the specter of "mass society" rendered unstable by the prevalence of anomie and alienation, and the brighter side of which raised the prospect of a new era of cosmopolitanism, urbanity, and tolerance.[18] And while the same mode of thought permitted the existence of territorial subcommunities within the larger and basic territorial community, of little subcommunities within the larger metropolitan community, it did not posit the existence of neighborhood as a primordial social force.[19]

Indeed, disillusionment with the earlier twentieth-century emphasis on the significance of neighborhood in urban life received its most salient expression in the 1920s from the Chicago-school sociologists. By the end of the decade, Robert Park and Louis Wirth had abandoned it entirely, and, as early as 1926, Ernest Burgess began to express his doubts.[20] In that year, he complained that the city had become "the 'happy hunting ground' of movements," all of which lacked a "basic understanding or conception of the city. Even the community organization movement, theoretically grounded upon the conception of the city as a unit," he added for emphasis, "had the misfortune to stake its program upon an assumption of the supreme value of the revival of the neighborhood in the city instead of upon a pragmatic, experimental program guided by studies of actual conditions and trends in urban life." Burgess remained optimistic about the urban prospect, however, for he felt that with

> the dawning perception of the breakdown of our traditional institutions of social control, and of the failure of many promising makeshifts for them, a disposition is emerging to base fundamental changes

in these institutions upon a more fundamental understanding of the city as the product of the interplay of economic and cultural forces.[21]

It was in that mood that Harvey Warren Zorbaugh, a student of Park and Burgess, undertook the study of Chicago's Lower North Community Council and the diverse population it served. He published the results in 1929 in a volume entitled *The Gold Coast and the Slum*, which stands as perhaps the most comprehensive and direct attack on the first neighborhood organization movement and which neatly highlights dominant notions of the city and of American society between 1920 and 1940. Zorbaugh, like Park and Burgess, still considered the city an appropriate unit of study and action within the metropolis, and still viewed it as an organism. They, however, saw it as essentially pluralistic in its composition, as much the product of competition as of cooperation. And they manifested a new and special interest in the individuals who inhabited the city, particularly because of the way in which the process of city growth impinged upon personality and seemed to be producing a new way of life, one very different from the informal, gemeinschaftliche, neighborly small community that they associated with the rural community, the village, or with pre-modern cultures generally, and that they believed the leaders of the first neighborhood organization movement mistakenly read into urban residential areas in the late-nineteenth- and early twentieth-century American big city.

For Zorbaugh, neighborhood, in the traditional sense, could not and did not exist in local areas of big cities, which consisted of mosaics of mobile economic and cultural groups in conflict and in transition. That basic fact, he contended, undermined the neighborhood organization movement, which rested upon an assumption of permanence, stability, common territorial interest, and cooperation at the local level. By 1929, that same basic fact had turned the Lower North Community Council, which itself grew out of the CND's community organization effort, into "merely" a social agency staffed by professionals with a program determined by an executive committee composed of residents of the Gold Coast, who also contributed the money to pay its secretary and social workers and to fund its programs. And he ranked the transformed council as one of many promising and "interesting" experiments to meet the problems associated with the growth of the city.[22]

Though various other techniques for handling urban problems pleased Zorbaugh, those he cited all considered the city as a whole, not the neighborhood, as the proper point of departure, and he frequently moved out from it to consider the metropolis and its region. He agreed, for example, with the "advocates of 'pluralism'," who argued that proportional representation "makes the city more nearly articulate" by basing "the vote on membership in social groups rather than on residence." He also regarded the commission and city manager forms of government as "realistic" because "city government is becoming increasingly a matter of business administration rather than of the crystallization and definition of opinion," and its proponents "attempt, with the aid of bureaus of municipal research, to introduce into city government the standardization and scientific management already found in industry."

Zorbaugh found even more interesting, "and perhaps more significant," the comprehensive city plan, including those like the Regional Plan of New York, which encompassed the entire region around the city. A comprehensive plan's significance, he wrote, was twofold.

> It tends toward an increasingly realistic conception of city life. But beyond this, as city plan commissions resort to publicity to arouse public interest, the plan begins to give the city a conception of itself— a self-awareness, a sense of its history and role, a vision of its future— in short, a personality. And only when the city has achieved self-consciousness, only when the mosaic of cultural worlds which compose it come to think of themselves, not as over against one another, but as related to a vision of the city as a whole, can the city adequately act.[23]

Finally, Zorbaugh looked to an alliance of what he called "social politics" with civic leadership from the Gold Coast as the most influential coalition in the city's future. By "social politics" he meant the process by which experts from citywide and statewide social and research agencies and foundations formulated the mass of social legislation enacted by cities and states. He saw it as "a movement away from the local urban community and in the direction of the standardization characteristic of other aspects of city life."[24] As for the civic leaders from the Gold Coast, the residential center in the 1920s of Chicago's high society, they composed the element most closely in touch with social politics and "the only element in the city's life that sees the city as a whole, dreams dreams for it as a whole." The Gold Coast, moreover, contained the wealth, " 'good will'," cosmopolitan perspective, and the expertise and leadership to realize those dreams; and its wealthy elite, "as no other group," had a historically self-conscious "sense of its role in the life of the city, and of its responsibility for the future."[25] Other local areas could not help, for, in Zorbaugh's view, the tendency in other inner-city districts ran to disorganization and an absence of a sense of either local or citywide community, while the suburbs, though potential and often real allies of the Gold Coast, carried, because of their stable and " 'traditionally' American" culture, the old, idealistic, "rural," "uplift," spirit of reform.[26]

Though Zorbaugh saw the city and American society as organic, pluralistic, and in a perpetual state of process, he felt confident that "social politics" and the expertise and leadership concentrated in the Gold Coasts of the nation, not the advocates of neighborhood democracy, would control and shape the urban future. "Great changes are impending in the life of the city," he wrote in the last paragraph of *The Gold Coast and the Slum,* and what "the city's future will be, it is hard to predict."

> But a study of the areas of the inner city cannot but give us a clearer and more realistic appreciation of the character of the city's life and the city's problems, a more accurate evaluation of the roles that various groups have played and are playing in controlling the city's destiny. And it seems probable that the role of the Gold Coast will be more significant than that of the street meeting in Bughouse Square, the discussions in the garrets of Towertown, or the political club over the shop of Romano the barber.[27]

Zorbaugh's study amounts to a virtual compendium of the conventional wisdom of the 1920s, 1930s, and 1940s on the city, and principal actors in urban life during the period behaved as if they had read it. Cincinnati's civic leaders, for example, who won for the Queen City its reputation as the nation's best-governed city through reforms enacted in this period, seemed to have taken its message literally. After the abandonment of the social unit experiment, and under the aegis of the elite-dominated Charter Committee, the city, under a home-rule charter, changed to the city manager form of government, eliminated the ward system in favor of a small council elected at large on a nonpartisan ballot, adopted proportional representation, and installed civil service as the method of selecting municipal employees. In that period, too, the new City Planning Commission promulgated and the City Council approved a comprehensive city plan, the first in a city of Cincinnati's size. The plan rested on the premise that the city functioned as a social organism. It ignored the question of neighborhood, took existing residential areas and specialized land districts as "givens," and sought to control their growth, to protect, and to rationalize them by the application of the new legal device of zoning. And implicit in the plan lay the assumption that the city, as an expanding social organism, should be subject to a central government, either by annexing newly populated territory or through metropolitan government.[28]

Some twenty years later, Cincinnati planners made explicit their metropolitan assumptions in the city's *Metropolitan Master Plan 1948,* although they skirted the still-controversial subject of metropolitan government. The document, developed by the City Planning Commission under the auspices of a metropolitanwide civic committee, contained the transportation, central business district, and slum-clearance proposals characteristic of the period. And it also proposed to merge the metropolitan area's ninety-two "traditional" neighborhoods into twenty-two "communities," noteworthy less for their "natural" tendency for social cohesion than for their utility as a locus for the delivery of services and amenities and for the development among some of their inhabitants of a sense of attachment both to the locality and to the metropolis. Each community, for example, would be virtually interchangeable with the others, for each would contain a battery of elementary schools anchored by a junior high, a branch post office and a library, perhaps a community center, a population sufficiently large to support a local shopping district, but no local government. Instead of seeking to revive a sense of neighborhood, in short, the metropolitan plan of 1948 envisaged the entire "reorganization" of the metropolis to

> reintroduce . . . in Cincinnati . . . the advantages of . . . cities of about 20,000 to 40,000 population, self-contained in respect to the everyday life of their inhabitants except for such facilities and services as will continue to be located in or supplied by Cincinnati as the central city, and by institutions serving the metropolitan area.[29]

In a variety of ways, events elsewhere fell into this general scheme of things. Saul Alinsky, the country's premier community organizer between the two world wars, who shared Zorbaugh's concern for the individual uprooted in a larger, pluralistic, and competitive organic complex, talked more about "people's" than he did about neighborhood organizations.

He mobilized and organized local groups with reference less to territoriality than to those forces outside the circle of local interest with whom his clients competed for existence.[30] This period, too, represented the heyday of the Regional Planning Association of America, which saw big cities as the central force in larger metropolitan regions and which strove for balanced "organic" growth at the regional level. During these years, moreover, housing reformers and city planners sought to bring functional, organic coherence to the city as a whole—the metropolitan community, they increasingly called it—by advocating federally subsidized public housing for the inner-city poor and the construction of model, moderate-income suburbs for workers and for the lower- and middle-income white-collar classes. And before the end of the 1930s, the New Deal undertook a public housing program and responded through the resettlement and greenbelt town programs and the TVA to the new concern for regionalism and comprehensive city planning. "Our Cities," the 1937 report of the Urbanism Committee of the National Resources Board, produced not only "the first inquiry of national, official, and comprehensive scale into the problems of the American urban community," but also a catalogue of those problems drawn in the Chicago-school mold, including a gloomy account of the deplorable consequences of the rampant localism built into the patchwork quilt of competing intrametropolitan political jurisdictions.[31]

Yet, "Our Cities" stood toward the end rather than at the beginning or the middle of a movement, for it came from the work of a distinctive generation of urban professionals with a distinctive perspective on the city. Put together by presidential advisor Charles E. Merriam, a University of Chicago political scientist, the Urbanism Committee's members included C. A. Dykstra, city manager of Cincinnati during the depression years, and Louis Wirth, the University of Chicago sociologist who produced his classic paper "Urbanism as a Way of Life" from research carried out under his direction for the committee. Ladislas Segoe, a planner and resident of Cincinnati, served as the committee's staff director, and Cincinnati was the staff's base of operations.[32] By 1945, those men had made their major original contributions to the study of the city, municipal administration, and city planning. Within that decade, moreover, a new cohort of urban professionals had rediscovered the local community, though they conceived of it in terms alien both to the turn-of-the-century neighborhood organization movement and to the first generation of Chicago urbanists.

CITIES, SUBURBS, AND THE COMMUNITY OF
LIMITED LIABILITY, 1950-1968

The rediscovery of the local community took place within the framework of a new conception of the city and of American society. By mid-century, the most influential students of the city had given up on the organic metaphor and, with it, the view of either the city or the metropolis as a natural, albeit man-made, component of the natural order. In its stead, they placed a more mechanistic conception of society, which drew on physics rather than biology for its analogue in the hard sciences.[33] This form of analysis held that individuals constituted the fundamental units of society and thus comprised the only "real" and therefore appropriate entities of study and objects of concern. The clash of individual interests, values, and aspirations, to be sure, produced classes, associations, institutions, organizations, and even communities of a sort, but nothing similar to the turn-of-the-century formulation of neighborhood and city, or to the subsequent casting of city, metropolis, and region as "natural" elements in the social order. The new "behavioral" research orientation in the social, policy, and managerial sciences centered on the individual and created a theoretical context in which the city, not to mention the neighborhood or community, seemed almost an illusory construct veiling the greater and real process of interaction among classes, institutions, and organizations. Through these interactions, thousands or millions of individuals with conflicting desires, values, and aspirations worked out terms of mutual accommodation for survival, producing an equilibrium expressed in a social order.

In this scheme, moreover, individuals possessed autonomy of the sort that David Riesman and his colleagues wrote about in *The Lonely Crowd,* the ability to become what they wanted to become as a consequence of personal decisions insignificantly influenced by their associations, residences, and histories. In territorial terms, this meant that where you came from no longer determined who you were. Instead, who you were—or decided to be—determined where you went, and wherever you went, you sought a degree of autonomy sufficient to maintain your security and self-defined sense of your self. You deserved, in other words, to be consulted about what happened to you and your chosen environment.

This new view, with its emphasis on the individual, on personal needs, and on their variety, implied a new respect for diversity and a new toler-

ance for socioeconomic, racial, ethnic, and land-use mixes and for
separatism. The new view drew a sharper distinction particularly between
the city and its suburbs, and that differentiation characterized the city
in such terms as heterogeneity, concentration, specialization, tension,
and drive, and placed suburbs toward the opposite ends of those descriptive categories. In this context, in the words of William H. Whyte, Jr.,
there could be "people who like cities," just as there indubitably existed people who liked silk-stocking or industrial suburbs or exurbia. In
this view, too, a slum need not be a mere hotbed of pathology that en-
trapped and demoralized its victims; it could be either a staging ground
for mobility or a location chosen by people because it fit their self-
defined needs. Similarly, the central business district need not be exclusively a place of business or entertainment; it could also be a place of
residence, like New York's Fifty-Seventh Street, which seemed particularly
suited to those for whom downtown epitomized the prototypically desirable characteristics of "the city." And while some people could and
did continue to use the word "community," the term no longer designated
a powerful social and cultural force; it merely represented a place in which
people chose to live for the purpose of satisfying their personal needs,
whether economic, psychological, career, civic, or a combination of the
four.[34]

The emergence of this new approach to society had profound consequences.[35] First, it created a rift in the ranks of urban professionals
that would have seemed strange to the Zorbaugh-Wirth-Merriam generation. Stated in extreme terms, the division placed on one side "academic"
students of the city, who saw their primary task as the resolution of
problems defined by and within the boundaries of their disciplines,
and who dealt more in the realm of probabilities than with certainties
on which policy could be confidently based. On the other side stood
"practical" students of the city, who concerned themselves with
"applied" research and with the training of students to treat urban problems defined by society itself. Instead of working together, these two
groups saw their relationship as analogous to that between the "basic"
and "applied" hard sciences, a connection in which the work of the
"academics" would occasionally, and essentially coincidentally, produce
something of utility for the practitioners and society but that marched
to a logic of its own.

Second, the new approach placed different subjects of enquiry on the agenda of both the "academic" and "practical" students of the city. It led to an essentially ahistorical concern with the condition of individuals in mass society; with the problem of how consensus developed in mass society; with the degree to which the melting pot melted in mass society; and with measuring the exact degree of residential and occupational mobility and of class stratification. More specifically, power—the question of who governs and how—became a lively issue of debate among political scientists and sociologists, with positions ranging roughly along a continuum represented by C. Wright Mills and Floyd Hunter on one end and Robert Dahl, Nelson Polsby, and Wallace Sayre on the other. And the field of human ecology, which had been pioneered by the first-generation Chicago-school sociologists, now centered on Amos Hawley and his students, who, in the company of some geographers and economists, sought to explain the functioning of the national system of cities by observing the behavior of individuals acting in response to a web of influence created by the variables of population, social organization, environment, and technology. But the new approach also sparked a new interest in the local community.[36]

Ironically, Scott Greer credited Morris Janowitz of the University of Chicago with the rediscovery of local community, though Janowitz might have selected Frank Sweetzer or William F. Whyte.[37] In any case, Janowitz, in *The Community Press in an Urban Setting* (1952), argued that local community existed within what he conceded to be a mass society, and that the community press exerted an influence on the behavior of individuals by seeking to maintain local consensus through an "emphasis on common values rather than on the solution of conflicting values."[38] He opened the book, moreover, with an assault on the model of the city and society that his predecessors at Chicago had done so much to develop and disseminate.

After documenting the existence of more than one hundred eighty-one community newspapers in the Chicago metropolitan district—a phenomenon that, according to that "variety of sociological theory . . . oriented toward viewing our modern mass society as movement from the simple to the complex, from the small scale to the large scale," should have ceased to exist—Janowitz attacked that social scientific outlook which stressed "the impersonality and disorganization of urban life. . . . The 'obvious fact' of a decline in the importance of local community . . . ," he continued, "precludes understanding how some measure of consensus persists at the lowest levels, or, in short, how it is that urban society persists at all." Indeed, he contended that

> If society were as impersonal, as self-centered and barren as described by some who are preoccupied with the one-way trend from "gemeinschaft" to "gessellschaft" seem to believe, the levels of criminality, social disorganization and psychopathology which social science seeks to account for would have to be viewed as very low rather than as alarmingly high.[39]

Janowitz preferred another perspective and another model, one that recognized that "the large city involves an intricate balance between the relative use of local and non-local facilities, and a complex of social institutions for integrating the individual into his 'residential' community as well as his 'employment' community." Within that context, he argued, the community press operated, and its analysis in those terms "might help clarify the character of the 'residential' community, and in particular, help answer the question of actually how rootless is the resident of the metropolis."[40] And the model he proposed, while it failed to resurrect the spirit of neighborhood and neighborliness in the turn-of-the-century sense of those concepts, provided a role for local community unacknowledged by what he described as conventional social science wisdom.

Janowitz argued, in short, for the persistence of local community orientation among some people. He posited the existence of the metropolis, not as a basic territorial unit of community, but as a congeries of localities, each of them functioning as a "community of limited liability." Within this kind of community, individuals and families with social and psychological commitments to a variety of other "communities"—churches, fraternal and social organizations, ethnic and labor groups, businesses and professions—could identify and interact, participating or withdrawing, whether by moving or by adopting a passive attitude to local affairs, as their interests, perceptions of community conditions, and stage in the family cycle dictated. "Our community," Janowitz wrote,

> is clearly not one of completely bureaucratized and impersonalized attachments. In varying degrees, use of local facilities is accompanied by community orientations. The extent and character of these attachments are in good measure linked to the individual resident's predispositions and acts. Raising a family and, to a lesser extent, length of

residence and local social contacts predispose him to an acceptance
of local community institutions and social controls. In the process,
purely "rational" and "instrumental" relations are modified. In this
regard, individuals vary in the extreme; some are more capable (or
have more need) than others of developing these orientations.[41]

This mode of thought about the significance of local community in
the metropolis, combined with some unforeseen consequences of urban
renewal, set off another community organization movement. Before the
end of the 1950s, the large-scale removal of people involved in the massive
expressway, slum-clearance, and central business district refurbishment
projects had created widespread resentment among those who had to
move out. Given the assumption of the importance of autonomy and
the consensus that a real public opinion could exist in local areas, their
complaints struck a responsive chord, and soon a variety of projects
appeared that aimed to elicit citizen participation in urban renewal.

Though we often associate this movement with the Kennedy-Johnson
urban programs, as early as 1953, the President's Advisory Committee
on Government and Housing Policies recommended the formation of
"a broadly representative private organization . . . with congressional
and/or Presidential sponsorship to mobilize public opinion in support
of vigorous and responsible action by communities in urban renewal
activities." In 1954, a group of business leaders and national civic leaders
established the American Council to Improve Our Neighborhoods
(ACTION). Before the end of the decade, President Eisenhower and
Adlai Stevenson had addressed the organization; Senator Joseph Clark
joined its board; General Electric and Sears, Roebuck set up discussion
groups on community development; and grants from the Ford Foundation supported an intensive and lengthy ACTION-sponsored study of
government and housing in metropolitan areas.[42]

The ACTION idea caught on quickly at the local level, and its manifestations ranged from the formation of local groups dominated by
business to organizations controlled by area residents, or to some mix of
the two, while its sponsors included city planning departments, churches,
and nonprofit corporations. In Pittsburgh in 1957, for example, leaders
of its "Renaissance" set up ACTION-Housing, a nonprofit corporation
that, among other things, encouraged neighborhood (by this time, the
terms "community" and "neighborhood" were often used interchange-

ably and synonymously) citizen participation in renewal activities. To facilitate the process, ACTION-Housing hired as associate director James V. Cunningham, who had been executive director of Chicago's Hyde Park-Kenwood Community Conference since 1956, and whose experience there convinced him that neighborhood renewal could be accomplished without resort to the bulldozer and that renewal constituted a continuing process requiring organization for broad citizen participation in making decisions. Yet, his objective was not narrowly parochial. "At stake" in the urban renewal process and neighborhood reconstruction, Cunningham claimed, was the "nature of urban life itself. Is there to be local community life, or merely the big, impersonal metropolis?"[43]

Clearly, Cunningham worked with a set of assumptions compatible with the community of limited liability notion, a notion that linked the individual, the local community, and the metropolis, and that posited civic activity—in this case, citizen participation in planning—as an indispensable prerequisite for the democratic and humane functioning of mass society. For him, the "responsible citizen," rather than the neighborhood or metropolis, represented the starting point in planning, the "basic ingredient in neighborhood improvement" who functioned as "both the chief agent for achieving improvement and the chief client to benefit from improvement. When the citizen plans and acts, he becomes a man of dignity." And Cunningham, as a "neighborhood professional,"[44] saw his role, in effect, as a surrogate for a community press or for one of the other variety of community organizations, motivating people to act by emphasizing common values rather than local conflicts in order to link more effectively and meaningfully individuals to the local community, the metropolis, and mass society.

The credibility of the metropolis conceived as a collection of communities of limited liability depended basically on two factors. First, it relied on the ability of the system to meet the demands of most of its organized groups for the advance, welfare, and mobility of their constituents. Only then would individuals adhere to the code of work and civic responsibility, and only under conditions of prosperity would the community of limited liability's safety valve—the promise that one could always withdraw from one arena of competition to another in the hope that success and security might be found in another context—work effectively. Second, it rested on a definition of the metropolis and society that, while taking individuals as the basic units of the social order, allowed for their integration into a civic network of communities, including the local community.

THE COMMUNITY OF ADVOCACY, 1968-

Both factors disappeared in the late 1960s and early 1970s, and their collapse signalled the end of the post-World War II community organization movement and the beginning of the contemporary neighborhood organization revolution. And the latter, while it rhetorically invoked the idea of neighborhood, rested, in the final analysis, on the turning inward tendency, an intensely privativistic individualism more concerned with one's self-fulfillment, or careerism, or property values than with a genuinely public policy. People, as columnist Ellen Goodman put it, seemed to have "lost faith in public solutions" and turned "to what they can control." That category, she added, included vegetable gardens, where

> friends are as obvious as the sun. Enemies are as real as the root borer. The goal is as tangible as a head of cabbage. You don't need a consultant to assess failure or success.[45]

Nor, she might have added, a professional neighborhood organizer.

The conviction that the community of limited liability system no longer worked stemmed from several sources.[46] At the heart of the crisis of confidence, however, lay the disjunction between the conventional definition of urban society and its functioning. The system proved tolerable and credible to the poor so long as a son, a next-door neighbor, or a friend down the block managed to gather the resources to move out of the central-city slum to a dwelling in a "better neighborhood" of their choice. During the 1950s and into the 1960s, that process—and abundance and belief in abundance that supplied its dynamic—buoyed the hopes and sustained the incentive of thousands of newcomers to the metropolis. But when large numbers met the social imperative to secure an education, get a job, build a family, invest in a home, and become an autonomous and "responsible citizen," yet failed to receive the rewards of socioeconomic security and mobility into a better neighborhood, the incentive to conform to the civic demands of the community of limited liability waned.

That defect in the system first hit blacks, who, after the massive civil

rights campaign of the 1950s and early 1960s, still found themselves confined to the ghetto. Their response, the assertion of black power and the
demand for "community" control, helped incite a revival of white ethnic
consciousness and the contemporary neighborhood organization revolution. In the context of inflation and limited economic growth that
emerged from President Johnson's guns-and-butter policy, and the perception in the late 1960s and early 1970s of energy and resource shortages,
black power translated readily into mimetic cries for white ethnic power,
women's power, gay power, blue-collar power, white-collar power, consumer power, taxpayer's power, senior-citizen power, suburban power,
and neighborhood power. In short, because the system no longer seemed
to work in their welfare, discontented individuals saw their temporary
disadvantages as permanent, and sought to reformulate the terms and
modes of conflict by transforming the definition of the city into a community of advocacy for access to scarce resources and jobs and for
personal, group, and local autonomy.

Perhaps affirmative action ranks as the most characteristic policy of
the new mood, for, in the name of advancing disadvantaged groups, it
serves the interest of individuals seeking a position in society to facilitate
their pursuit of essentially personal goals. But the new way of conceiving
society manifested itself in other ways. The critical question became,
Who governs in private as well as in public institutions? The protest took
the form of a pervasive demand for self-management, and the managers
of public and private bureaucracies and other key institutions became
the special targets of the upheaval. Women revolted against their sub-
servient role in the family and on the job; workers sought more control
of factories and offices; dissenting professionals rewrote the constitutions
and bylaws of their organizations in an effort to root out the "old boy"
network; students pushed for more control of their education; professors
asserted their superiority to administrators who now seemed managers
of universities rather than servants of the faculty; and across the face of
the metropolis, leaders in local communities pressed for "neighborhood"
control of political functions that just a few years before they had shared
in the spirit of compromise with delegated or elected officials, professional planners, and department or agency heads. In this context, the demand of the 1950s and early 1960s for citizen participation in planning
became an assertion of the right of localities to zone for themselves and
to make their own budgets. And while democracy retained its allure, in

the late 1960s and 1970s, a resort to demonstrations, litigation, arbitration, and initiative and referendum procedures challenged politics as usual and the legislative process as preferred means of issue resolution and problem solving.

Pluralism also remained in vogue, but appeals to it in the new context sounded ritualistic. Pluralistic rhetoric in the 1970s veiled a longing for separation, for the division of the metropolis into homogeneous groups and areas in which, as in Ellen Goodman's vegetable garden, individuals could pursue self-fulfillment in a static environment where the patent visibility of friends, enemies, and goals eliminated from life doubt, uncertainty, and fear. And some, like the members of the Institute for Local Self-Reliance, even wanted to make neighborhoods self-sufficient. They sought, for example, to induce the residents of the South Bronx to "green" their area through the manufacture of compost from garbage, tree leaves, and pulverized brick, the product of which they spread on two hundred acres of community vegetable gardens, which might also be used to farm Christmas trees for cash income.[47]

In the new world of the 1970s, not only neighborhood, but also metropolis conveyed an uncertain meaning. Though still in common parlance, the term "metropolis," with its connotations of interdependence, community, and public polity, seemed awkward, and gradually a rival, the neologism "metroplex," entered the vocabulary. It simply meant an area for the provision of services to individuals, whether health care, air transportation, or radio and television programs. Metroplex boundaries, in addition, did not necessarily coincide with local political jurisdictions or traditional socioeconomic definitions of the kind utilized by the Federal census. Thus, the Dallas metroplex originally referred to the entire territory from which the city's new airport drew local outbound passengers. A health-care metroplex, on the other hand, might encompass all the hospitals and medical clinics in parts of two or three counties, while a radio station's metroplex might extend from its transmitter in a circle of thirty miles, the length of its signal. In any case, what had once been seen as a coherent metropolitan region now began to take on the appearance of a maze of overlapping metroplexes, a concept that accorded with the new view of neighborhood as itself nothing more than a service area for a collection of individuals in pursuit, not of community, but of their own varied and quite personal goals.

THE CONTEMPORARY CONDITION

While this account of metroplex and the new notion of neighborhood may read like a caricature of emerging tendencies in urban society, it seems clear that new conceptualizations are in the process of being made, or at least that students of urban life are groping for a new formulation of the relationship between individuals, community, and space in the metropolis. In this sense, neighborhood, city, and metropolitan policymakers occupy a position similar to that described by E. J. Hobsbawm as the contemporary "secular crisis."

> Once upon a time, say from the middle of the nineteenth century to the middle of the twentieth, the movements of the left—whether they called themselves socialist, communist, or syndicalist—like everybody else who believed in progress, knew just where they wanted to go and just what, with the help of history, strategy, and effort, they ought or needed to do to get there. Now they no longer do. In this respect they do not, of course, stand alone. Capitalists are just as much at a loss as socialists to understand their future, and just as puzzled by the failure of their theorists and prophets. . . . At the end of the most extraordinary period of transformation in human affairs, old landmarks have disappeared, new ones are not yet recognized as such, and intellectual navigation across the suddenly estranged landscapes of human society becomes unusually puzzling for everybody.[48]

This analysis of the contemporary metropolitan crisis, then, suggests that another redefinition of the city, and with it of neighborhood, is in the making, even though the symptoms of change may be more evident than its content and direction. In this view, nostalgia, and especially that which longs for the allegedly lost world of the small community, may be one of our most pressing yet sadly neglected problems, for it inhibits our ability to perceive with precision and therefore to make significant breaks with what is taken as a successful past, a past that is all the more intensely cherished because of its assumed successes. We need to recognize, in short, that the past is past, that the cities of Jane Addams, Harvey Zorbaugh, and Morris Janowitz are gone. It then remains, in the last quarter of the twentieth century, to get on with those social, economic, political, and institutional adjustments, analyses, and innovations that

seem appropriate to a society haunted by the specter of scarcity. Out of
the experimentation may emerge a definition of the city sufficiently
compelling to restore the trust, confidence, credibility, vision, and sense
of public policy required to dispel in a democratic way the paralysis of
will and action that grips contemporary metropolitan politics in a period
when the perception of scarcity threatens to circumscribe our opportunities and to impose upon us a new despotism.

NOTES

1. See Warren G. Bennis, "Chairman Mac in Perspective," *Harvard
Business Review* 50, no. 5 (September-October 1972): 139-43; Philip
Roth, *My Life as a Man* (New York: Holt, Rinehart and Winston, 1974);
Richard Sennett, *The Fall of Public Man* (New York: Alfred A. Knopf,
1977). Also see Leon Botstein, "The Children of the Lonely Crowd,"
Change (May 1978): 16-20; Zane L. Miller, "The Neighborhood
Organization Revolution: Neighborhood, Community, and the Con-
temporary Metropolitan Crisis," in Ralph Pearson, ed., *Ohio in Century
Three: Quality of Life* (Columbus, Ohio: The Ohio Historical Society,
1977), pp. 18-24.

2. For an explication of this construction of the perception of cities
in the early and mid-nineteenth century, see Alan I. Marcus, "In Sick-
ness and in Health: The Marriage of the Municipal Corporation to Public
Interest and Problems of Public Health, 1820-1890. The Case of Cincinnati" (Ph.D. diss. University of Cincinnati, 1979), Introduction-Ch. IV.

3. Ibid., Chs. IV-V. The nineteenth-century ward, unfortunately,
has yet to find its historian. For a start, however, see Joseph S. Villari,
"Cincinnati Wards: Their Usages, 1819-1925," typescript, May 1978,
Laboratory in American Civilization, Department of History, University
of Cincinnati.

4. Zane L. Miller, "Scarcity, Abundance, and American Urban
History," *Journal of American History* 4, no. 2 (February 1978): 142.

5. For a fuller exposition of this view of society, the city, and
neighborhood, see Patricia Mooney Melvin, "Neighborhood in the
'Organic' City: The Social Unit Plan and the First Community Organization Movement" (Ph.D. diss., University of Cincinnati, 1978), Introduction. I have drawn heavily on her study for this section of the essay.

6. Henry C. Adams, ed., *Philanthropy and Social Progress* (New York:
Thomas Y. Crowell, 1893), p. xi.

7. Josiah Strong, *The Twentieth Century City* (New York: Baker and Taylor, 1898; reprint edition, New York: Arno Press, 1970), pp. 117, 123-24.

8. M. P. Follett, *The New State: Group Organization, the Solution of Popular Government,* 2d ed. (New York: Longmans, Green, 1923), p. 715.

9. Edward T. Devine, "Some Elementary Definitions," *Charities,* June 4, 1904, p. 597.

10. Frederic C. Howe, *The City, The Hope of Democracy* (New York: Charles Scribner's Sons, 1905), pp. 23, 280.

11. Robert A. Woods, "The City and Its Local Community," in *The Neighborhood in Nation Building,* ed. Robert A. Woods (Boston: Houghton Mifflin, 1923; reprint edition, New York: Arno Press, 1970), p. 196.

12. Patricia Mooney Melvin, "Neighborhood in the 'Organic' City"; on Dabney, see Zane L. Miller, *Boss Cox's Cincinnati: Urban Politics in the Progressive Era* (New York: Oxford University Press, 1968), pp. 155-56.

13. Henry D. Shapiro and Zane L. Miller, *Clifton: Neighborhood and Community in an Urban Setting. A Brief History* (Cincinnati: Laboratory in American Civilization, Department of History, University of Cincinnati, 1976), pp. 36-38.

14. The standard source for the late-nineteenth- and early twentieth-century settlement house movement is Allen F. Davis, *Spearheads for Reform: The Social Settlements and the Progressive Movement, 1890-1914* (New York: Oxford University Press, 1967).

15. See, for example, Mooney Melvin, "Neighborhood"; and Thomas Lee Philpott, *The Slum and the Ghetto. Neighborhood Deterioration and Middle-Class Reform, Chicago 1880-1930* (New York: Oxford University Press, 1978), pp. 62-68, 293-313.

16. For discussion of the social center movement, see Sidney Dillick, *Community Organization for Neighborhood Development: Past and Present* (New York: William Morrow, 1953); Eduard C. Lindeman, *The Community* (New York: Association Press, 1921).

17. Mooney Melvin, "Neighborhood," Epilogue.

18. Louis Wirth, "Urbanism as a Way of Life," *American Journal of Sociology* 44 (July 1938): 1-24.

19. See, for example, Harlan Paul Douglass, *The Suburban Trend* (New York and London: Century Co., 1925); and R. D. McKenzie, *The Metropolitan Community* (New York and London: McGraw-Hill, 1933).

20. See Albert Hunter, with the assistance of Nancy Goldman, "Introduction," in *Ernest W. Burgess on Community, Family and Delinquency*, ed. Leonard S. Cottrell, Jr., Albert Hunter, and James F. Short, Jr. (Chicago: University of Chicago Press, 1973), pp. 3-9; Jean B. Quandt, *From the Small Town to the Great Community: The Social Thought of Progressive Intellectuals* (New Brunswick, N.J.: Rutgers University Press, 1970), pp. 152-55.

21. Ernest W. Burgess, *The Urban Community: Selected Papers from the Proceedings of the American Sociological Society, 1925* (Chicago: University of Chicago Press, 1926), p. viii.

22. Harvey Warren Zorbaugh, *The Gold Coast and the Slum: A Sociological Study of Chicago's Near North Side* (Chicago: University of Chicago Press, 1929, Phoenix Edition, 1976), pp. 200-220, 272.

23. Ibid., pp. 272-73.

24. Ibid., pp. 261, 273-74.

25. Ibid., pp. 274, 277.

26. Ibid., p. 269.

27. Ibid., p. 279.

28. William A. Baughin, "Murray Seasongood: Twentieth Century Urban Reformer" (Ph.D. diss., University of Cincinnati, 1972), passim; Cincinnati City Planning Commission, *Official Plan of the City of Cincinnati* (Cincinnati: Cincinnati City Planning Commission, 1925), pp. 7-38.

29. Cincinnati City Planning Commission, *Metropolitan Master Plan 1948* (Cincinnati: Cincinnati Planning Commission, 1948), pp. 7-34.

30. Saul D. Alinsky, *Reveille for Radicals* (New York: Random House, 1946, Vintage Book Edition, 1969), pp. 53-190; Robert Bailey, Jr., *Radicals in Urban Politics: The Alinsky Approach* (Chicago: University of Chicago Press, 1974). Also see Michael J. Austin and Neil Betten, "Intellectual Origins of Community Organization, 1920-1939," *Social Service Review* 51 (March 1977): 155-70; Roy Lubove, *The Professional Altruist: The Emergence of Social Work as a Career, 1880-1930* (Cambridge, Mass.: Harvard University Press, 1965), pp. 157-219.

31. Charles N. Glaab and A. Theodore Brown, *A History of Urban America* (New York: Macmillan, 1976), pp. 27-279; Roy Lubove, *Community Planning in the 1920s: The Contributions of the Regional Planning Association of America* (Pittsburgh: University of Pittsburgh Press, 1964); Roderick McKenzie, *The Metropolitan Community* (New York: McGraw-Hill, 1933).

32. Mark I. Gelfand, *A Nation of Cities: The Federal Government*

and Urban America, 1933-1965 (New York: Oxford University Press, 1975), pp. 82-96.

33. The "mechanistic" notion is adapted from Werner Stark, *The Fundamental Forms of Social Thought* (New York: Fordham University Press, 1963).

34. See the essays, including Whyte's, in The Editors of *Fortune, The Exploding Metropolis: A Study of the Assault on Urbanism and How Our Cities Can Resist It* (New York: Anchor Books, 1958).

35. This paragraph and the next rest principally upon Barry D. Karl, *Charles E. Merriam and the Study of Urban Politics* (Chicago: University of Chicago Press, 1974); Elizabeth Wirth Marvick and Albert J. Riess, Jr., eds., *Community Life and Social Policy: Selected Papers by Louis Wirth* (Chicago: University of Chicago Press, 1956), parts III and IV; Philip M. Hauser and Leo F. Schnore, eds., *The Study of Urbanization* (New York: John Wiley, 1965); Leo F. Schnore, ed., *Social Science and the City: A Survey of Urban Research* (New York: Frederick A. Praeger, 1968); David W. Minar and Scott Greer, eds., *The Concept of Community* (Chicago: Aldine Publishing, 1969), especially pp. 287-316; Stephan Thernstrom, *Poverty and Progress: Social Mobility in a Nineteenth Century City* (Cambridge, Mass.: Harvard University Press, 1968), pp. 255-59.

36. For symptoms of the rediscovery of local community, see Maurice R. Stein, *The Eclipse of Community: An Interpretation of American Studies* (New York: Harper & Row, 1964); Robert C. Wood, *Suburbia: Its People and Their Politics* (Boston: Houghton Mifflin, 1958); Roland L. Warren, *Studying Your Community* (New York: The Free Press, 1965, originally published by The Russell Sage Foundation, 1955); Willis D. Hawley and Frederick M. Wirt, eds., *The Search for Community Power* (Englewood Cliffs, N.J.: Prentice-Hall, 1968); Arthur J. Vidich, Joseph Bensman, Maurice R. Stein, *Reflections on Community Studies* (New York: John Wiley, 1964); Scott Greer and Ann Lennarson Greer, eds., *Neighborhood and Ghetto: The Local Area in Large-Scale Society* (New York: Basic Books, 1974); Horace Cayton and St. Clair Drake, *Black Metropolis: A Study of Life in a Northern City* (New York: Harcourt, Brace, 1945).

37. Morris Janowitz, *The Community Press in an Urban Setting: The Social Elements of Urbanism,* 2d ed. (Chicago: University of Chicago Press, 1967), pp. 6, 245.

38. Ibid., p. 11.

39. Ibid., pp. 1-7.

40. Ibid., p. 7.

41. Ibid., pp. 210-13.

42. Gelfand, *A Nation of Cities,* p. 280.

43. Roy Lubove, *Twentieth Century Pittsburgh: Government, Business and Environmental Change* (New York: John Wiley, 1969).

44. Ibid., pp. 163-64.

45. *Newsweek,* July 17, 1978, p. 90.

46. Miller, "Scarcity, Abundance and American Urban History," pp. 149-50.

47. Membership solicitation letter, Institute for Local Self-Reliance, 1718 18th Street NW, Washington, D.C. 20009, n.d. [1978].

48. E. J. Hobsbawm, "Should the Poor Organize?" *New York Review of Books* 25, no. 4 (March 23, 1978): 44.

From Grass-Roots Organizing to Community Service: Community Organization Practice in the Community Center Movement, 1907–1930

ROBERT FISHER

Little of the voluminous literature on community organization published since the 1960s has been written from a historical perspective or by historians.[1] It is not that community organizations are simply a current phenomenon or that historians have ignored the study of social reform or social welfare organizations.[2] Quite the opposite is true. Social change organizations abound in the history of the United States, and they have interested historians at least as much as contemporary efforts intrigue social scientists. But historians prefer to view neighborhood-based, social change programs, such as social settlements, as urban reform efforts. They do not define the efforts as community organizations and, thus, have ignored, until recently, a rich literature on the subject compiled by sociologists and social work scholars since the 1920s.[3] It is time the resources of community organization literature were used by historians and integrated into the study of social movements in the past.

One place to begin is with a typology of community organization practice developed by Jack Rothman.[4] According to Rothman, there

───────

Note: The author wishes to express his thanks to Bayrd Still, Terry Weiner, and Robert Wells for their especially helpful comments on an earlier draft delivered before the Organization of American Historians, April 1978.

are at least three distinguishable approaches to community organization. The first type, called "locality development," seeks to develop or improve the sense of community by gathering neighborhood residents together and assisting them in determining and solving their own problems. Social settlements and overseas community development projects fit most closely this type of organizing effort. Rothman's second type, called "social planning," seeks to solve specific problems by initiating or coordinating community projects for the benefit of community residents. This type would be characterized by a local planning board or social service agency. The third type, called "social action," seeks to achieve community control, neighborhood power, and radical social change by crystallizing issues and organizing residents to take direct action against enemy targets. Many of the neighborhood organizing efforts of the civil rights and New Left movements of the 1960s reflect this approach.

Though the work of Rothman and others supplies evidence of the varieties of community organization practice, their studies do not address sufficiently the question of how community organization practice changes over time. For example, given the diversity of practice types, do organizations use more than one approach over a span of time, and, if so, what causes the shift from one type to another? Do changes in practice follow a distinguishable pattern given certain conditions or developments? Is there a sequential relationship between these types of practice? Such questions of organizational development are a natural province for historians, who have always studied change over time and who are now willing to use social science theory and case studies in a more or less formal way.

In this vein, this conceptual essay seeks to establish a typology of community organization practice by focusing on the community center movement—an effort to use public schools after hours as neighborhood centers— during the years 1907-1930. Special attention is given, in the earlier years, to the pioneering local efforts in Rochester, New York, and to the People's Institute in New York City; for the later years, case studies from a number of cities and surveys of the national movement form the data. To establish typologies of practice, four questions are addressed: What did organizers assume were the community problem conditions? What were the stated goals of community organizers? What were their strategies? How did they structure the organization?[5] The results suggest that this early community organization effort experienced four different, if overlapping, types of practice, which I call Community Development

(1907-1914), Professional Planning (1915-1917), Community Mobilization (1918-1919), and Community Service (1920-1930).[6]

But this essay also seeks to go beyond this typology in order to develop a model of change in community organization practice. As the title suggests, the sequence of practice in the community center movement went from efforts to get residents involved in grass-roots community development to programs designed by organizers to deliver services to neighborhood residents. Thus, what began as one type of community organization evolved relatively quickly into something very different. This transformation to a more formal structure and service function is not uncommon in community organization; the specifics, however, are unique to the community center movement in the early twentieth century.

COMMUNITY DEVELOPMENT: 1907-1914

The roots of the community center movement lie deep in the urban social reform movements of the 1890s and early 1900s. The first centers were founded by social settlement workers, public recreation advocates, and civic reformers. Settlement workers such as Mary Simkhovitch and Mary Follett saw in community centers the essence of the settlement idea: using the neighborhood as an organizational unit for counteracting urban problems.[7] Recreation proponents viewed community centers as a logical extension of their efforts to expand the use of public schools beyond traditional academic functions.[8] Similarly, multifaceted urban reform organizations such as the People's Institute in New York City sought, in public-school community centers, appropriate and inexpensive sites for organizing neighborhood social and civic clubs.[9]

Edward Ward, who initiated the first social centers in Rochester, New York, in 1907, aptly expressed many of the underlying assumptions of problem conditions in his work *The Social Center*. Ward believed that neighborhood-based, democratic, "home-like" civic clubs could counteract the lack of effective and intelligent urban government and the disconnecting qualities of urban life.[10] Five years later, the People's Institute, a multifaceted reform organization, established the first social center in New York City in response to what its leaders perceived as the pressing problems of contemporary urban society: the prevalence of class segregation with its potential for dramatic class conflict; the large numbers of unassimilated, impoverished immigrants; and the rapid growth of "harmful" commercial leisure-time recreations, such as burlesque, pool halls, bars, and motion pictures.[11]

The stated goal of community centers in this initial phase was to assist community self-expression. Rothman and others would refer to this as a "process goal." A process goal seeks to foster collaboration, cooperation, and participation in self-help neighborhood projects. This differs from a task goal, which seeks to complete a concrete task or solve a community problem that is predetermined by community organizers.[12] The espousal of process goals is evident in a pamphlet written by Clinton Childs, the community organizer of the first social center in Manhattan.

> A community clubhouse and Acropolis in one; this is the Social Center.

> A community organized about some center for its own political and social welfare and expression; to peer into its own mind and life, to discover its own social needs and then to meet them, whether they concern the political field, the field of health, or recreation, of education, or of industry; such community organization is necessary if democratic society is to succeed and endure. There must be an [sic] unifying social bond of feeling, tradition, experience, belief and knowledge, a common meeting ground, spiritually and concretely speaking. But there must also be a community expression through activity, self-government and self-support.[13]

While organizers continued to voice process goals throughout this period, they never adopted the neutral role Childs suggests. Organizers hoped to guide as much as stimulate community development. Moreover, process goals reflected more than the organizer's preference for a truly democratic community program. Being outsiders, organizers needed resident involvement in order to develop the new community institution and they sought to legitimize their work by emphasizing concepts of neighborhood self-help and citizen participation.[14]

The organization of each center followed a relatively similar pattern. First, a voluntary reform group secured limited funds and permission from local officials to use a public school as a test site. Next, a trained organizer was sent into the designated community to develop support for the social center idea and to arrange for use of the school by clubs, organizations, and individuals. The organizer would help form a "neighborhood group" composed of local representatives appointed by the clubs that met at the center and "of prominent residents of the district who manifested an active interest in the project." The group would be under the direction of a "community secretary"—usually the initial outside organizer—who would plan, govern, and administer center activities with the assistance of the neighborhood group.[15]

Programs varied from city to city and from center to center. In Rochester, the school served as the site of a number of activities, but organizers there placed emphasis on "the importance of the school as a public forum where citizens of the neighborhood could discuss civic questions with absolute freedom."[16] In New York City, the People's Institute envisioned a wide-ranging program that included civic clubs, neighborhood information bureaus, literary clubs, ethnic pageants and festivals, motion pictures, amateur concerts, dramatic presentations, and athletic programs held in the school playground or gymnasium. As in Rochester, civic forums were established for the discussion of "subjects related to the everyday life of the People" and of "matters of intimate importance to the neighborhood," such as labor struggles and socialism.[17] But generally, activities at centers did not encourage fundamental social change or social action. This was partly the product of the organizers' limited goals and partly the result of using a public facility as the organizing site. Where center programs hinted at social action, as in Ward's effort in Rochester to develop centers into neighborhood-based reform groups, local officials cut appropriations and tightened supervision. Accordingly, the approach adopted was what sociologists label a "consensus strategy"—a reformist, socially approved method that does not threaten existing power relationships.

The organizational structure of these early efforts was designed, at least in theory, to promote process goals and to develop programs that would reflect the self-expression of the neighborhood. Centers were to be funded by neighborhood residents with a minimum of public assistance and democratically governed "from the bottom up" through the neighborhood group. At first, public support, not self-support, was the goal of organizers. In Rochester, Ward's initial center was begun with a $5,000 allocation by the City Council to be expended by the Board of

Education. But, with the victory at the polls some three years later of a faction opposed to "socialistic centers," appropriations were drastically cut.[18] Because of such political problems and because of the penchant of New York City progressives for fiscal austerity when considering public, social programs, the People's Institute advocated privately initiated and supported centers. Such centers combined dues from local residents and donations from upper-class-financed groups like the Institute with a limited allocation from the Board of Education to cover rent and maintenance of the building.[19]

The extent of resident participation in leadership of the centers is uncertain. Many contemporary commentators active in the movement trumpeted centers as self-governing and applauded the amount of resident participation in center decision making. But the lack of any concrete evidence of citizen participation in the neighborhood groups, and the comments of more detached observers, suggest strongly that organizing from the bottom up remained, at best, an unfulfilled ideal. Governance structure more closely resembled what Sherry Arnstein calls "partnership"—an organizational structure where professionals and citizens work together for community improvement.[20] But partnership was never very equal. Citizen participation was limited primarily to membership in the clubs and participation in center activities. While club and organization leaders may have participated in the neighborhood group, all concerned seemed willing to leave planning at the centers to the professional organizers who initiated the centers.

Community center organizers were strong proponents of the neighborhood ideal and of decentralization. They felt their goal of promoting solidarity between potentially conflicting groups in the metropolis could be achieved most simply at the neighborhood level. And the public school was the natural site for establishing community organizations in each neighborhood. Community centers, accordingly, were administratively and physically decentralized; that is, each center administered its programs, and all activities were based in a local public school and oriented to the surrounding neighbors.[21]

By 1915, social centers had attracted considerable attention. Charles Evans Hughes, then governor of New York, told center organizers in 1910: "I am more interested in what you are doing than anything else in the world. You are witnessing the foundations of Democracy." The 1912 national campaign platforms of the Democrats, Republicans, and

Progressives all endorsed the social center movement. At the local level, many centers prospered; by 1915, the center initiated at PS 63 in Manhattan became independent of direct financial ties with the People's Institute, achieving, to a noteworthy, if limited, degree, the goal of self-support and self-government.[22]

PROFESSIONAL PLANNING: 1915-1917

A few developments around and after 1915 point to an emerging second stage in the community center movement. The change in community organization practice is most apparent with the formation in 1916 of the National Community Center Association (NCCA) and in the multifaceted efforts of the People's Institute in the Gramercy district of Manhattan. But all centers initiated after 1915 were affected.[23]

Ideological assumptions of community problems shifted subtly. Fear of class conflict and concern with the "leisure-time problem" and the stratified, poorly integrated urban society remained. But organizers were now more concerned with the lack of coordinated social programs and services in neighborhoods, the lack of professional organizations to direct and develop community efforts, and the need to expand community programs beyond the public school in order to plan effectively for the entire community.

Goals shifted accordingly. Organizers now emphasized the need to coordinate social service resources, improve communication between existing services and potential consumers, and train professional community workers.[24] Task goals became more important than process objectives. Concern with community planning and professionalization superceded the earlier objective of neighborhood self-expression. Process goals were not suddenly dropped; nor was the emphasis on integrating neighborhood residents into community institutions forgotten. Community participation remained an ideal. But service delivery and professional coordination of activities took precedence over self-help goals in the years 1915-1917. This is illustrated in a description of the Community Clearing House, an effort designed by the People's Institute to support community center activities in the Gramercy neighborhood.

Through this "neighborhood gateway to all the city's resources of helpfulness" any man, woman, or child, rich or poor, American or alien, can be placed in immediate touch with the service which he needs. He can discuss his trouble, register his complaints at the effective point, and enlist himself as a nonpaid civil servant, helping his nearby or remote neighbors.[25]

Types of programs at community centers continued relatively unchanged. Forums and club meetings, for instance, continued to provide necessary recreational services for neighborhood residents. Additional programs that ultimately preoccupied organizers, however, best exemplify the change in practice to professional planning. The People's Institute, for example, organized a community center in 1915 at PS 40 as but one aspect of a larger project—a model neighborhood in the Gramercy district of Manhattan. The neighborhood plan included coordinating existing social service programs, establishing the Training School for Community Workers and the Community Clearing House, conducting an investigation by health-care professionals into neighborhood health conditions and facilities, as well as running the community center.[26] Furthermore, in 1916, the institute and representatives of other organizations founded the National Community Center Association, a professional group of community organizers and social workers. The association sought to improve the practice of community work and provide direction and unity to decentralized local efforts. But it also reflects clearly the new types of professional-oriented activities that occupied the interests and energies of leaders in the movement.[27]

Changes in organizational structure mirrored the rising professional concerns of organizers. The new emphasis at the centers called for expert and scientific management of community centers. As John Collier, a leader of the People's Institute organizing efforts, declared, "Democracy needs science, and the community movement aims to put science—which means experts—into the people's hands."[28] In practice, however, professionals were supervisors, not advisors. When neighborhood groups were initiated at new centers, professionals and persons prominent in reform efforts, not neighborhood residents, were appointed to fill the positions. New programs, such as the Training School, Clearing House, and NCCA, were service-oriented and were administered and governed completely by professionals. Mary Simkhovitch, a prominent leader of the social settlement movement, saw the trend clearly. In 1917, at the annual meeting of the NCCA, she admonished the audience by noting that only social workers, not center participants, were attending the conference.[29]

Increased administrative centralization was also evident in both the newly developed community centers and the effort to develop a national professional association. In the Gramercy district, People's Institute representatives played an increasingly larger role in the direction of center activities. This was partly attributable to the broader goals and widespread programs in Gramercy; community planning for the entire neighborhood demanded centralized control of all aspects of the plan. The development of the NCCA also reflects the increased centralization. While the association was not intended to supercede the local autonomy of neighborhood centers, the NCCA was initiated by community organizers who saw a need to coordinate and unify neighborhood efforts at the national level. While most community organizers during this period idealized the neighborhood as the natural organizational unit, they were not parochial localists. Rather, they felt that coordination at the national level and increased central direction of local efforts were critical to the success of both the national movement and the local centers.[30]

The third trend in organizational structure was the growing conflict between advocates of privately initiated and funded community centers and those who demanded that these activities be controlled by the public, that is, local government. The NCCA conference of 1916 pivoted on this single issue. Edward Ward, the speaker for the public-support side, attacked the voluntary, self-support advocates, who were led by John Collier of the People's Institute. Influenced by the appeal of Margaret Wilson, the President's daughter, for public support, the conference endorsed Ward's position.[31] But Collier was not completely adverse to or unfamiliar with the trend toward public control of centers. In 1915, the New York City Board of Education established a position of director of community centers. Most community organizers, Collier included, felt that more public supervision of community centers was necessary in view of the rapidly increasing number of centers throughout the city. But despite the decision in favor of public support at the NCCA conference and the expanding role of local governments, centers in New York City remained largely the product of voluntary organizations working under the limited supervision and with the permission of city authorities. Public officials were simply not that interested in community centers at this point.[32]

By 1917, community centers, no longer referred to as social centers, existed throughout the nation.[33] But community organization practice in the centers was distinctly different from the earliest efforts of Ward and Childs. In this second stage, the lack of effective service delivery and community planning replaced community solidarity as the central problem condition; task goals superceded process objectives; consensus strategies persisted, but with less focus on grass-roots organizing and political education; and organizational structure grew more centralized, professional, and bureaucratic.

Why did these changes occur? According to the People's Institute, the initial experiment in community development was a success, and, by 1915, it was necessary for the institute, as an innovator in the newly emerging field of community work, to move on to larger-scale projects such as the efforts in the Gramercy neighborhood and the formation of the NCCA. To some degree, this analysis is valid. As noted before, the social center begun by the institute at PS 63 achieved limited self-support by 1915. Funding from the institute was no longer necessary to maintain the center; the center was now paying for half of its costs, and the other half was paid for by the Board of Education. Based on their assumption that initial goals had been completed, institute professionals sought to expand their program. As Zald and Denton note in their examination of YMCAs, this broadening of goals over time is fairly common.[34]

But with the practice of professional planning, goals and programs were not simply broadened. The more professional and task-goal orientation was the result not only of completing prior goals, as the institute would have asserted, but of the organizers' seeking to implement changes more compatible with their actual goals and abilities.[35] Community development practice shifted to professional planning largely because the initial effort of organizers could not or did not seek to attract citizen participation at the level of decision making. Organizers thus had to shift their goals from developing self-help programs to creating professionally led, service-oriented programs. They shifted from seeking to work *with* to working *for* the neighborhood residents. Organizers undoubtedly sought to expand their programs and increase their effectiveness by adopting the more professional practice. But the shift of practice to professional planning was affected primarily by the lack of commitment to fulfilling the "from-the-bottom-up" goal of community development.[36]

COMMUNITY MOBILIZATION: 1918-1919

The entry of the United States into World War I introduced external factors into the community center movement that sealed certain trends begun in 1915 and altered the direction of others. In late 1917, the Federal Council of National Defense and local subsidiaries at the state and city levels organized a bureaucratic, centralized program to "nationalize neighborhoods" in support of domestic mobilization efforts. The community center movement enthusiastically supported this program, viewing it as official endorsement of the community center idea of organizing citizens and coordinating activities in cities at the neighborhood level.[37]

Obviously, the war altered basic assumptions of problem conditions. Neighborhood issues were de-emphasized as the more pressing national problem of war mobilization was made paramount. According to organizers, society was still too stratified, immigrants remained unassimilated and unrepresented, harmful commercial amusements continued to prosper, and community efforts lacked coordination. But the primary problem was the threat of Germany and the need to mobilize domestic resources against this enemy and in support of the U.S. war victory.

As the problem and the end became simpler and clearer than in prior years, goals became more focused. The mobilization effort demanded a type of community organization practice more dynamic and directed than simply community development or professional planning. Process goals became important again as the war mobilization sought to unite citizens and get them involved. But while organizers devoted much energy to getting residents active at the neighborhood level, the objective was not essentially one of process. Organizers did not encourage neighborhood determination of how or whether residents would support the war. Such activity would have been viewed as subversive. Rather, as before, but even more so now, process goals were designed to serve predetermined task goals. The task of center organizers was to coordinate local agencies and citizens in support of programs developed by the national, state, and city councils of defense.[38]

Programs were altered accordingly: recreation became less important; forums were watched more closely for subversive activities; patriotic propaganda dominated motion picture, civic club, and social club activities. Moreover, community centers became the sites for coordinating war-related activities such as Americanization, Red Cross relief, Liberty Loan drives, soldiers' aid work, and community thrift, food austerity, and nutrition programs.[39] Such programs again reflected the consensus strategy of community organizers—to unite all citizens in the "war to save democracy." But during the war period, the style of conflict tactics was introduced. Unlike a consensus strategy, which assumes a mutuality of interest in society, a conflict or confrontation strategy uses such tactics as protest and agitation to heighten the conflict between antagonistic and contending forces. During the war, an enemy target was the focus of activities, and organizers used extensive agitation and propaganda tactics to mobilize residents against the threat. This conflict style, however, is certainly different from the conflict strategy used by the Communist party in the 1930s or by Saul Alinsky in the 1940s, for example. For the community center movement, the enemy was not only outside the community, it was also beyond the borders of the nation; the goals were social stability and unity at home, not a restructuring of power and resources in the local community; and the programs were not only socially acceptable to, but initiated by the Federal government. The war period thus offers a unique use by the government of conflict style in the service of consensus goals.

Organizational structure reflected the vast changes stimulated by the war and the Council of National Defense. Administrative and political centralization was formalized. National, state, and city councils of defense provided personnel, direction, and supervision of neighborhood community center activities. One participant at the National Conference of Social Work in 1919 hoped, for example, that the "new community organization" of the war period would centralize and strengthen organizations, "swinging them in a solid front in one attack after another upon the pressing and urgent needs of the hour."[40]

Likewise, the move to public supervision of centers was accomplished during the war. In New York City, the Mayor's Council of Defense coordinated community programs on a citywide basis, and city officials were appointed to serve on neighborhood groups.[41] Self-support was still encouraged, but public funding achieved wider acceptance, and government control increased dramatically. During the war, thirteen states passed laws providing for the financing of community center activities by public taxation.[42]

The trend toward increased professional control of center activities was also furthered during the war. At PS 40 in the Gramercy district, twenty-eight professional representatives from public and private war-related agencies were appointed to the center's decision-making body. Community councils, the governing bodies at centers during the war, consisted of members appointed from above "and ratification by any more generally representative local body was said to be largely nominal."[43]

Centers prospered in a sense during the war years. Many commentators noted that the goals of developing "community action," "cooperative collectivism," and a concern for "mutual welfare" were facilitated at the local level by the demands and programs of the war.[44] Furthermore, the number of activities multiplied, and funds increased. The extent of co-ordination between agencies and recipients was unprecedented.[45] Community centers expanded throughout the nation. In 1919, one survey estimated, community centers were operating in more than 107 cities, not to mention the vast number of centers in communities with populations under five thousand people.[46] The whole "community movement" achieved widespread recognition and prestige during the war, recalled Jesse Steiner, the author of the first major study of community organization. While the word "community" was used infrequently prior to 1917, during the war it became a "magic talisman of value in dealing with social problems." As the power of government grew, Steiner added, "the local community took on a new significance for a democratic people unaccustomed to the inevitable centralization of the war period."[47]

Organizing practice had changed quickly and noticeably since 1917. Entry into the war altered assumptions of problem conditions and goals; strategy remained reformist, but the demands of mobilizing citizens to support the war encouraged a conflict-style approach; and, continuing and accelerating trends since 1907, organizational structure became highly centralized, professional, and bureaucratic. But whereas earlier shifts in practice were the result largely of internal developments, the shift from professional planning to community mobilization reflected the effect of a national, supralocal event.

COMMUNITY SERVICE: 1920-1930

The end of the war ushered in a new stage in organizing practice. Despite the hopes and efforts of reformers, postwar social reconstruction never became a national priority. The Council of National Defense bureaucracy was quickly dismantled, and voluntary organizations returned to more private and charitable activities. In 1920, the People's Institute, faced with declining funds and new leaders with little interest in social reform, withdrew completely from community organization work.[48] Nevertheless, the community center movement continued to expand; the number of cities operating centers more than doubled, from 107 in 1919 to 240 in 1924. Throughout the 1920s, community centers remained a significant element of community organization work from coast to coast. But the practice of community organization continued to change.

After the war, organizers viewed "urban disorganization" as the central problem condition. Urban disorganization was a catchall term for the negative social products of urban-industrial growth.[49] Among those problems noted most often were rapid social and geographic mobility, unassimilated immigrants, the superficiality of personal contacts, the decline in importance of neighborhood-based activities, the breakdown of community solidarity, and the growth of "crowd behavior."[50]

This "tangled web of modern urban life" required the "conscious organization of social forces," Eleanor Glueck asserted in her 1924 study of school centers.[51] As in the initial stage of community development, organizers in this period encouraged process goals to counteract urban stratification. Reacting against wartime experiences, organizers wanted to de-emphasize the service-oriented, bureaucratic trends of professional planning and community mobilization. Echoing the earlier sentiments of Clinton Childs, center organizers said that the function of centers "was not so much to hand down traditions, values, principles nor morals, but rather to form a matrix in which new values could be worked out by neighbors facing a new social situation."[52] But, as before, though certainly less so than during the war, organizers entered the community with specific goals in mind. While community work in the 1920s was labeled an "essential and continuous process," the primary goal of organizers was not to encourage self-help but actually to integrate, coordinate, and adjust groups of people "in the interest of efficiency and unity of action."[53]

Program offerings in the 1920s differed markedly from those of the war years: school community centers became synonymous in the public's mind with athletic programs; and activities related to social and political issues were few and far between.[54] In New York and other cities, two types of centers developed after the war: government "official centers" and private "permit centers." Official centers concentrated on athletic programs and typified the movement in the 1920s and thereafter. Permit centers were open fewer evenings each week, but tended to sponsor more political discussions and social clubs. Neither, however, initiated or supported local efforts to "organize the community comprehensively." While the programs of the 1920s emphasized "expressive releasing" activities more than ever before, this approach was consistent with the consensus strategies and programs of earlier years.[55]

From its inception, activists in the community center movement were ambivalent about organizational structure. Like most professionals, they preferred autonomy, decentralized authority structures, and limited standardization and bureaucratization. They wanted as much personal freedom as possible. But they also wanted the resources and power that came with centralized, government support of centers. Local officials were equally uncertain. They liked the power and standardization that accompanied their active participation, but preferred the cost-saving features of center self-support and self-government.[56] In the 1920s, fresh from the bureaucratic experience of World War I, local officials came to accept community centers as part of city government's responsibility to supply social and recreational services. While community organizers remained ambivalent, local officials implemented a highly centralized and bureaucratic structure run by professionals who were appointed by city politicians. Meaningful grass-roots participation was nonexistent.

As local governments expanded their control and support of centers, the role of private groups declined. Private groups wholly administered only 7 percent of all centers in cities. Public funds supported all activities at 44 percent of urban community centers, while 89 percent were financed at least partially by tax revenues. In New York City, while the number of permit centers exceeded official centers 225 to 68 in 1927 and 351 to 118 in 1930, the total aggregate attendance at the permit centers declined from 1,126,955 to 1,095,058; whereas, at the official centers, there was a striking increase in attendance from 3,356,312 to 4,379,792. Official centers were better staffed and organized, but the primary reason for the large attendance was that they possessed the physical resources to offer many more activities, especially athletic programs.[57]

Many commentators found this trend distressing. They felt that the relative decline of privately controlled centers ran counter to the goals of developing cooperation and democracy at the community level. They were upset as well by the standardization and restrictions that accompanied bureaucratization. And yet, community organizers writing about these developments knew that the expanded public role was critical to maintaining centers and providing extensive recreational services in urban areas.[58]

Centralization accompanied bureaucratization. Centers were physically decentralized, but administrative and political centralization was the norm, continuing the pattern formalized by World War I. Decision making, especially at official centers, remained highly centralized as boards of education or parks and recreation departments assumed ever-greater control over community centers.[59]

Reflecting general attitudes of the decade, practitioners of community organization were skeptical and critical of earlier efforts. They ridiculed the simplistic, idealistic notions of "uplifters" prior to 1920. They sought to develop a more sophisticated, scientific approach—a more professional approach—to the practice of community organization. Community organization began to be viewed as a subdiscipline of the emerging field of social work, complete with its own extensive literature, methodology, and theoreticians such as Clarence Perry, Leroy Bowman, and Jesse Steiner.[60] In theory, organizers still sought to develop a partnership with community residents. But, as Bowman suggested, serving the complex needs of communities now superceded the question of democratic decision making. Professional community workers remained open to resident participation in leadership

> if the need is felt and the leadership arises [from the community]. This is a far cry from the community religion of a few years ago when the drive was on to go out and get people into community organizations, democratic in the extreme and supposedly dominated by neighborly sentiments.[61]

What Bowman viewed as the religion of ultrademocracy was replaced, in the 1920s, by the ideal of an efficient and effective community organization led by sensitive and responsive professionals. Indigenous leadership in most types of community organizations, one "ultrademocrat" reported, was nonexistent or, at best, nominal. And the same was true for community centers. The process of formalization, especially at official centers, was accompanied by an increase in the number and role of paid professional staff. Organizers were aware of at least some of the problems inherent in both increasing professionalism and declining resident participation, but in the 1920s most accepted professional leadership as a fait accompli.[62]

In many ways, the school community center movement had come full circle by 1930. The first social centers were initiated by Ward and the People's Institute in response to the limits of school recreational centers. Recreational centers provided only recreational facilities and were governed, administered, and financed by reluctant and unpredictable local officials. Social centers were intended to develop a broader program rooted in resident participation and support. Now, altered by developments in the 1920s, centers were again largely recreational facilities administered and supported by local government bodies.[63]

Why these changes occurred in the 1920s defies simple explanation. Many of the developments reflect an oft-noted tendency of organizations to bureaucratization and formalization; in this case, both were stimulated by the war and were institutionalized in the 1920s. But there was more at work here than a natural order of organizational development. Of primary importance was the conservatism of the decade. The postwar years were generally hostile to social reform efforts. Organizers found little support, financial or otherwise, for their social change programs. Government-sponsored programs, even more than private ones, encouraged athletic, not political, activities. Community center goals, programs, and structures mirrored the "return to normalcy." The same was true in the social work profession. As Lubove notes, social work in the 1920s was characterized by the bureaucratic goals of efficiency and expert leadership. Of all social welfare practitioners, community workers were most inclined to criticize such goals. Glueck asserted, for example, that the one-dimensional, bureaucratic center of the 1920s opposed "the ideals set for it by leaders of the community organization movement." But most community workers were imbued with the new professional and more conservative values, and they were either unaware of or unwilling to challenge the departure from earlier objectives of the community center movement.[64]

CONCLUSION

The general sequence of community organization practice illustrated by the community center movement is as follows. Community development changed into professional planning as centers achieved legitimacy, began to broaden goals, but failed to enlist meaningful citizen participation. Professional planning developed into community mobilization as a drastic change occurred in objective conditions—namely, U.S. entry into World War I—and as a national bureaucratic structure was imposed on the community center movement. Community mobilization practice shifted into community service as the maintenance of centers became an accepted and expected responsibility of local government and as the climate for social reform efforts deteriorated. In sum, efforts quickly developed into professionally run, social service organizations, and, except for a deviation caused by World War I, that pattern continued from 1915 through the 1920s.

While the specifics of the sequence and the causes for the changes in practice are unique to the community center movement, other studies describe a similar shift from a grass-roots, democratic organizing practice to a bureaucratic community service function. Of Rothman's three types of community organization practice noted at the outset of this paper, the community center movement demonstrates a shift from a practice resembling "locality development" to one similar to "community planning." Philip Selznick, in his study of the Tennessee Valley Authority, sees a similar pattern resulting from both the need to co-opt local constituents and the power struggle that ensued. Piven and Cloward, in their recent work on four social movements since 1930, describe comparable changes produced by the dislike of organizers for spontaneous social movements and their preference for formal, structured organizations.[65] The Community Action programs of the 1960s supply a more recent example. CAPs, like community centers, failed in their stated objective to organize residents and to promote community self-development. The final product in the Community Action programs was the formal acceptance of the social service functions of the program, not the initially stated grass-roots organizing of "maximum feasible participation."[66]

The pattern underlines the essence of this type of community organization program. Organizations initiated by liberal, social welfare professionals serve a primary role as interest groups on behalf of and as test cases for the official adoption of social service programs. When the value of the program is acknowledged, the social change, grass-roots orientation is replaced by an almost complete preoccupation with delivering the social services. Community workers such as those who organized the first community centers may have hoped to do more in the way of community organizing, but social service delivery best suited their reformist vision and goals, consensus strategies, scanty resources and power, and professional orientation.

NOTES

1. A representative sample could include George Frederickson, ed., *Neighborhood Control in the 1970s* (New York: Chandler Publishing, 1973); Howard Hallman, *Neighborhood Control of Public Programs* (New York: Praeger Publishing, 1970); Hans Spiegel, ed., *Citizen Participation in Urban Development* (Washington, D.C.: National Training Laboratories Institute for Applied Behavioral Science, 1968); and David Morris and Karl Hess, *Neighborhood Power: The New Localism* (Boston: Beacon Press, 1975).

2. Secondary sources with a pre-1950s historical perspective of community organization include: Fred M. Cox and Charles Garvin, "Community Organization Practice, 1865-1973," in *Strategies of Community Organization: A Book of Readings,* ed. Fred Cox et al. (Itasca, Ill.: F. E. Peacock Publishers, 1974); James Dahir, *The Neighborhood Unit Plan: Its Spread and Acceptance* (New York: Russell Sage Foundation, 1947); Sidney Dillick, *Community Organization for Neighborhood Development: Past and Present* (New York: William Morrow, 1953); Arthur Dunham, *The New Community Organization* (New York: Thomas Y. Crowell, 1970); Howard Hallman, "The Neighborhood as an Organizational Unit: A Historical Perspective," in *Neighborhood Control,* ed. Frederickson; Douglas Yates, *Neighborhood Democracy: The Politics and Impacts of Decentralization* (Lexington, Mass.: Lexington Books, 1973); Michael J. Austin and Neil Betten, "Intellectual

Origins of Community Organizing, 1920-1939," *Social Service Review* 51 (March 1977): 155-70.

3. For an invaluable historical overview of the process of defining community organization, see Meyer Schwartz, "Community Organization," in *Encyclopedia of Social Work*, ed. Harry Lurie (New York: National Association of Social Work, 1965), pp. 177-89.

4. I have found the work of Jack Rothman especially helpful, most specifically, "Three Models of Community Organization Practice," in *Strategies*, ed. Cox et al., pp. 22-39. Also see Rothman, *Planning and Organizing for Social Change: Action Principles from Social Science Research* (New York: Columbia University Press, 1974). Other valuable essays that address the problem of developing models of community organization practice include: Arthur Hillman and Frank Seever, "Elements of Neighborhood Organization," in *Strategies*, ed. Cox et al., pp. 273-88; Martin Rein and Robert Morris, "Goals, Structures and Strategies for Community Change," *Social Welfare Forum, 1962, Proceedings of the National Conference on Social Welfare* (New York: Columbia University Press, 1962); and Jesse Steiner, *Community Organization: A Study of Its Theory and Current Practice* (New York: D. Appleton-Century, 1930).

5. Studying only four variables is limiting. Rothman, "Three Models" examines twelve variables without attempting to address, as I do, questions of organizational structure.

6. Two qualifiers to this proposed periodization should be noted. First, while each period is relatively distinct, as Rothman notes for his typology, a degree of mixing and overlapping of types of practice is apparent throughout the case study. Second, this study generalizes from the case studies and national surveys used. Experiences of individual centers varied: not all went through the four stages. For those that did, the time period for each type was not as neat as this paper seems to suggest. Nevertheless, while there is a good deal of diversity in the history of each center, most followed a pattern similar to the one outlined here.

7. For example, see Mary Parker Follett, *The New State: Group Organization, the Solution of Popular Government* (New York: Longmans, Green, 1918). Follett served as vice-president of the National Community Center Association in 1917.

8. On the development of the recreation movement in public schools, see Clarence Rainwater, *The Play Movement in the United States: A Study of Community Recreation* (Chicago: University of Chicago Press, 1921).

9. On the work of the People's Institute, see Robert Fisher, "The

People's Institute of New York City, 1897-1934: Culture, Progressive Democracy, and the People" (Ph.D. dissertation, New York University, 1974).

10. Edward Ward, *The Social Center* (New York: Appleton, 1913); Eleanor T. Glueck, *The Community Use of Schools* (Baltimore: Williams and Wilkins, 1927), p. 20. For a similar analysis, see City of New York, Superintendent of Schools, *Fourteenth Annual Report* (1911-1912), p. 9.

11. Fisher, "People's Institute," Chapters IX and X. Woodrow Wilson, speaking in 1911 before a conference on social center development, noted that, while "the study of the civic center is the study of the spontaneous life of communities," the goal was to solve the problem of modern "disconnected" society, which lacked communication mechanisms between "portions of the community" and democratic problem-solving capacities to eliminate "misunderstanding," "hostilities," and "deadly rivalries." Arthur Link, ed., *The Papers of Woodrow Wilson,* vol. 23, *1911-1912* (Princeton: Princeton University Press, 1977), pp. 481-82.

12. See Rothman, "Three Models"; Rein and Morris, "Goals, Structure . . ."; Irving Spergel, *Community Problem Solving* (Chicago: University of Chicago Press, 1968).

13. Clinton S. Childs, "A Year's Experiment in Social Center Organization: An Account of the Activities Conducted in Public School 63, Manhattan" (pamphlet printed by the New York Social Center Committee for the Wider Use of School Properties, 1912). See also Jean Quandt, *From the Small Town to the Great Community: The Social Thought of Progressive Intellectuals* (New Brunswick, N.J.: Rutgers University Press, 1970), p. 49.

14. For a discussion of the role of legitimation and "informal cooptation" in a community organization, see Philip Selznick, *TVA and the Grass Roots: A Study in the Sociology of Formal Organizations* (Berkeley: University of California, 1949).

15. Clarence Perry and Marguerita Williams, *New York School Centers and Their Community Policy* (New York: Russell Sage Foundation, 1931). Childs and Ward were community secretaries in their respective centers. Childs was elected; Ward was appointed by the Board of Education.

16. Steiner, *Community Organization,* p. 183.

17. People's Institute of New York City, *Annual Reports,* 1913-1915.

18. Ward, *Social Center,* pp. 199-200; Blake McKelvey, *Rochester: The Quest for Quality, 1890-1925* (Cambridge, Mass.: Harvard University Press, 1956), pp. 102-107. Within three years after the inception of social centers in Rochester, public appropriation for centers had in-

creased to $20,000, and centers had been established in eighteen public schools. The cuts in appropriations by the "boss" faction were so severe that, in March 1911, centers were closed in Rochester because of a lack of funds. Steiner, *Community Organization,* p. 184.

19. Steiner, *Community Organization,* p. 187. This was especially true after the election in 1913 of the fiscal conservative John P. Mitchel as mayor of New York City.

20. Sherry R. Arnstein, "A Ladder of Citizen Participation," *Journal of the American Institute of Planners* 35 (July 1969): 216-24.

21. For a discussion of varieties of decentralization, see Howard W. Hallman, *Small and Large Together: Governing the Metropolis* (Beverly Hills: Sage Publications, 1977), especially pp. 113-14.

22. Harvey W. Zorbaugh, *The Gold Coast and the Slum* (Chicago: University of Chicago Press, 1948), p. 202; Allen Davis, *Spearheads for Reform: The Social Settlements and the Progressive Movement* (New York: Oxford University Press, 1967), p. 81.

23. The "Gramercy district," according to the People's Institute, included School District 10, extending from 9th St. to 29th St. on the east side of Manhattan. Clinton Childs said the area had a population of some eighty-five thousand. PS 40, the institute's community center in this district, was located in the northern part of the area, on East 20th St.

24. From the first use of the term "community organization" in the early 1910s, community organizers sought the correlation of organizations and activities as one of their major goals. Initially, in the community center movement, this goal was played down in favor of process objectives. See Monna Heath and Arthur Dunham, *Trends in Community Organization: A Study of Papers on Community Organization Published by the National Conference on Social Welfare, 1874-1960* (Chicago: University of Chicago Social Service Monographs, 1963), especially p. 33.

25. People's Institute, *Annual Report,* 1918, p. 40.

26. Fisher, "People's Institute," pp. 322-23 as well as Chapters 9 and 10. In addition, the institute conducted a large-scale survey in the Gramercy district into the causes of juvenile delinquency in order to convince the NYC Board of Estimate of the need for play streets and community centers. This demonstrates, again, the planning and service orientation of the organizers during this period. Surveys were conducted by the institute before 1913 as a method of supporting planning objectives; thus, even in the period of community development, community recreational planning was a major facet of the institute's neighborhood work. It was, however, more pronounced after 1915 and especially so in the Gramercy "model" neighborhood.

27. See Robert Fisher, "Community Organizing and Citizen Participation: The Efforts of the People's Institute in New York City, 1910-1920," *Social Service Review* 51 (September 1977), for more information on the founding of the NCCA.

28. John Collier, "The Dynamics of the Community Movement," *The Community Center* (February 1917), p. 12. *The Community Center* can be found in the New York Public Library.

29. Fisher, "Community Organizing," p. 480; *Proceedings of the National Community Center Association,* 1917, Leroy Bowman MSS, Columbia University.

30. While most organizers saw the neighborhood as the ideal local unit, they were not "parochial localists." This interpretation runs counter to Quandt, *From Small Town.* Quandt details the limitation of the "neighborhood vision" held by such intellectuals and activists as Mary Parker Follett, Charles Horton Cooley, Jane Addams, and John Dewey.

31. *New York Times,* April 21, 1916, p. 118. For a more complete statement of the goals of conference organizers, see "National Conference on Community Centers and Related Problems: Summary of the Tentative Findings of Special Committees" (pamphlet printed by the New York Training School for Community Workers).

32. By 1918 there were eighty or so community centers in New York City. People's Institute, *Annual Report,* 1918, p. 19; Perry and Williams, *New York School Centers,* p. 26.

33. It is difficult to determine the number of community centers nationally because the best source of statistics for this period includes all school center activities held in public schools after hours. See Clarence A. Perry, *School Extension Statistics* (Washington, D.C.: Government Printing Office, 1917).

34. Initially, the institute funded the PS 63 effort. By 1915, the center was paying for half its costs and the other half was picked up by the Board of Education. Mayer N. Zald and Patricia Denton, "From Evangelism to General Service: The Transformation of the YMCA," *Administrative Science Quarterly* 8 (September 1963): 214-34.

35. Rothman, *Planning and Organizing,* pp. 438-39.

36. There is no evidence to suggest that organizers turned to professional planning out of frustration with trying and failing to get resident participation in these working-class neighborhoods. Regarding the nature of the neighborhoods in which the institute organized community centers, the area around PS 40 on East 20th St. had a much higher percentage of natives and middle-class professionals than did the PS 63 neighborhood on East 4th St. Both neighborhoods, however, had sizable foreign-born,

working-class populations. While many centers in urban areas may have
been based in middle-class neighborhoods, the large majority were situated
in poorer areas where organized activities and associations were less
common or less accessible and where organizers felt they could have a
greater impact.

37. Fisher, "Community Organizing," p. 482.

38. See John Collier, "Community Councils: Democracy Every Day,"
The Survey 40 (August 31, September 21, and September 28, 1918),
pp. 604-606, 689-91, 709-11, 725; Heath and Dunham, *Trends in Community Organization,* p. 31. As Clarence Perry noted, Collier had a
tendency to credit centers with abilities not demonstrated in actual
practice. Letter, Clarence A. Perry to Mr. Glenn, May 8, 1916, Russell
Sage Foundation, Perry MSS.

39. Wingate Community Center, *Annual Report,* 1917-1918, pp. 1-2;
Fisher, "Community Organizing," pp. 482-83.

40. Heath and Dunham, *Trends in Community Organization,* p. 31.
Also, see Mildred V. Bennett, "Community Council Study for New York
City" (March 1919), in *Proceedings,* ed. Leroy Bowman MSS, Columbia
University.

41. The New York City Council of National Defense had a general
director based in the Municipal Building, a director for each borough,
boroughs divided into zones, and zones divided into local councils.
In addition, close public supervision of center activities was exercised.
See Bennett, "Community Council"; Fisher, "Community Organizing."

42. Glueck, *Community Use,* p. 32. The states included: Minnesota,
New Hampshire, Massachusetts, New York, Delaware, Alabama, West
Virginia, Ohio, Michigan, North Dakota, Iowa, Utah, and California.

43. People's Institute, *Annual Report,* 1918, p. 25; Dillick, *Community Organization,* p. 74.

44. Glueck, *Community Use,* p. 133; Quandt, *From Small Town,*
pp. 141-44; Zorbaugh, *Gold Coast,* pp. 204-06.

45. Jesse Steiner, "Community Organization: A Study of Its Rise
and Tendencies," *Journal of Social Forces* 1 (November 1922): 15.

46. Glueck, *Community Use,* pp. 36-40.

47. Jesse Steiner, "An Appraisal of the Community Movement,"
Journal of Social Forces 7 (March 1929): 336.

48. Fisher, "Community Organizing," pp. 483-84.

49. Arthur Hillman, *Community Organization and Planning* (New York:
Macmillan, 1950), p. 137; Quandt, *From Small Town,* pp. 152-53.

50. Leroy Bowman, "Population Mobility and Community Organiza-

tion: Sources and Methods," in *The Urban Community*, ed. Ernest W. Burgess (Chicago: University of Chicago Press, 1926); Zorbaugh, *Gold Coast*, especially p. 16; Steiner, "Appraisal of the Community Movement," pp. 338-41; Glueck, *Community Use*, especially p. 2; Jesse Steiner, "Community Organization and the Crowd Spirit," *Journal of Social Forces* 1 (March 1923): 221-26.

51. Glueck, *Community Use*, pp. 2, 124.

52. "One Difference Between the Community Center and the Other Community Organizations," *Social Forces* 7 (September 1928): 97.

53. Steiner, *Community Organization*, p. 170.

54. Glueck, *Community Use*, pp. 113-14, 134. For example, in 1919-1920, the center at PS 40 in Manhattan was sponsoring five types of activities on six evenings per week. By 1930, the center had only two types of activities—athletics and club meetings—and was open only two evenings per week. Clarence A. Perry, *School Center Gazette, 1919-1920* (pamphlet published by Russell Sage Recreation Department); Clarence A. Perry and Marguerita Williams, *New York School Centers*, p. 56. Also, Glueck's survey recorded that in cities of over five thousand people, recreational activities occurred in 72 percent of the centers, civic activities in 15 percent, and educational/cultural activities in approximately 12 percent.

55. Perry and Williams, *New York School Centers*, pp. 44-48; Clarence Perry, "Ten Years of the Community Center Movement" (pamphlet printed by Russell Sage Foundation, 1921), pp. 4-5; Steiner, *Community Organization*, pp. 393-94.

56. Rothman, *Planning and Organizing*, p. 165; Quandt, *From Small Town*, pp. 146-49; Steiner, *Community Organization*, p. 199.

57. Glueck, *Community Use*, pp. 82-84, 100-101; Perry and Williams, *New York School Centers*, pp. 44-49.

58. Glueck, *Community Use*, p. 83; Perry and Williams, *New York School Centers*, p. 28.

59. "Policy of New York City Board of Education in Reference to Forums," *NCCA Members Bulletin*, February 1926, p. 7, Bowman MSS.

60. Glueck, *Community Use*, pp. 35-38; Roy Lubove, *The Professional Altruist: The Emergence of Social Work as a Career, 1880-1930* (New York: Atheneum, 1975); Leroy Bowman, "The 1929 Content of the Community Concept," *Journal of Social Forces* 7 (March 1929): 407-09; Leroy Bowman, "Community Progress: Developments in Community Organization," *Social Forces* 5 (September 1926): 91-94; Zorbaugh, *Gold Coast*, pp. 211-18.

61. *The Community Center,* January-February 1921, p. 6; Leroy Bowman, "Community Organization," *American Journal of Sociology* 35 (May 1930): 1008.

62. Glueck, *Community Use,* p. 84; Steiner, *Community Organization,* p. 384; John Daniels, *America via the Neighborhood* (New York: Harper and Brothers, 1920).

63. Leroy Bowman, "Community Centers," in *Social Work Yearbook,* 1933, ed. Fred Hall (New York: Russell Sage Foundation, 1933), pp. 91-93; Jesse Steiner, "Community Centers," in *Encyclopaedia of the Social Sciences,* vol. 4, ed. Edwin R. A. Seligman (New York: Macmillan, 1931), pp. 105-06.

64. Lubove, *Professional Altruist;* Glueck, *Community Use,* pp. 145-46. Other sources point to efforts of local officials, businessmen, and religious leaders to dilute or abolish political orientation of centers. Zorbaugh, *Gold Coast,* pp. 215-20; Steiner, *Community Organization,* pp. 67-72, 345.

65. Rothman, "Three Models"; Philip Selznick, *TVA and the Grass Roots;* Frances Fox Piven and Richard A. Cloward, *Poor People's Movements* (New York: Pantheon Books, 1977).

66. Personal experience as neighborhood representative, Cambridge Economic Opportunity Committee, 1974-1976; Frances Fox Piven and Richard A. Cloward, *Regulating the Poor: The Functions of Public Welfare* (New York: Random House, 1971); Marcie Laden, "The Great Society's Anti-Poverty Program: A Case Study of the Schenectady Community Action Program" (unpublished B.A. thesis, Union College, 1978).

"A Cluster of Interlacing Communities": The Cincinnati Social Unit Plan and Neighborhood Organization, 1900-1920

PATRICIA MOONEY MELVIN

The "urban crisis" of the 1960s generated concern about the urban environment as a whole as well as its component parts. Part of this concern manifested itself in a fascination with utilizing the neighborhood as a "testing ground" for solutions to contemporary problems. As part of Lyndon Johnson's War on Poverty, numerous "community action programs," designed to stimulate resident participation in neighborhood affairs and to foster "working relationships" among the different groups active in the neighborhood, sprung up in a variety of American communities. But interest in the neighborhood as a base to promote "maximum feasible participation" is not new; its roots reach back to the first decades of the twentieth century. During those years, individuals concerned about urban conditions labored to involve all neighborhood residents in local organizations that promised fuller services as well as the potential for social change. Adopting the organic analogy that was popular in descriptions of society, activists viewed the city as an interdependent system of complementary parts. Guided by a biological conception of interdependence, they sought to translate their beliefs into a workable system of urban organization. Their attempt to organize cities and neighborhoods along the lines of interdependence and cooperation constitutes the first community organization movement.

Late-nineteenth-century America experienced extraordinary urban growth, geographic specialization of land use, and high rates of internal migration. The convergence of these trends "disrupted" society, and stimulated many Americans to search for a way to cope with the "new society."[1] They wanted a conceptual resolution for what they perceived as a lack of harmony between the different groups and interests jockeying for secure positions. They began to look for an organized body of ideas through which to understand and to direct society. By the 1880s, the notion of interdependence had captured their imagination.[2] Interdependence, generally expressed in terms of an organic analogy, soon dominated turn-of-the century thought. While not everyone championed the new beliefs, many Americans began to accept the idea that no part of life could be viewed in isolation, and that all parts were interrelated in a larger whole.[3]

Students of urban areas began to see the city as an organically interdependent unit as well. They groped for a new image or definition of the urban landscape to replace the older and seemingly inapplicable image that described urban areas as collections of amorphous groups of individuals. They abandoned the notion of the city as a residential community composed of congeries of densely settled individuals joined together by a "quest for economic expansion and social improvements,"[4] and began to see the city as an interdependent system of differentiated but complementary parts. While each of these parts, or neighborhoods, exhibited differences, proponents of the organic view stressed the existence of a symbiotic relationship between the local units and the city as a whole. According to Boston's South End House director, Robert A. Woods, the organic city was

> a cluster of interlacing communities, each having its own vital ways of expression and action, but all together creating the municipality which shall render the fullest service through the most spirited participation of all its citizens.[5]

Insisting that the well-being of the whole depended upon the health of the parts, numerous groups, among them public-health activists, settlement workers, and community organizers, attempted to organize neighborhoods and to establish systems designed to facilitate communication between the city and its constituent parts.

Advocates of the organic, or interdependent, city believed that city life could not be understood, nor its problems met, unless the process began in the neighborhood. Just as the city was seen as a distinct unit within a larger organic society, it was also viewed as being composed of a "bunch of communities," or units. As the fundamental social unit, the neighborhood was seen as an "elaborate nexus of interrelations, needs, and ambitions." Sufficiently small enough to be comprehensible to and manageable for the average citizen, it was at the same time large enough "to include, in essence, practically all the problems of the city, state, and nation.[6] As epitomes of the city, the neighborhoods were believed to provide "handy laboratories for social inquiry."[7]

Those working in the neighborhoods, arguing that once Americans "knew how to be one neighborhood they would then know how to be one nation,"[8] championed a variety of programs designed to develop more fully the neighborhood as a vital part of the city, and to foster a high degree of concern for the city and, ultimately, the nation as a whole. These programs, which were loosely covered by the term "community organization," represented an attempt to effect the "reconstruction, expansion, and integration" of neighborhood and community life.[9] The activities all sought resident participation in discovering and solving neighborhood problems, and included the establishment of settlement houses, school centers, community councils, and social unit organizations.[10]

Of all the activities that focused on organizing neighborhoods, Wilbur C. Phillips's Social Unit Organization represents the quintessential example of the attempt to organize neighborhoods "to function properly as a part of the city."[11] More than most of his contemporaries, Phillips tried to bring the neighborhood into the "stuff of American life," and to provide residents with the potential to better the community.[12] On the basis of his experiences with the New York Milk Committee and the Milwaukee Child Welfare Commission, Phillips devised an organizational scheme built around grouping experts and citizens on the neighborhood level in order to foster the continual interaction between the "forces of democracy" and those of "specialism."[13] He proposed to divide the neighborhood into occupational and citizen groups that would meet regularly to ascertain needs and allocate community resources to meet those needs, making the neighborhood unit into a "well-constituted community" within the larger city. From 1917 to 1920, Phillips attempted to demonstrate the feasibility of organizing neighborhood residents in this way, as citizens and experts, in the Mohawk-Brighton district of Cincinnati.

Phillips first began his neighborhood work in New York City,

with the New York Milk Committee (NYMC).[14] As secretary of the
organization from 1906 to 1911, he helped to mobilize community resources for a campaign against infant mortality. Like many others who
were active in the early twentieth-century crusade against infant mortality,[15] Phillips found that programs that focused narrowly on cleaning up
the physical environment in which milk was produced failed to bring
down the high rates of infant mortality. He began to look beyond the
physical environment, and started to concentrate on the people within
that environment.[16] Once he realized that infant mortality resulted from
more than "dirty milk," Phillips transferred his emphasis from "milk
to motherhood."[17]

Stressing social, personal, and environmental aspects of community
health, under Phillips's direction, the NYMC infant milk stations not
only dispensed "clean" milk, but also offered maternal education in the
principles of child hygiene. The work in the NYMC's milk depots exem-
plified the shift from milk to motherhood, and helped to publicize the
fact that concerted programs focusing both on the environment and on
the child could help in lowering the infant death rate and in promoting
infant health and welfare.[18] The activities undertaken in the milk stations
in the fight for human welfare pointed to the interdependence of the
environment and the child.

But Phillips soon became restive working within the confines of the
New York Milk Committee. Unfortunately for Phillips, the committee's
program consisted of more than the milk depot work; it also included
cleaning up the milk environment, which required Phillips to devise programs for securing a pure and inexpensive milk supply and for regulating
milk standards. Because of this twofold program, the committee could
not divert all its resources to the milk depots. As a result, and despite
the new direction taken in the stations, the NYMC's work fell short of
Phillips's growing expectations.

While caring for those infants whose mothers sought help or who
were accidently brought to the attention of the depot workers, the New
York Milk Committee failed to seek and reach every mother and every
baby in the areas served by each milk station. Phillips wanted the depot
personnel to contact every mother and infant, and to attack infant health
problems on the basis of the community rather than by focusing only
on random individual cases. If it were able to establish a close and continuing relationship with the mothers, Phillips believed, the depot would

grow into a social center and, as he told members of the Child Welfare Conference for Research and Development in 1909, would "radiate the influences of education and social betterment," thus improving the whole environment of the child. On the basis of his work with the NYMC, he also looked beyond efforts in a single neighborhood. He felt that such work, if duplicated in neighborhoods across the city, would provide the base for a thorough, citywide child-welfare program. Each part of the city would contribute to the well-being of the larger whole.[19]

When an opportunity came to organize a child-welfare program in Milwaukee in 1911, Phillips left the New York Milk Committee and traveled west. In Milwaukee, as secretary of the Child Welfare Commission, a semiprivate organization under the aegis of the municipal government, Phillips attempted to construct a child-welfare program that more closely matched his desire for a "total" child-health program. Building upon the lessons learned in New York City, Phillips sought to organize a neighborhood—St. Cyril's Parish—for community-oriented infant-health services. This service operated from the commission's baby station located in the heart of the parish. He and his corps of local doctors, nurses, midwives, and residents tried to bring knowledge of proper infant care into every home, to coordinate the activities of the numerous organizations that touched on child welfare in the neighborhood, and to involve the local residents in planning their own health programs. No other agency in the country provided such intensive preventive care as did the health center in St. Cyril's Parish.[20] A change in the municipal administration, however, resulted in the creation of a Division of Child Welfare under the auspices of the Health Department, and in the dissolution of the Child Welfare Commission.[21] Phillips returned to the East, reviewed his experiences, and pondered the possibilities and techniques of both health and community organization.

On the basis of his experiences with the New York Milk Committee and with the Child Welfare Commission, Phillips developed his theory of community organization. In his 1914 treatise, entitled "The Plan for Social Organization or the Unit Method of Gradually Building Up a Complete System for Studying and Meeting Social Needs," Phillips laid out his organizational scheme.[22] The plan centered around the establishment of a "democratic" structure through which citizens could participate directly in the control of community affairs while at the same time making use of the highest technical skills available. According to Phillips's plan, this structure was to be set up first in "the basic unit of national life, the neighborhood."[23] He visualized the nation as a grand union of neighborhoods, which, when linked together, comprised cities, counties, states, and, ultimately, the nation as a whole. Learning to function "intelligently" and democratically within the confines of the neighborhood allowed Americans to understand society, to participate more fully in its operation, and to enjoy the fruits of living in a democracy.[24] Believing, as did many of his contemporaries, that the neighborhood was small enough to be manageable and comprehensible, and large enough to reflect the needs of the entire community, Phillips devised a system that utilized the neighborhood as a "laboratory unit" to coordinate needs and resources for all.[25]

Although the organization Phillips proposed in his Social Unit Plan was more developed than those of many of his contemporaries, the thrust of his proposals reflected a general fascination, among Progressive reformers, with the notion of a cooperative society. During the early twentieth century, political theorists, most particularly Herbert Croly, argued that the American political system failed to meet the American citizens' particular needs while at the same time remaining, in a general fashion, responsive to their collective wishes. Most people had only sporadic and superficial contact with their chosen leaders; there existed little interaction between the representatives and their constituents. In addition, Croly, like Phillips, believed that most legislators did not base many of their decisions upon "technical knowledge," voting, instead, on the basis of "interests." As a result, those in power failed to provide the basis for real social "progress."[26]

Croly argued for cooperation most persuasively in *Progressive Democracy,* published in 1915. His general theme in this treatise was cooperation and participation. "Democracy," he wrote,

> implies and needs some method of representation which will be efficient and responsible enough a . . . policy but which does not imply the delegation of its ultimate discretionary power to any [fixed] body of men or law.[27]

Active, popular participation created responsible and creative citizens, who then relayed their needs to experts capable of devising suitable programs. Such a communion between the citizens and the experts constituted, according to Croly, a "fundamentally whole and sound society."[28]

From his Milwaukee experience, in particular, Phillips arrived at similar conclusions about the importance of cooperative interplay between citizens and experts. He found that if he generalized about the people he worked with, he was dealing with two groups in the social structure: those who supplied human service, such as the doctors and the nurses, and those who sought service, the consumers of health and social programs. The Social Unit Plan represented an attempt to formulate a method for resolving these two "separate but complementary forces of supply and demand." Because Phillips believed that everything was "inextricably related to and dependent upon each other," he wanted his system to provide for the expression of all people, be they producers or consumers.[29]

But, in order to effect such interaction, there had to be complete and continuous contact between both groups. Cooperation demanded some mechanism that encouraged the collection of all necessary information concerning consumer needs, and then provided for its transmission to the experts for resolution. Again, on the basis of his experience, Phillips believed that the neighborhood represented the ideal arena for this interchange between consumers and producers.[30]

Based on neighborhood units, the plan depended upon four fundamental instruments designed to stimulate people to define and meet their own needs and to interact as consumers and producers. These integral components were the Block Councils, the Citizens' Council, the Occupational Council, and the General Council. In essence, the plan called for subdividing the neighborhood into block associations to promote face-to-face contact among the residents. Then, to provide vehicles for the expression and resolution of block ideas, needs, and aspirations, Phillips set up a Citizens' Council and an Occupational Council. Representatives from each Block Council sat on the Citizens' Council to advance the needs of the locale, and representatives from the area's professional sector sat on the Occupational Council to suggest ways to meet neighborhood needs.[31] And finally, Phillips wanted both groups to meet together regularly to seek, through consensus, practical resolutions of the neighborhood's needs. (See figure 1.)

Phillips believed that the formulation of a sound program necessitated a well-grounded knowledge of each neighborhood and its needs. In order

Figure 1. Phillips's Social Unit Plan

Together the Citizens' Council and the Occupational Council form the General Council. Neighborhood decisions are made during sessions of the General Council.

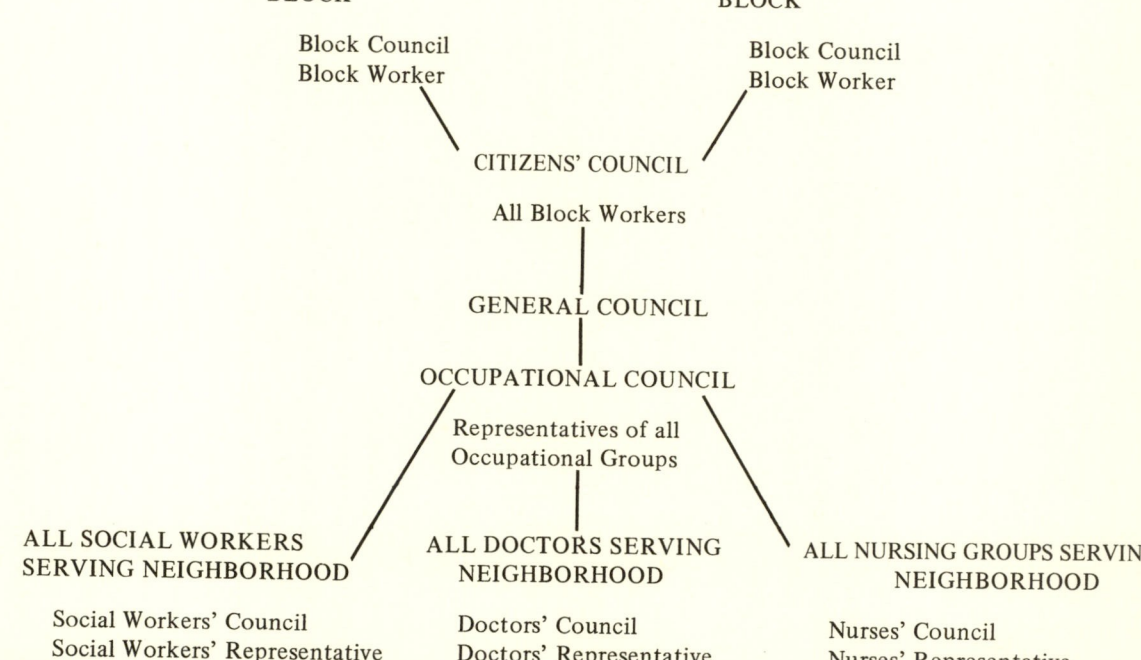

BLOCK

Block Council
Block Worker

BLOCK

Block Council
Block Worker

CITIZENS' COUNCIL

All Block Workers

GENERAL COUNCIL

OCCUPATIONAL COUNCIL

Representatives of all
Occupational Groups

ALL SOCIAL WORKERS
SERVING NEIGHBORHOOD

Social Workers' Council
Social Workers' Representative

ALL DOCTORS SERVING
NEIGHBORHOOD

Doctors' Council
Doctors' Representative

ALL NURSING GROUPS SERVING
NEIGHBORHOOD

Nurses' Council
Nurses' Representative

to secure more than just nominal representation, Phillips thought that it was essential to reach all neighborhood residents and to solicit their ideas and demands. Based on his work in St. Cyril's Parish, where a group of eight residents assisted the doctors and the nurses of the child-welfare station, Phillips felt that if the resident group were expanded, it would provide an ideal way to secure information about neighborhood residents' needs. But, instead of merely being adjuncts to the health station's staff, as were the eight residents in St. Cyril's Parish, the neighborhood residents, under the Social Unit Plan, would actually be part of the work team. They would be "representatives of the people." Thus, Phillips reasoned, "nothing could be done in their neighborhood that they [the residents] didn't want."[32]

Phillips selected the block as the unit to represent the neighborhood residents. Those over eighteen years of age in each block were to meet together and select, first, a Block Council and, then, a block worker. After some instruction by the "directors" of the plan, each block worker would serve as an educational agent who instructed the residents of his or her block about the work and the principles of the Social Unit Plan. Phillips wanted each worker to establish a friendly acquaintance with all the residents of the block. Then, each block worker was to solicit the concerns of his or her constituents and, after "neighborly" discussion, compile information concerning the needs of the area. One fact collector, known to the residents of each block, could secure more information and explain its importance far better, Phillips believed, than all the volunteers and paid agents from numerous organizations who combed the city making intimate inquiries and duplicating both questions and services.[33] The block worker, as Courtenay Dinwiddie, a Cincinnati Social Unit Organization executive, said later, "was in the best sense of the word, a neighbor, familiar with the conditions and needs and responsive to the wishes of other residents."[34]

The block worker represented his or her block in the Citizens' Council, and presented the problems and needs of their respective blocks at regular meetings. The council then studied the data presented by the various block workers. From this information, the Citizens' Council prepared complete and accurate statements outlining the needs of the neighborhood residents.[35] Phillips, in a 1919 outline of the Social Unit Plan, compared the relationship between the block workers and the Citizens' Council to the nervous system of the human body. Just as the "body had a system which notifies every part of it as to what the needs of the body are," the block workers were to serve as the nerves of the district, knowing whenever a need existed, and then transmitting that need to the central node of the system—the Citizens' Council—making the need felt until it was satisfied.[36]

The third component of the Social Unit Plan was the Occupational Council. Comprised of representatives from the "skilled groups," or "experts" such as doctors, nurses, and social workers who served the neighborhood, the members of the Occupational Council were charged with the formulation of "sound and efficient" programs for meeting the needs discerned by the Citizens' Council. In theory, each skilled group in the neighborhood organized and elected from its number a representative to serve on the Occupational Council. If the Citizens' Council desired a plan to meet a need identified by the block workers, the council contacted the Occupational Council. Once the need was presented to the Occupational Council, all groups that were able to provide supportive services collaborated on the plan, which was sent back to the Citizens' Council for consideration and, hopefully, for adoption. Phillips believed that this collaboration would develop a well-rounded program that would cover all aspects of a need. By studying new opportunities for better and wider service to meet the needs disclosed by the Citizens' Council, Phillips felt that the neighborhood would be able to have at its disposal the "skill, judgement and experience of the service sector of the population."[37]

To ensure a close relationship between those who possessed specialized knowledge and those who needed expert service, Phillips capped his plan with a General Council. Based on the premise that citizen participation, combined with expert analysis, produces a "working democracy," the General Council represented the union of the people (the Citizens' Council) and the experts (the Occupational Council). With individuals separated according to their special activities into occupational and citizens' groups, the General Council provided the arena where the experts and the people worked together to develop practical plans for meeting neighborhood needs. In such a way, all groups would work together to solve the problems of the neighborhood and promote, by implication, a healthy society.[38]

Once this plan was functioning in neighborhoods throughout the city, Phillips hoped to achieve intracity cooperation. He wanted each neighborhood to send delegates to a citywide Citizens' Council and a citywide Occupational Council. These groups were to articulate city needs and strategies for action, the actual programs to be decided upon in joint meetings of the two bodies at the citywide General Council. Phillips envisioned the eventual reproduction of this organizational form at the county, state, and federal levels. He felt that such a structure permitted more group participation in the decision-making process, provided a sense of order throughout the city, and trained neighborhood inhabitants to be responsible citizens.[39] It was to be a total plan for community betterment.

By late 1915, Phillips had interested a number of people, such as the *New Republic* editor, Herbert Croly, Dr. Richard Cabot of the Massachusetts General Hospital, Dr. S. S. Goldwater, former health commissioner of New York City, and John L. Elliott, head worker of the Hudson Guild, a New York City settlement house, in backing his plan. Together, they established the National Social Unit Organization (NSUO), with headquarters in New York City, and voted to sponsor a three-year demonstration of Phillips's social unit scheme, focusing on a preventive health program for young children to illustrate the plan's feasibility.[40] Soon after the announcement, sixteen cities offered to host the NSUO's demonstration. In November 1916, following a vigorous campaign led by Courtenay Dinwiddie, superintendent of the Cincinnati Tuberculosis League, and Dr. John Landis, health officer of Cincinnati and chairman of the Municipal Tuberculosis Committee, the NSUO selected Cincinnati as the host city for the social unit experiment. According to the NSUO, Cincinnati possessed the best facilities of all the interested cities for carrying out the social unit demonstration. These included a high degree of enthusiasm displayed by the general public in the Social Unit Plan; the promise by Cincinnati's social- and public-health agencies to support the experiment, and to relinquish their own work within the section of the city selected for the demonstration; and the pledge of $15,000 per year to help finance the operation. At the end of December, Phillips left New York City and arrived in Cincinnati on January 2, 1917, ready to "set to work."[41]

Phillips spent all of 1917 working with Cincinnatians to select a district, or neighborhood, for the social unit demonstration, and then to organize the area following the Social Unit Plan guidelines. First, Phillips concentrated on explaining the plan to the public through a series of public lectures, and on laying the necessary groundwork for a Cincinnati Social Unit Organization. Such an organization, Phillips believed, composed of "representative citizens," would stimulate competition among the various neighborhoods, and would allow those areas of the city not involved in the experiment to familiarize themselves with the general principles of social unit organization.[42] On March 22, 1917, at a meeting held in Exchange Hall at the Chamber of Commerce, over six hundred people gathered to vote the Cincinnati Social Unit Organization (CSUO) into existence.[43] This organization, composed of a Citizens' Council and an Occupational Council, was to oversee the social unit experiment, to advise the unit laboratory, and, at the conclusion of the experiment, to assist the NSUO in the evaluation of the demonstration.[44] The CSUO's first task, after its formation, was to select an appropriate neighborhood for the social unit demonstration.

For the next two months, the CSUO concentrated on choosing the experimental district. It announced in the daily newspapers that it intended to select as the laboratory district the neighborhood of the city that proved most eager for the plan. From May 14 through May 21, all the major newspapers carried a daily column on "What the Social Unit Experiment Means for You and Your Neighborhood." Randall J. Condon, superintendent of Cincinnati's public schools, authorized the distribution of five thousand ballots throughout the public-school system to collect information concerning neighborhood interest in the demonstration.[45]

By the beginning of June, five neighborhoods emerged as leading contenders. Residents in these areas sent the CSUO numerous petitions and letters urging the selection of their neighborhood as the social unit district. At a meeting held in Exchange Hall on June 7, 1917, the CSUO announced that it had selected Mohawk-Brighton as the demonstration neighborhood, and that organization of the neighborhood would begin at once.[46]

This Cincinnati neighborhood lay slightly west of the center of the city. Described by Phillips as "a picturesque area that lay both at the foot and the side of one of those many hills of Cincinnati,"[47] Mohawk-Brighton was part of the "Zone of Emergence," a term used by Robert A. Woods and Albert J. Kennedy for that area of the city inhabited by city residents who "had emerged from the slum into the mainstream of American life."[48] It nestled between the belt of land surrounding the central business district, which contained the central city slums, and the fashionable hilltop suburbs of Cincinnati.[49] With the movement of industries up the Millcreek Valley in the late-nineteenth century, and the rapid settling of the peripheral area of the old walking city, Mohawk-Brighton, like most areas in the zone, emerged as both a residential and an industrial neighborhood. By the turn of the century, it had grown into an "industrial beehive," containing perfumeries, brass founderies, machine shops, and a flour mill. A wide variety of small enterprises, such as tobacconists, groceries, dry goods shops, and saloons, located primarily along Central Avenue, the main artery into Mohawk-Brighton, provided the necessary services to the neighborhood residents.[50] And the majority of these residents, whether laborers or small entrepreneurs, were predominantly first- or second-generation Germans or Irish.[51]

While it remains unclear precisely why Mohawk-Brighton residents sought the Social Unit Plan so strenuously, one peculiarity of the zone perhaps provides a general reason for the interest of Mohawk-Brighton in securing the social unit demonstration. By definition, the Zone of Emergence consisted of people with only marginal economic security who feared engulfment or reengulfment by the slums. To combat this threat, one characteristic of most of the areas comprising the Zone of Emergence was the "penchant for organization." Residents of zone neighborhoods tended to be "joiners" and organization builders. By banding together in groups, whether social, economic, or religious, "zone residents sought to realize their aspirations," however imprecisely defined, and "to control their community." The other four neighborhoods in the social unit competition, all part of the Zone of Emergence, exhibited different levels of organization-making in their attempt to secure the unit demonstration. While Mohawk-Brighton residents set up a 145-member committee to canvass all the blocks in their neighborhood, and to sponsor public meetings about the unit plan, the other neighborhoods only established "small" committees that were relatively inactive.[52] Evidently, the residents of Mohawk-Brighton, and more particularly the neighborhood leaders of this community, on the cutting edge of the slums, were more interested in pursuing an activity that they viewed as an opportunity for neighborhood betterment.

Once Mohawk-Brighton had been selected as the experimental district, the committee in charge of the campaign to secure the unit met and voted to remain active as a Temporary Organizing Committee for the neighborhood. The committee turned its attention first to the establishment of definite boundaries for the social unit area. It constructed a spot map showing the residences of all who had signed petitions urging the selection of Mohawk-Brighton. Then, since the NSUO budget only allowed for a district of fifteen thousand people, the committee "fixed the geographical center and eliminated those blocks on the border of the district which contained the smallest number of petitioners."[53] Emming Street bounded this area on the north; Liberty Street, on the south; West and Colerain avenues, on the west; and Linn, Renner, Manchester, and Central streets, on the east. The committee divided this area into thirty-one blocks, with approximately five hundred people per block.[54]

Once the district was divided, the committee began to set up Block Councils by visiting supporters from each block and securing their help. After a series of talks by committee members and by Phillips with block residents, each Block Council elected a block worker as representative to the Citizens' Council. Without exception, all the block workers were women. According to Phillips, the committee urged the selection of women for two reasons: first, the initial service planned for the social unit district, an infant health program, directly affected women as mothers; second, Phillips, as well as the committee, believed that men would not have the time to devote the "kind of attention" necessary during the initial organizational phase of the Social Unit Plan.[55] Once the blocks selected their representatives, the committee and Phillips worked tirelessly with them. They acquainted the women with the plan of organization, outlined their duties as block representatives, and placed them on the social unit payroll. Because Phillips strongly believed in the importance of the block workers' role as block representatives, the women received $8.00 a week to compensate them for the time spent on social unit activities.[56]

Concurrent with the formation of the Block Councils, Phillips worked with the Temporary Organizing Committee to organize groups to be represented on the Mohawk-Brighton Occupational Council. They approached various occupational groups in the neighborhood, and attempted to familiarize them with the plan's basic ideas. Because the NSUO recommended that the initial program undertaken by the selected district focus on child welfare, Phillips and the committee concentrated primarily on organizing physicians, nurses, and social workers. However, they also spent time with teachers, businessmen, and clergymen, acquainting them with the plan, and enlisting their help in encouraging neighborhood participation and in disseminating information about the Social Unit Organization's activities. Once it was organized into a council, each occupational group elected an executive to serve on the neighborhood Occupational Council, through which they would contribute their special knowledge or skill to the community.[57]

The three most active councils during the life of the social unit demonstration were those of the physicians, the nurses, and the social workers. The Physicians' Council consisted of nine men, who represented the twenty-six physicians active in Mohawk-Brighton. The Nurses' Council included a representative from each of the four nursing organizations active in Mohawk-Brighton and a nursing aide to handle the paperwork. The Social Workers' Council organized in a similar fashion. Most of the social-service agencies active in Mohawk-Brighton assigned workers to the social unit district, and these workers constituted the Social Workers' Council.[58]

By the middle of September 1917, as a result of the organizational activities carried on by the Temporary Organizing Committee and by Phillips, the residents of Mohawk-Brighton grew impatient for action. On September 27, the committee called a meeting to discuss the neighborhood's progress. Those who attended the meeting voted for the creation of the Mohawk-Brighton Social Unit Organization (MBSUO), consisting of a neighborhood Citizens' Council, an Occupational Council, and a General Council. Immediately, the MBSUO General Council established a neighborhood bulletin to serve as a "medium for the expression of the community's thought," and to assist in the exchange of information between the various groups active in the neighborhood organization. The council then announced the location of the headquarters for the district operation, and explained the NSUO's projected budget for 1918, which consisted of the funds raised by the NSUO from private donations plus the $15,000 promised by various Cincinnati social and health organizations.[59]

During the next six weeks, the block workers held block meetings to discuss the proposed budget, and the General Council held several general informational sessions. On December 4, 1917, the residents approved the neighborhood budget of $35,049, which represented approximately three-fourths of the total money collected by the NSUO. This budget covered the rental of the headquarters, the health-center physicians' fees, the salaries of the executives and their assistants, the salaries of the block workers, all operating expenses, and a number of miscellaneous expenses. At a meeting in early December, following the wishes of the NSUO, the MBSUO adopted a preventive child-health program as its pilot project. On December 17, 1919, the MBSUO launched its infant-welfare program.[60]

After the preparatory training sessions on the importance of preventive health care, the block workers held a number of discussions with the members of their blocks on the subject of infant health care. Then they canvassed their blocks, house by house, to locate the infants in their area. Nurses followed the block workers, met with each infant's mother, and encouraged her to attend the examination sessions.[61] The health center soon became very popular. As babies were born, they automatically came under the station's care. By the end of 1918, the nursing staff had made 5,388 visits to 576 babies, and, of the 576, over two-thirds had received full medical examinations. By 1919, there existed in Mohawk-Brighton, one observer noted, "a markedly greater interest and intelligence about child care."[62]

The success of the postnatal medical service affected the medical and nursing services offered at the health station. The enthusiasm of the MBSUO's staff, and the apparent success of the infant-health campaign, heightened the neighborhood mothers' receptiveness to the advantages of preventive health care. During 1918, block workers reported an increasing number of requests to extend health programs. By 1920, in response to this demand, the MBSUO offered prenatal care, general bedside nursing, medical examinations of all preschool children, and supervision of local tuberculosis cases, in addition to postnatal examinations.[63]

Two unforeseen events in 1918 tested the efficiency of the Social Unit Organization: the Children's Year campaign and the influenza epidemic. Early in 1918, the U.S. Children's Bureau announced its decision to sponsor a nationwide campaign, Children's Year, to direct public attention to the problem of correctible defects and to the advantages of periodic medical examinations. In cooperation with the Women's Committee of the Council of National Defense, the Children's Bureau launched its campaign on April 6, 1918, to weigh and measure as many preschool children as possible. After discussing the national program with their block members, block workers announced their support for the Children's Year crusade. To generate even more enthusiasm for the weight and measurement program, and to promote the goal of 100 percent participation in preschool examinations, the MBSUO General Council sponsored a Children's Year Parade, complete with ponies, marching bands, and floats. Because of the enthusiasm generated by the festivities, and the familiarity of the block workers with their constituents, the MBSUO was able to send a complete list of the district's preschool population to the Children's Bureau by the end of April. By July, 1,075 of the 1,173 children under six had received medical examinations. And, in accordance with the social unit's attempt to work with the doctors of the neighborhood, the 640 children who were found to have physical difficulties were referred to their family physicians for the proper treatment.[64]

The outbreak of the influenza epidemic in the fall of 1918 provided the second opportunity for the MBSUO to demonstrate the efficiency of its organizational apparatus. Influenza first appeared in a mild form in the East during the spring. By the beginning of September, Massachusetts health officers noted an increasing number of cases of "Spanish influenza" in Boston. Following the main east-west lines of transportation, the virus soon began to spread throughout the rest of the country. Before the epidemic officially hit the Midwest, the block workers and the nurses had reported to the MBSUO health station an alarming increase in the number of colds and sore throats. On the advice of the Nurses' and Physicians' councils, the General Council decided to initiate preventive measures against the influenza-like symptoms before the virus "officially" hit Cincinnati. The Nurses' and Physicians' councils drafted a handbill announcing the possible danger of an outbreak of influenza in the Cincinnati area, giving instructions on the prevention and treatment of grippe, and stressing the importance of prompt medical attention.

Within twenty-four hours, the block workers delivered a copy of the handbill to each family in the Mohawk-Brighton district. Armed with this information, the neighborhood residents were better prepared than were most Cincinnatians when the epidemic struck the Queen City in late September.[65] After a study of all the influenza cases reported to the Health Department, the social unit's medical and nursing staffs found that the "percentage of cases per thousand population was great, if not greater, in the Mohawk-Brighton district than in the city as a whole." But, despite the large number of cases reported in the social unit neighborhood, the area had a lower death rate than that of the city as a whole.

The mortality rate from influenza and pneumonia per thousand population for the rest of the city of Cincinnati, for the months of October, November, and December, stood at 4.10 per thousand compared with 2.26 per thousand for the social unit district. Although the medical and nursing staffs recognized that they could not say with absolute certainty that the unit organization was responsible for the lower death rate, the fact that the district organization "proved to be more efficient in the prompter and more complete reporting of cases, in the quick dissemination of information about the epidemic, and in the care provided by the nurses, block workers and physicians indicated that the neighborhood organization, if nothing else, certainly facilitated the saving of lives."[66]

During 1918 and 1919, the Mohawk-Brighton Social Unit Organization established one of the most comprehensive neighborhood health-care programs in the country. From the establishment of its initial infant-health service, the neighborhood Social Unit Organization brought trained health personnel into a "working relationship" with the citizens of the district and stimulated a "local health consciousness." The MBSUO demonstrated that geographical localization and administrative coordination, complemented by the social organization of the neighborhood, resulted in a health-care program that could meet the needs of a community. By focusing on the interaction between health experts and the "people," the MBSUO fostered nearly 100-percent health care, and revealed the importance of mobilizing the entire community in the pursuit of health and, more broadly, social welfare.[67]

By nourishing the interaction between medical and social-welfare personnel and residents, the MBSUO helped to improve significantly the overall health of the Mohawk-Brighton district. Courtenay Dinwiddie and Dr. A. G. Kriedler, head of the MBSUO's Physicians' Council, concluded that the "unusual features" of the social unit's health-care operation were responsible for the improved level of neighborhood health care. According to Dinwiddie and Kriedler, the fact that the necessity for many of the services offered at the social unit center was not determined "by an outside group," but rather by neighborhood-based medical and social-welfare personnel in conjunction with neighborhood residents, increased local participation in the social unit's programs. In addition, because the nurses and the physicians spent a great deal of time explaining the nature of the services offered and their expected effect on the health of the community, many residents understood and appreciated the importance of preventive health care.[68]

In his study of the health programs offered by the MBSUO, Haven Emerson, a former health officer of New York City, found that the neighborhood organization had produced a number of "tangible accomplishments." Emerson noted that the MBSUO provided necessary prenatal advice to a very high percentage of expectant mothers and supervised all babies born in the district. He found that the physical examinations of the neighborhood preschool population uncovered a number of "correctible defects," and that many of the children with the "defects" received corrective treatment. Emerson reported that during the influenza epidemic, the "prompt and efficient nursing service" of the MBSUO helped to reduce the number of deaths from the virus. In general, he concluded that the mothers and fathers of the district had become "educated to an alertness, an understanding, and an interest in the relation of health and its maintenance to their children's welfare, and that the medical needs of the district had been better met than before."[69]

But, despite the social unit's success in the area of neighborhood health care, it failed to survive the antiradical hysteria that followed World War I. In March 1919, Cincinnati's mayor, John Galvin, accused the MBSUO of expressing an alien political philosophy, and declared that, as such, it represented "a menace to our municipal government and was but one step removed from Bolshevism."[70] Investigations by the Council of Social Agencies and the Helen S. Trounstine Foundation, made during the previous summer when Director of Public Welfare James White questioned the "Americanism" of the social unit experiment, exonerated the MBSUO of these charges.[71] At the same time, Cincinnati's health officer, William Peters, after observing the work of the social unit health center, feared that the health programs sponsored by the MBSUO would undercut the work of the Health Department. Peters withdrew his support from the social unit experiment and campaigned actively against the expansion of this type of health-care program. These charges slowed the neighborhood work as the MBSUO battled for its existence. Despite the favorable outcome of a referendum held to determine support for the plan in Mohawk-Brighton, the city withdrew its support. Without increased expenditure forthcoming from the NSUO, the MBSUO could not survive. Despite a gallant effort on the part of the residents to raise enough money to support the MBSUO health center, in November 1920, the Babies Milk Fund Association,[72] an agency concerned with the reduction of infant mortality, assumed control of the MBSUO's headquarters, equipment, and infant health work.[73]

When Phillips left Cincinnati, he did not abandon the social unit idea. The National Social Unit Organization remained intact, and Phillips began to work closely with the NSUO in New York City to promote the establishment of more social unit-style community organizations. In December 1919, the NSUO entered into an agreement with the New York City Community Councils (New York City's reorganized Community Councils of National Defense)[74] and made plans to establish another social unit laboratory in New York City. But, within little more than a year, both the New York City Community Councils and the NSUO disbanded after a series of financial disagreements.[75] The dissolution of the NSUO and of the New York City Community Councils in 1921 represented more than just the end of an experiment; it marked the beginning of a major shift in community organization practice, from democratic, collaborative neighborhood schemes to task-oriented, problem-solving activities led by professionals.

The Social Unit Organization illustrated, according to social-welfare historian Roy Lubove, "community organization in the years when its exponents believed literally in the possibility of a social harmony that transcended the fragmentation of American life."[76] It represented that part of the larger community organization movement that constituted, according to Eduard C. Lindeman, a prominent social-welfare theorist,

> a conscious effort on the part of the community to control its affairs democratically and to secure the highest service from its specialists, organizations, agencies and institutions by means of recognized interrelatedness.[77]

Like other community organizations of that period, such as the settlements, the school centers, and the Community Councils of National Defense, the social unit theory of organization rested upon two basic premises: the "wholeness of the environment," and the importance of "neighborhood in nationbuilding." Community organizers during the first two decades of the twentieth century stressed the totality of the world around them. And, like others who promoted community organizing during that period, Phillips based his plan on the belief that "America was made up of the sum total of thousands of neighborhoods," and that "neither the city nor the nation could be understood nor their problems met" unless the process began in the neighborhood.[78] Moreover, they emphasized not what the social technician could do for the citizen, but, instead, the joint responsibility of the citizen and the specialist in discerning local needs and meeting them through consultation and cooperation.[79] Theoretically, the city and its neighborhoods represented a "cluster of interlacing communities."

Of all the attempts to organize communities during the first two decades of the twentieth century, Phillips's Social Unit Plan represents the most celebrated attempt to facilitate communication and cooperation between the "interlacing communities," despite the fact that the experimentation period proved too short to yield conclusive results. Probably in no other community were plans and policies for the neighborhood so painstakingly submitted in advance to the people of a neighborhood. Most decisions rested on public understanding and approval. The residents of Mohawk-Brighton studied some of their own problems, determined community needs, and conducted the proposed services themselves. The unit organization stimulated local initiative so that, as the life of the unit progressed, the establishment of some of the services, such as the prenatal service and the bedside nursing program, was not initiated by the founders of the plan.[80]

In theory, the experiment sought to demonstrate the feasibility of cooperation between "specialists" and "citizens," and to illustrate the practicality of democratically run health services. The novel feature of the organization, the division of function between the Occupational Council and the Citizens' Council, made it possible for various elements of the community to make substantial contributions. The Citizens' Council encouraged a general community consciousness and neighborhood spirit. The block workers developed an ability to diagnose needs and then to direct, when called upon, the implementation of the programs. And the Occupational Council brought together the skilled groups in the area and fostered an understanding of the interrelatedness of their services. It eliminated duplicated efforts and overlapping services, and tended to elevate the standards of service rendered to the community.[81]

In operation, however, the social unit fell short of success. The project had some serious deficiencies. The Block Councils, while supporting the block workers, failed to operate as an effective part of the organizational machinery. The councils rarely assumed responsibility for carrying out policies for the block workers. For the most part, the block workers bypassed the councils and dealt directly with the residents of their block. This only added to the block workers' inordinately heavy burden, which included canvassing the neighborhood and developing programs and policies in the Citizens' Council. On the occupational side, not all groups were as well integrated into the organizational structure as were the physicians, nurses, and social workers. The project never achieved widespread acceptance. Cooperation was hampered, especially near the end of the experiment, by those groups, such as the Health Department, that felt threatened by social unit-style activities. Ultimately, and most importantly, the unit organization failed to sustain itself financially.[82]

Despite these and other organizational problems, the Social Unit Organization demonstrated that it was possible to democratically organize a neighborhood to facilitate the identification and resolution of local needs. Residents did discover neighborhood problems and did participate in the solutions of those problems as never before. The social unit stands as a "bold effort" to achieve neighborhood organization through the nurturing of an "organic" relationship between the citizen and the specialist, and it attempted, although with mixed success, to foster a civic consciousness that identified with and yet transcended the neighborhood and incorporated it into the whole of the American experience.

NOTES

1. Robert H. Wiebe, *The Search for Order, 1877-1920* (New York: Hill and Wang, 1967); David J. Russo, *Families and Communities: A New View of American History* (Nashville, Tenn.: American Association of State and Local History, 1974), p. 292; David P. Thelen, *The New Citizenship: Origins of Progressivism in Wisconsin, 1885-1900* (Columbia, Mo.: University of Missouri Press, 1972), p. 56.

2. Jean B. Quandt, *From the Small Town to the Great Community: The Social Thought of Progressive Intellectuals* (New Brunswick, N.J.: Rutgers University Press, 1970); A. H. Lloyd, "The Organic Theory of Society," *American Journal of Sociology* 6 (March 1901): 577.

3. Henry C. Adams, ed., *Philanthropy and Social Progress* (New York: Thomas Y. Crowell, 1893), p. xi; Josiah Strong, *The Twentieth-Century City* (New York: Baker and Taylor, 1898; reprint ed., New York: Arno Press, 1970), pp. 117, 123-24. For a discussion of the impact of the "organism" on late-nineteenth and early twentieth-century American social thought, see Quandt, *Small Town to Great Community;* Stow Persons, *American Minds: A History of Ideas* (New York: Henry Holt, 1958), pp. 225-29; Merle Curti, *The Growth of American Thought,* 3d ed. (New York: Harper and Row, 1964); Stow Persons, ed., *Evolutionary Thought in America* (New Haven: Yale University Press, 1950); Sidney Fine, *Laissez-faire and the General Welfare State: A Study of Conflict in American Thought, 1865-1901* (Ann Arbor: University of Michigan Press, 1956); Richard Hofstadter, *Social Darwinism in American Thought* (Boston: Beacon Press, 1955).

4. Zane L. Miller, "Scarcity, Abundance, and American Urban History," *Journal of Urban History* 4 (February 1978): 142.

5. Robert A. Woods, "The City and Its Local Community," in *The Neighborhood in Nationbuilding,* ed. Robert A. Woods (Boston: Houghton Mifflin, 1923; reprint ed., New York: Arno Press, 1970), p. 196; Blaine Brownell, *The Urban Ethos in the South, 1920-1930* (Baton Rouge: Louisiana State University Press, 1975), pp. 39-43; Scott Greer, *The Emerging City: Myth and Reality* (New York: Free Press, 1962), pp. 6, 21.

6. Robert A. Woods, "The Neighborhood in Social Reconstruction," *American Journal of Sociology* 19 (March 1914): 579.

7. Susan E. Foote, "The Settlement as a Social Laboratory," *Ethical Record* 4 (February-March 1903): 83.

8. Quandt, *Small Town to Great Community,* pp. 1, 48; Robert A. Woods, "The Neighborhood and the Nation," *Proceedings of the National Conference of Charities and Correction* 36 (Buffalo, 1909), p. 106; Graham Taylor, "The Neighborhood and the Municipality," *Proceedings of the National Conference of Charities and Correction* 36 (Buffalo, 1909), pp. 156-63.

9. Amos Griswold Warner, Stuart Alfred Queen, and Ernest Bouldin Harper, *American Charities and Social Work* (New York: Thomas Y. Crowell, 1930), pp. 456-57; Dwight Davis, "The Neighborhood Center: A Moral and Educational Factor," *Charities and the Commons,* February 1, 1908, p. 1506.

10. Jesse Steiner, *Community Organization* (New York: Century Press, 1925), p. 195.

11. Strong, *Twentieth-Century City*, pp. 117, 123-24.

12. "The Expert and American Society," *New Republic*, May 4, 1918, pp. 7-8.

13. Eduard C. Lindeman, *The Community* (New York: Association Press, 1921), pp. 139-40.

14. The New York Milk Committee, one of the many committees of the New York Association for Improving the Condition of the Poor, was founded in 1907. The NYMC sought to improve the milk supply of New York City, and "to educate the public to the proper use of milk for infant feeding and other purposes" in an attempt to reduce the high rate of infant mortality. See Phillip Van Ingen and Paul Emmons, "Infant Mortality and Milk Stations" (New York: New York Milk Committee, 1912); New York Milk Committee, *Ten Years Work, 1907-1916* (New York: New York Milk Committee, 1916).

15. One of the most common causes of infant deaths was infantile diarrhea, which resulted largely from "dirty" milk. Late-nineteenth- and many early twentieth-century public-health workers believed that once the milk environment was cleaned up, the rate of infant mortality would drop.

16. R. L. Duffus and L. Emmett Holt, Jr., *L. Emmett Holt: Pioneer of a Children's Century* (New York: D. Appleton-Century, 1940), p. 166; George Rosen, *A History of Public Health* (New York: MD Publications, 1958), pp. 238-39; Van Ingen and Emmons, "Infant Mortality," p. 24.

17. John Spargo, *The Common Sense of the Milk Question* (New York: Macmillan, 1908), p. 144; Michael M. Davis and Andrew R. Warner, *Dispensaries: Their Management and Development* (New York: Macmillan, 1918), p. 304.

18. Ernest C. Meyer, *Infant Mortality in New York City: A Study of the Results Accomplished by Infant Life-Saving Agencies, 1885-1920* (New York: Rockefeller Foundation, 1921), p. 82; Wilbur C. Phillips, *Adventuring for Democracy* (New York: Social Unit Press, 1940), p. 44.

19. Wilbur C. Phillips and Elsie C. Phillips, "A Plan for Social Organization or the Unit Method of Gradually Building Up a Complete System for Studying and Meeting Social Needs," unpublished ms., (1912-1914), p. 188, Wilbur C. Phillips Papers, Social Welfare History Archives Center, University of Minnesota, Minneapolis, Minn.; Phillips, *Adventuring*, pp. 46-48; Wilbur C. Phillips, "The Achievements and Future Possibilities of the New York Milk Committee," *Proceedings of the Child Conference for Research and Development* 1 (Worcester, Mass., 1909), pp. 191-92.

20. Phillips pioneered in the establishment of the urban health center. It was an institution designed to tackle health problems from the

standpoint of a neighborhood, and to consider all the different yet related factors that contributed to the maintenance of good health. As the health centers developed during the period from 1911 to 1920, they sought to provide service determined by the needs of each neighborhood, and to mobilize local participation in the programs for health conservation. After Phillips's Milwaukee demonstration, health centers opened in Cleveland, Philadelphia, Buffalo, and New York City. By 1920, the health-center mania had spread to other cities east of the Mississippi River. For a fuller discussion, see Patricia Mooney Melvin, "Make Milwaukee Safe for Babies: The Child Welfare Commission and the Development of Urban Health Centers, 1911-1912," *Journal of the West* 17 (Spring 1978): 83-93; George Rosen, "The First Neighborhood Health Movement: Its Rise and Its Fall," in *From Medical Police to Social Medicine: Essays on the History of Health Care,* ed. George Rosen (New York: Science History Publications, 1974), pp. 304-27.

21. Sally M. Miller, "Milwaukee: Of Ethnicity and Labor," in *Socialism and the Cities,* ed. Bruce M. Stave (Port Washington, N.Y.: Kennikat Press, 1975), pp. 48-50; *Milwaukee Free Press,* April 14, 1912, p. 5; Milwaukee, Wisconsin, *Proceedings of the Common Council of the City of Milwaukee for the Year Ending April 14, 1913,* File # 2262, June 17, 1912, p. 270.

22. Phillips and Phillips, "Plan for Social Organization."

23. Wilbur C. Phillips, "The Need of Community Planning in Child Welfare Work," *Transactions of the Fifteenth International Congress on Hygiene and Demography* (Washington, D.C., 1912), pp. 291-93; Wilbur C. Phillips, "A New Design for Democracy or the Social Unit Theory and Plan for Evolving a Functional Consumers and Producers Democracy," unpublished ms. p. 37, Wilbur C. Phillips Papers, Social Welfare History Archives Center, University of Minnesota, Minneapolis, Minn.

24. Phillips, *Adventuring,* pp. 162-65.

25. Robert A. Woods, "The Recovery of the Parish," in *The Neighborhood in Nationbuilding,* ed. Robert A. Woods (Boston: Houghton Mifflin, 1923; reprint ed., New York: Arno Press, 1970), p. 135; Phillips, *Adventuring,* p. 93; Phillips, "New Design," p. 37.

26. Phillips and Phillips, "Plan for Social Organization," pp. 429-51; Charles Forcey, *The Crossroads of Liberalism: Croly, Weyl, Lippman, and the Progressive Era, 1900-1925* (New York: Oxford University Press, 1961), p. 41.

27. Herbert Croly, *Progressive Democracy* (New York: Macmillan, 1915), p. 283.

28. Ibid., p. 301; Forcey, *Crossroads of Liberalism,* pp. 27, 157, 165; Wiebe, *Search for Order,* pp. 161-62; David W. Noble, "Herbert Croly and American Progressive Thought," *Western Political Quarterly* 7 (December 1957): 547-50.

29. Phillips and Phillips, "Plan for Social Organization," pp. 431-56; Phillips, *Adventuring,* pp. 84-85.

30. Phillips and Phillips, "Plan for Social Organization," pp. 271, 451-56.

31. Phillips used "consumer" and "citizen" interchangeably. The citizen was the consumer of produced goods and services.

32. Phillips, *Adventuring,* pp. 94-104.

33. Ibid., pp. 64-104; Phillips and Phillips, "Plan for Social Organization," pp. 277-318.

34. Courtenay Dinwiddie, *Community Responsibility: A Review of the Cincinnati Social Unit Experiment* (New York: New York School of Social Work, 1921), p. 2.

35. Phillips, *Adventuring,* pp. 167-69; Phillips and Phillips, "Plan for Social Organization," p. 306.

36. National Social Unit Organization, *Description of the Unit Plan,* Bulletin 4 (Cincinnati: National Social Unit Organization, 1919), pp. 6-7.

37. Phillips, *Adventuring,* pp. 169-70.

38. Ibid., pp. 103-104, 150-51; Phillips and Phillips, "Plan for Social Organization," p. 177; NSUO, *Description of Unit Plan,* p. 7; James Weinstein, *The Corporate Ideal in the Liberal State, 1900-1918* (Boston: Beacon Press, 1968), p. xiv. See also Roy Lubove, *The Progressives and the Slums: Tenement Housing Reform in New York City, 1890-1917* (Pittsburgh: University of Pittsburgh Press, 1962; reprint ed., Westport, Conn.: Greenwood Press, 1974); and Samuel Haber, *Efficiency and Uplift: Scientific Management in the Progressive Era, 1890-1920* (Chicago: University of Chicago Press, 1964).

39. Phillips and Phillips, "Plan for Social Organization," p. 355; Phillips, *Adventuring,* pp. 153, 160, 163.

40. National Social Unit Organization, *History of the Unit Plan,* Bulletin 1 (Cincinnati: National Social Unit Organization, 1917), pp. 3-7; "Health Centers as an Aid to Democracy," *The Survey,* April 22, 1916, p. 93; *New York Times,* April 12, 1916, p. 5.

41. N. A. Nelson, "Neighborhood Organization vs. Tuberculosis," *Modern Medicine* 1 (October 1919): 516; Cincinnati *Commercial Tribune,* October 22, 1916, p. 6; Phillips, *Adventuring,* pp. 175-77; *New York Times,* November 20, 1916, p. 6; NSUO, *History of Unit Plan,* pp. 7-10.

42. National Social Unit Organization, *Creation and Purpose of the*

Cincinnati Social Unit Organization, Bulletin 3 (Cincinnati: National Social Unit Organization, 1918), pp. 5-7.

43. Cincinnati *Commercial Tribune,* March 22, 1917, p. 8.

44. National Social Unit Organization, *The Social Unit Experiment from the Standpoint of Popular Control, Theoretical Soundness, Efficiency, Educational Value and Cost,* Bulletin 6 (Cincinnati: National Social Unit Organization, 1919), p. 2.

45. Phillips, *Adventuring,* pp. 179-80; *Cincinnati Enquirer,* May 14 through May 21, 1917; Cincinnati *Commercial Tribune,* May 14 through May 21, 1917; "Will You Vote Yes or No?" Wilbur C. Phillips Papers, Social Welfare History Archives Center, University of Minnesota, Minneapolis, Minn.

46. Cincinnati *Commerical Tribune,* June 8, 1917, p. 1; "Social Unit District Choses Itself," *The Survey,* July 21, 1917, p. 355; Wilbur C. Phillips, "Health and Commonwealth," *Proceedings of the National Conference of Social Work* 44 (Pittsburgh, 1917), p. 255.

47. Phillips, *Adventuring,* p. 183.

48. For a discussion of the notion of the Zone of Emergence and its use as a descriptive term for city structure, see Robert A. Woods and Albert J. Kennedy, *The Zone of Emergence,* ed. Sam Bass Warner (Cambridge: MIT Press, 1962).

49. See Zane L. Miller, *Boss Cox's Cincinnati: Urban Politics in the Progressive Era* (New York: Oxford University Press, 1968), pp. 3-55, for a fuller discussion of the Circle, Zone, and Hilltop sections of Cincinnati during this period.

50. Zane L. Miller, "Boss Cox and the Municipal Reformers: Cincinnati Progressivism, 1880-1914" (Ph.D. dissertation, University of Chicago, 1966), pp. 58-96; *Historic Brighton* (Cincinnati, 1902), p. 91; William C. Smith, *Queen City Yesterdays: Sketches of Cincinnati in the Eighties* (Crawfordsville, Ind.: R. E. Banta, 1959), p. 3.

51. Miller, "Boss Cox," pp. 72-78; according to the fourteenth census of the United States, the population of the three wards comprising Mohawk-Brighton stood at 39,835. Of this number, the native white population totaled 33,355, and the foreign-born population accounted for 5,918 people. Of the foreign-born population, the census registered 967 Hungarians, 283 Rumanians, and 2,929 Germans. United States, Bureau of the Census, *Fourteenth Census of the United States, 1920: Population.*

52. Report of the Secretaries. Wilbur C. Phillips Papers, Social Welfare History Archives Center, University of Minnesota, Minneapolis, Minn.; Miller, *Boss Cox's Cincinnati,* pp. 25-40.

53. National Social Unit Organization, *The Beginning of Work in the Social Unit,* Bulletin 5 (Cincinnati: National Social Unit Organization, 1918), p. 3.

54. Ibid.; Cornelius J. Petzhold, "The Social Unit," pp. 5-6, Social Unit Organization Papers, Cincinnati Historical Society, Cincinnati, Ohio.

55. Petzhold, "Social Unit," pp. 7-8; Cincinnati *Commercial Tribune,* August 2, 1918, p. 6; NSUO, *Beginning of Work,* p. 5.

56. NSUO, *Beginning of Work,* p. 6; Phillips, *Adventuring,* p. 186.

57. Dinwiddie, *Community Responsibility,* p. 40; NSUO, *Experiment from Standpoint of Control,* p. 10; Phillips, *Adventuring,* p. 187.

58. NSUO, *Beginning of Work,* pp. 6-7.

59. Ibid.

60. Ibid., p. 10; "Financial Report of the National Social Unit Organization from February 9, 1916, to January 1, 1918," pp. 2-6, Wilbur C. Phillips Papers, Social Welfare History Archives Center, University of Minnesota, Minneapolis, Minn.; Phillips, *Adventuring,* pp. 193-200.

61. At these sessions, the physicians on duty weighed and measured each child and gave each mother a full report on the child's health. The doctors referred all cases requiring medical attention to either the family physician or the appropriate agency. These sessions were followed up promptly by the nurses who provided instruction in the home on the proper nursing techniques required for the child's condition. Abbie Roberts, "Report of the Nurses' Council for the Year 1918," n.d., p. 7, Wilbur C. Phillips Papers, Social Welfare History Archives Center, University of Minnesota, Minneapolis, Minn.

62. Ibid.; Nelson, "Neighborhood Organization," p. 519.

63. Courtenay Dinwiddie and A. G. Kriedler, "Community Self-Organized for Preventive Health Work," *Modern Medicine* 1 (May 1919): 27-29; Dinwiddie, *Community Responsibility,* pp. 146-48.

64. Anna Rude, "The Children's Year Campaign," *American Journal of Public Health* 9 (May 1919): 346; Mary Hicks to Julia Lathrop, April 20, 1918, U.S. Children's Bureau Records, National Archives, Washington, D.C.; Dinwiddie, *Community Responsibility,* pp. 78-79; *Social Unit Bulletin,* July 20, 1918, p. 1; Roberts, "Nurses Report," p. 9.

65. Alfred W. Crosby, Jr., *Epidemic and Peace, 1918* (Westport, Conn.: Greenwood Press, 1976), pp. 53, 203; Robert S. Katz, "Influenza, 1918-1919: A Study in Mortality," *Bulletin of the History of Medicine* 48 (Fall 1974): 418; "Flu," Wilbur C. Phillips Papers, Social Welfare History Archives Center, University of Minnesota, Minneapolis, Minn.; Phillips,

Adventuring, p. 244; "The Social Unit Plan in the Epidemic," *The Survey,* January 11, 1919, p. 503.

66. Roberts, "Nurses Report," p. 11; NSUO, *Experiment from Standpoint of Control,* p. 34; "The Social Unit Plan," *The Outlook,* July 23, 1919, p. 460. None of the figures for the influenza epidemic are complete, so actual totals cannot be fully ascertained. Especially during the early months of the epidemic, many cases of influenza were listed as pneumonia. U.D. Department of Commerce, Bureau of the Census, *Mortality Statistics, 1919,* pp. 28-29; Louis I. Dublin, *Twenty-five Years of Health Progress* (New York: Metropolitan Life Insurance Co., 1937), pp. 127-28.

67. Dinwiddie, *Community Responsibility,* p. 152; Rosen, "First Neighborhood Health Center Movement," pp. 304-27; C. E.-A. Winslow, "The Health Center Movement," *Modern Medicine* 1 (August 1919): 328.

68. Dinwiddie and Kriedler, "Community Self-Organized," p. 27; Dinwiddie, *Community Responsibility,* p. 47.

69. Haven Emerson, "The Social Unit and Medical Organization," *National Social Unit Conference* (Cincinnati, 1919), p. 4.

70. *Cincinnati Enquirer,* March 11, 1919, p. 7.

71. William J. Norton, *The Social Unit Organization of Cincinnati,* report of the Helen S. Trounstine Foundation, Cincinnati, Ohio, February 1, 1919, pp. 183-86; Council of Social Agencies, *Investigation of the Charges Against the Social Unit Organization* (Cincinnati, 1919).

72. Organized in 1909 under the direction of Dr. Benjamin K. Rachford, the Babies Milk Fund Association established infant milk clinics throughout the city of Cincinnati to help combat milk-related infant deaths. In 1919, the Babies Milk Fund Association became part of the newly formed Community Chest.

73. Dinwiddie, *Community Responsibility,* pp. 109, 124-25; *Cincinnati Enquirer,* March 13, 1919, p. 4; *Social Unit Bulletin,* April 16, 1919, p. 1; Phillips, *Adventuring,* p. 355; Mary Hicks to Wilbur C. Phillips, November 6, 1920, Wilbur C. Phillips Papers, Social Welfare History Archives Center, University of Minnesota, Minneapolis, Minn.

74. After the outbreak of World War I, the Council of National Defense organized state, county, and city councils to aid in the mobilization of the nation's resources. On the city level, the council fostered the creation of numerous Community Councils through which "all people in the neighborhood could gradually assume some responsibility for the prosecution of the War." New York City was one of the earliest cities to institute the Council of National Defense's Community Council Plan.

For further information, see Lindeman, *Community Organization,* pp. 168-69; Sidney Dillick, *Community Organization for Neighborhood Development—Past and Present* (New York: William Morrow, 1953), pp. 71-73.

75. *New York Times,* December 8, 1919, p. 12; John Collier, "Community Councils—Democracy Everyday: III," *The Survey,* September 28, 1918, p. 710; Jesse Steiner, "Community Organization: A Study of Its Rise and Recent Tendencies," *Social Forces* 1 (November 1922): 15; "Plan of Cooperation Between the Community Councils of Greater New York, Community Service, Inc., and the National Social Unit Organization" (1919), pp. 1-2, Wilbur C. Phillips Papers, Social Welfare History Archives Center, University of Minnesota, Minneapolis, Minn.; *New York Times,* March 30, 1921, p. 18.

76. Roy Lubove, *The Professional Altruist: The Emergence of Social Work as a Career, 1880-1930* (New York: Atheneum Press, 1971), p. 177.

77. Lindeman, *Community,* p. 173.

78. Hart, *Community Organization,* pp. 6, 15; Holden, *Settlement Idea,* pp. 193-94.

79. Lubove, *Professional Altruist,* pp. 177-78; Lindeman, *Community,* p. 173.

80. Dinwiddie, *Community Responsibility,* pp. 33-36.

81. Ibid., p. 39; Seba Eldridge, "Community Organization and Citizenship," *Social Forces* 7 (September 1928): 139; NSUO, *Community from Standpoint of Control,* pp. 36-45.

82. Dinwiddie, *Community Responsibility,* pp. 23-24, 37-38, 97; Lubove, *Professional Altruist,* p. 177.

Harlem Communists and
the Politics of Black Protest

MARK NAISON

To people who were politically awakened in the 1960s, to speak of Communist party activity under the heading of "community organizing" seems like a contradiction in terms. Partisans of the sixties tradition of community mobilization, whether civil rights activists, poverty program staffers, or graduates of the Alinsky schools, saw their primary goal as awakening the poor to a sense of their own power rather than recruiting them into specific organizations. For American Communists, the priorities were precisely reversed. Yet, if depression-era Harlem is indicative, Communists may have done more to inspire self-confidence and militancy in the urban poor than did any group of New Left organizers committed to popular democracy.

This experience is so contrary to received wisdom that it is worth looking at in some detail. On the eve of the Great Depression, the Communist party (CPUSA) launched a dramatic effort to expand its following in Afro-American communities. Though such an effort had long been advocated by black Communists (who numbered no more than fifty in 1928), the major impetus came from the Communist International. Following the Sixth World Congress of the Comintern in 1928, the Comintern drew up a resolution on the American "Negro Question" that

Note: An earlier version of this article originally appeared in *Marxist Perspectives,* No. 3 (Vol. I, No. 3), New York 1978.

defined the recruitment of blacks as a matter of top priority. The moral and political force of this resolution impelled American party members, overwhelmingly immigrants and children of immigrants, to enter black communities and try to enroll blacks into campaigns against segregation and discrimination, to recruit them into unions, and, in the process, to draw them into the Communist party.[1]

The political goals of their organizing were defined by the Communist International, and were further elaborated and refined by the Politburo and the Central Committee of the CPUSA. There was no effort to enlist the people being organized into a decision-making process. Unlike most New Left organizers, Communists came to people with a prearranged set of tactics and objectives and tried to mobilize them for action. Local party units, whether in neighborhoods or workplaces, did make decisions on certain matters: which person in an apartment building should be made the leader of a rent strike; on what corner should a soapbox be set up; how should hecklers be handled; which church should be used for a meeting hall. As any organizer knows, these issues are important and time-consuming, and it represents a misreading of Communist activity to assume its cadres were automatons. Nevertheless, it is also true that rank-and-file Communists were not encouraged to think independently about major policies such as the party's approach to the Garvey movement; its relationship to the Democratic party; its approach to trade-union organizing in an industry where there was already an AFL union; its position on the foreign or domestic policies of the Roosevelt administration. On such issues, initiative flowed from the top down, and a recruit who challenged the party line could find himself or herself censured or expelled.

That this party, undemocratic even by Leninist standards, could arouse a significant popular response in the thirties speaks to a high degree of working-class and black disfranchisement in American society on the eve of the depression. In a society where the overwhelming majority of the working class was nonunionized, and where blacks were isolated from their fellow workers by a formidable wall of prejudice, the party's strategy of black-white unity, and its organization of protest against depression conditions, had considerable impact. Communists succeeded in convincing their white followers that the American working class could not progress unless blacks were included in all movement activities, and that blacks would not join unless whites conscientiously fought racial discrimination. In turn, the party's mobilization of whites for the struggle against

Jim Crow, which extended considerably beyond its membership, had a catalytic effect on the black community.

The range of Communist-led activity in depression-era black communities was immense.[2] From 1929 on, Communists organized eviction resistance, relief bureau sit-ins, protests against job discrimination, rent strikes, consumer boycotts, and demonstrations against segregated hotels, restaurants, and recreation facilities. In some cities, their activities broke ground; in others, they trailed behind that of non-Communist protest leaders. But their influence was widespread and helped shape the world view of a generation of black trade unionists, politicians, social workers, and civil rights leaders. "Even conservative leaders agree," a journalist studying Harlem wrote in 1938, "that it is Communist agitation and Communist activity that have been largely responsible for the awakening of the upper class Negro community to the plight of the poorest."[3]

This activity, despite its breadth, failed to meet many of the objectives that Communists had set out for it. Though Communists organized tens of thousands of blacks into protest movements, they failed to attract a stable black mass membership or a large black following at the polls. The party's organizational work helped make many blacks militant, but it turned relatively few into disciplined Communists. By the standards of the 1960s (which were *not* Communist standards), Communists proved to be excellent "community organizers"; they helped awaken a spirit of resistance in the black population without determining all the forms that that resistance took.

To shed light on this paradox, let us take a close look at Communist activity in a black community where Communists concentrated a great deal of energy: Harlem. Four main conclusions emerge from that experience, though they must be tested against the experience of black communities in other cities. First, the Communist party provided the single most energetic force in the black community, applying mass protest techniques to depression conditions and civil rights issues. Communists not only used direct action tactics on a scale previously unknown in Harlem, but they directed such protests toward the government rather than toward the private sector. They thereby differed sharply from community leaders in Harlem and other cities who tried to form "Don't Buy Where You Can't Work" movements. Second, the strategic viewpoints that Communists expressed, virtually alone, in the early 1930s, became widely accepted by non-Communist black leaders after 1935. Not only did the whole spectrum of Harlem's leadership come to endorse direct action techniques, but a sizable segment of the community (with the important exception of the Garveyites) began to view the white working class as an ally and to regard interracial unionism as essential to black progress. Third, Communist efforts to link all black protests to the organization drives of the CIO and the "united front against fascism," enthusiastically received at first, evoked considerable dissatisfaction among black leaders in the late 1930s. In the name of "unity of all progressive forces," Communists insisted that blacks subordinate their special interests when they conflicted (even tangentially) with labor's struggles for recognition, thereby sacrificing some of the credibility they had attained through their prior work. Finally, the party's abject reversal of its policies following the Nazi-Soviet pact impelled many of its black allies into open opposition. Communists found themselves isolated from much of the protest activity in Harlem after the pact, even from those activities that made use of symbols and tactics pioneered by the party.

THE EARLY DEPRESSION YEARS

The depression struck Harlem with exceptional force. Unemployment in Harlem rose to 66 percent of the labor force in 1933 and to 80 percent by 1935.[4] But local organizations did not respond to the crisis with militant action. In the face of unemployment, evictions, and widespread hunger, churches and civic groups organized collections to provide food and clothing for those in distress, sponsored delegations to private charities and city officials to urge them to increase aid to the needy, and approached store owners on 125th Street to ask for white-collar jobs for blacks. They did not use marches, boycotts, or picket lines to back up their requests until almost three years after the depression struck.[5] They did not challenge the philosophy of private charity; they did not insist that it was the government's responsibility to provide aid for the unemployed.

From 1930 to 1932, the Communist party alone in Harlem resorted to mass protest and direct confrontation with the government and the police. The party in Harlem was small and predominantly white, but it entered the depression on the heels of a dramatic reorganization that impressed upon its entire membership the importance of incorporating blacks into the movement and of fighting discrimination in all dimensions of American life.[6] Under the leadership of two black intellectuals, Richard Moore and Cyril Briggs, who had been in the party since the early 1920s, Harlem Communists seized upon depression conditions as an opportunity to win the Harlem masses away from "bourgeois" leaders who controlled the churches, fraternal organizations, political clubs, and nationalist groups that dominated Harlem life.[7] Sectarian, dogmatic, and insensitive to many of the nuances of black life, party organizers had one advantage over more established organizations and leaders: they understood that they were in a general crisis of capitalism in which traditional methods of self-help and private charity could not work. Only "persistent mass agitation," Communists insisted, could force the government to take action to ease the plight of the jobless, and they were determined to make blacks participants and beneficiaries of such an effort.

Communists made their first impact on Harlem with the organization of "hunger marches." Beginning with the great City Hall demonstration on March 6, 1930, Communists brought sizable contingents of unemployed Harlemites to mass marches on the mayor's office and on the Board of Estimate to demand the appropriation of funds for the unemployed.[8] These marches, which usually resulted in mass arrests, were held regularly from 1930 on, building up to national demonstrations in Washington, D.C., in December of 1931 and 1932.

The second tactic was eviction resistance. Beginning in the summer of 1930, interracial groups of Communists, organized in Unemployed Councils, would replace the furniture of Harlem residents evicted for nonpayment of rent.[9] These actions, initiated at street-corner meetings, sometimes attracted hundreds of community residents, though it was usually the Communists who risked arrest when the police came.[10] Eviction resistance reached its peak of effectiveness in the summer and the fall of 1931, shortly before the city set up home-relief bureaus that gave direct grants to the unemployed. Although it did not dramatically increase the party's black membership, eviction resistance helped the party recruit a small corps of street-wise black organizers, some with Garvey movement background, who could effectively present the party's views from soapboxes and stepladders and defend the party from the attacks (sometimes physical) of Harlem nationalists.[11]

The third tactic, the relief bureau sit-in, proved the most significant. In the spring of 1931, the Unemployed Councils developed a systematic way of acquiring food for their members. In addition to taking up collections for the starving, they would bring a delegation to sit in at private relief organizations until all those present were given aid.[12] Once the city opened its home-relief bureaus in December 1931, the Communists extended this same tactic to the city agencies. Although the bureaus tried to stay within their budgets and deal with cases individually, Communists, willing to risk arrest, insisted that entire delegations be given aid en masse. Sometimes, demonstrations became violent, with Unemployed Council members breaking furniture and fighting toe to toe with police; at other times, they were accompanied by sizable marches outside.[13] But the tactics did work. Large numbers of Harlemites willingly paid dues to Unemployed Councils that got their members on the relief rolls. In the mid-1930s, the councils had a membership varying between one and three thousand, and relief bureau sit-ins by large delegations occurred frequently.[14]

Despite the breadth of community participation in these protests— most participants were not Communists—I have been unable to find one recorded example of an eviction-resistance action or a home-relief bureau sit-in organized by a non-Communist group. These tactics remained the exclusive property of the Communist party throughout the depression. Part of the reason was ideological. Black community organizations, even those with militant rhetoric such as the Garveyite groups, traditionally preferred self-help efforts to organized mass protest. Imbued with a capitalist ethic, they looked to the private sector as the focal point of black advancement, and were most comfortable with forms of economic agitation that seemed consistent with the development of black business and a self-sufficient black economy.[15] The predepression mass protest that made the greatest impression on Harlem was the Chicago "Don't Buy Where You Can't Work" campaign, whose leaders defined the effort to force the employment of black clerks as a step toward the accumulation of business expertise as well as a solution to black unemployment.[16]

But even black spokespersons and organizations not enamored of capitalism were heirs to a deep-rooted caution stemming from years of persecution and isolation from the main currents of working-class protest. Black leaders feared that direct confrontations with government authority would be suicidal unless the community had powerful allies, and experience had taught them that such allies did not exist.[17] It remained for the Communists, with their militant interracialism, to show that some sections of the white working class would ally themselves with blacks around issues of common concern, and that confrontation tactics yielded results. Though party activities were not the only models of direct action available to black leaders—the NAACP's silent parade against lynching, the protests against *Birth of a Nation,* and the Chicago boycott movement were all within recent memory—their frequency, militancy, and practical effectiveness gave the tactics new legitimacy and helped encourage church, civic, and nationalist leaders to take a more activist stance.

Perhaps the most convincing evidence of the party's radicalizing effect on the Harlem community comes from the protests it organized on behalf of the Scottsboro boys. When the Communists fought the NAACP for control of the Scottsboro case in 1931, they argued that "mass action" rather than legal procedure would save the defendants' lives. In the spring of 1931, they organized three huge protest parades in Harlem, as well as several large indoor rallies and daily street-corner meetings featuring both black speakers and white speakers.[18] Harlemites nonetheless remained skeptical. The three protest parades, though they involved thousands of people, were overwhelmingly white, and few Harlem organizations endorsed the International Labor Defense's (ILD) efforts to "capture" the case.[19]

Throughout the winter of 1931 and the spring of 1932, Communists continued their program of marches, rallies, and street meetings without dramatically increasing community participation in the movement. Although the NAACP had dropped completely out of the defense, only intellectuals and performing artists in the Harlem community cooperated consistently with the ILD, helping to sponsor a large benefit at the Rockland Palace.[20] But when the Supreme Court agreed to hear the ILD's appeal in May 1932, the ILD's credibility increased markedly, and more and more Harlemites began to participate in movement activities, adopting the protest tactics as their own. One black clubwoman commented:

> I feel that it is amazing that in a situation of this kind, white citizens of this country have . . . demanded, in strong outspoken language, justice for these boys, and that Negroes would be reluctant to come to the front. I feel that this is, after all, a Negro fight, and that Negroes should put their shoulder to the wheel and carry on with as great, if not greater enthusiasm than their friends.[21]

In the party itself, black leadership also began to play a more prominent public role. Although the number of blacks in the organization remained small (seventy-odd in the summer of 1933), the Scottsboro case attracted a new group of talented street organizers and an equally impressive group of intellectuals and professional people.[22] With Richard Moore, William Fitzgerald, and Louis Campbell speaking from stepladders and soapboxes, William Patterson expounding legal strategy, and Louise Thompson charming and cajoling the Harlem elite in her salon, the Harlem party began to look less and less like an alien organization.[23] In addition, the party, even without the sanction of a new international line, openly began to seek the cooperation of church and fraternal organizations, though it remained unremittingly hostile to the leaders of the NAACP.[24] The shift in tactics and personnel helped to expand its influence.

When the Supreme Court overturned the Scottsboro convictions and sent the case back to Alabama for a new trial, the Scottsboro protests in Harlem began to assume an entirely different character. Harlem protest parades held during the trial, in April 1933, were overwhelmingly black, and community people lined the sidewalks contributing "pennies, nickels and dimes for the Scottsboro defense."[25]

The spontaneous community response to the conviction of Haywood Patterson, the first of the eight boys to come to trial, dwarfed all previous activity. When news arrived on Easter Sunday 1933, tens of thousands of Harlemites took to the streets in a "continuous mass meeting" in which Communists, Garveyites, ministers, and civic leaders spoke from the same platform.[26] The publisher of the *Amsterdam News*, William Davis, who had previously counseled extreme caution, called for a march on Washington to insure the safety of the defendants, and began circulating petitions asking President Roosevelt to intervene in their behalf. Within twenty-four hours, forty thousand people signed the petition.[27] The next day, three thousand Harlemites went downtown to greet the defense attorney, Samuel Liebowitz, on his return to New York, and five hundred of them tried to march up Broadway to Harlem, clashing with police at several points along the route.[28]

This level of activity continued unabated for the next month while the ILD prepared to appeal the conviction and went ahead with its plans for a Scottsboro march to Washington. Communist organizers, avoiding the culture shock that often confronted Harlemites when they joined

the party (both because of the unfamiliarity of party ideology and of
the disquieting presence of whites) recruited them en masse into virtually
all-black ILD chapters, which devoted their complete attention to
raising money for the defense and to preparing for the march.[29] Harlemites
participated in unprecedented numbers in local demonstrations, convey-
ing their strong support for the movement's tactics of mass action. "Yes
brother, a new thing is born," one protester commented. "It's a new people and we're a'marching for our rights."[30]

The ideological shift was dramatized by the division that took place
in the community over tactics for the Washington protest. In mid-April,
William Davis announced that he was no longer endorsing a mass march
to the capital and that he intended, instead, to organize a group of
"representative citizens" to present the petitions.[31] Many of Harlem's
most prominent civic leaders agreed to participate, including A. Philip
Randolph, Reverend Adam Clayton Powell, Sr., and Elks leader J.
Dalmus Steele. But, when the ILD denounced this action and proceeded
with its protest, it found support from several fraternal leaders and a few
key ministers, including Adam Clayton Powell, Jr.[32] A New York contingent of two thousand was sent to Washington, where they marched
outside the White House with protesters from other cities and forcibly
"integrated" several restaurants on their way back to the city.[33] For
many, the march decisively confirmed the effectiveness of mass pressure.
"We've never before attempted to fight our way through," one demon-
strator declared at a gathering of Harlem marchers, "we've always
attempted to pray our way through. We must go back to our churches
and lodges and put the spirit of fight in them."[34] Adam Clayton Powell, Jr.,
told the marchers that he was "losing a great many friends" because of
his repudiation of traditional tactics, but that he would "rather be
here with you humble people."[35] To achieve the things "we must and
shall have," Powell declared, "we must work together, and think together . . . until freedom is real, the world is uplifted, and we can say
the world is ours and everything that's in it."

In succeeding years, Scottsboro continued to be a focus of mass community protest and of ideological division among Harlem leaders. But
above all, it became a symbol of the community's growing resistance
to racial and economic abuse. Taken into every corner of Harlem life
by ILD and party organizers, adopted by a growing number of non-

Communist party leaders, the Scottsboro case not only sparked numerous marches, rallies, and street meetings, but it also provoked the first large-scale riot in Harlem's history.

In March 1934, at a Scottsboro protest meeting at which a mother of one of the defendants was speaking, Harlem police drove their cars into the crowd. As the demonstrators tried to fight back, thousands of Harlemites rushed into the streets to battle with the police, while others threw objects from the roofs and windows of buildings. For more than two hours, an estimated five thousand Harlemites battled with the police, finally dispersing only when police reinforcements came from other precincts.[36]

This spontaneous outburst, coming one year before the more publicized Harlem riot that began outside the Kress store on 125th Street, demonstrated the new kind of militancy emerging in the community. Stimulated and encouraged by the activity of Communist "cadre," it provided an atmosphere conducive to the development of numerous protest movements, many of them independent of party control.

THE COMMUNITY ERUPTS

The popular radicalization that the Communists had done so much to evoke had consequences that made the party deeply uneasy. During the spring and the summer of 1933, a former Garveyite calling himself Sufi Abdul Hamid had begun to organize a "Don't Buy Where You Can't Work" movement, along the lines of the Chicago boycott, in the 135th Street shopping district, and had forced a number of small stores to yield jobs to his suppporters. Party leaders, watching Sufi increase his following, feared that he might become the focal point of a massive nationalist upsurge aimed at "driving the white workers out of Harlem," a fear that Sufi fueled by periodic attacks on Jewish store owners and employees in the community.[37]

In addition, national leaders of the party had doubts about the willingness and ability of the party's Harlem leadership to counteract nationalist sentiment or to strengthen the party in a volatile situation. Briggs and Moore had shown remarkable skill as agitators, but the organization they headed seemed more like a mass movement than a disciplined Communist organization. Although the Unemployed Councils and the ILD each had over a thousand members, the party itself had only seventy blacks, and seemed incapable of developing coherent administrative procedures or eliminating personality conflicts and tensions between whites and blacks.[38] More seriously (to the Central Committee), some black Communists seemed susceptible to the nationalist moods sweeping the community. In July 1933, the Harlem leadership had initiated a campaign to force Harlem chain stores to hire black clerks, with an ultimate goal of a labor force that was at least 50 percent black. Although the campaign leaders also insisted that no white workers be fired, they aroused the ire of Central Committee leaders because they failed to involve white store employees in a supporting role, and because they defined the retail trades sector as a serious source of jobs at a time when only the government and the large corporations had the power to make concessions that would have a substantial impact on Harlem's unemployment problems.[39]

After an emergency party conference in the summer of 1933 (at which trade-union strategy and party building were the primary focus of attention), the Central Committee decided to change the Harlem leadership.[40] They demoted Briggs and Moore to secondary positions and brought in James W. Ford, a college-educated black Communist who had run for vice-president on the party ticket, to head the Harlem organization. Ford, unlike his predecessors, had never lived in Harlem and could not be easily swayed by community pressures to challenge party policies or question party discipline. An administrator rather than an agitator by temperament, Ford had a shrewd understanding of both the party apparatus and the inner workings of black community organizations.[41] He had the skills—and the ruthlessness—necessary to strengthen the party internally and to improve its bargaining power in the community at large.

To help Ford in his mission, the Central Committee initiated a policy of assigning some of its most talented black organizers from all over the country to the Harlem section. Ben Davis, Jr., an Amherst-educated black lawyer radicalized by the Angelo Herndon case, arrived from Georgia to be editor of the *Harlem Liberator;* James Ashford came from Detroit to head the Harlem Young Communist League; and Abner Berry came from Kansas City to serve as top party "trouble shooter" and negotiator with Harlem organizations.[42] To reinforce these black leaders, who set local party policy and defended the party line to the community and the membership, the Central Committee assigned to Ford a team of white Communists who would work behind the scenes to tighten up party administrative procedures and bring about a more efficient coordination of the party's diverse activities.[43] With this new leadership, the Central Committee hoped, the Harlem party would dramatically expand its black membership, minimize internal dissension, and move vigorously to prevent emerging community protest from assuming a nationalist direction.

Shortly after Ford's arrival, the party found itself face to face with a major challenge to its strategic outlook. During the spring and the summer of 1934, a coalition of Garveyites and middle-class church and civic leaders, few of whom had previously shown much enthusiasm for direct action tactics, began to picket stores on 125th Street in an effort to force them to hire black workers. The picketing had been initiated by Sufi, but a new campaign soon developed under the leadership of Harlem clergymen, who chose Blumstein's Department Store as their target. All the major churches, fraternal organizations, and political clubs supported the campaign, along with the editorial staff of the *New York Age,* and Arthur Reid and Ira Kemp of the African Patriotic League took charge of the picketing.[44] For sheer political breadth, the coalition surpassed anything the party had developed in the course of the Scottsboro campaign.

Although Communists welcomed the militancy displayed in the campaign, they were dismayed by its nationalist tone, particularly that expressed on the picket lines where the Garveyite influence was greatest. According to the party leadership, "Don't Buy Where You Can't Work" campaigns were dangerous and divisive unless they: (1) demanded that no whites be fired when blacks were hired; (2) welcomed whites on movement picket lines, especially white workers from stores being picketed; and (3) warned that jobs in black neighborhoods could not solve the problems of black unemployment.[45] The Harlem movement met none of these criteria; indeed, white Communists were regularly thrown off movement picket lines, and movement leaders, in their speeches and writings, described the campaign as a step toward black control of Harlem's economy.[46] "Race pride" and black unity were the movement's symbols, not "black and white unite and fight."

Harlem party leaders, though determined to undermine the nationalist character of the protest, quickly concluded that it would be politically disastrous to oppose a movement openly that had such broad-based community support. Instead, they decided to influence the movement indirectly by organizing parallel campaigns to win jobs for blacks through the joint effort of community groups and workers in those institutions that practiced discrimination. In August 1934, party organizations initiated a boycott of a large Harlem cafeteria and won the complete support of its unionized white employees. They mobilized large interracial picket lines and street demonstrations near the store to dramatize the effectiveness of black-white unity.[47] After a week and a half of protest, in which many arrests took place, the cafeteria agreed to hire four black countermen without firing any whites.[48]

In October 1934, a Communist-organized Home Relief Employees Association launched a campaign against discriminatory practices in the relief system. Supported by a number of Harlem churches and civic groups, the campaign helped force the promotion of several blacks to supervisory positions and was responsible for a large increase in the number of black investigators and clerks employed by the relief bureau.[49]

The effectiveness of these two campaigns did not persuade Harlem Garveyites to modify their strategy to win jobs. But they did help convince many moderate civic leaders that the party was fighting job discrimination more constructively than were such leading nationalist organizers as Sufi Abdul Hamid, Ira Kemp, and Arthur Reid. At the moment that the party's campaigns were winning victories, Reid and Kemp were fighting clergymen and editors over who should get the jobs at Blumstein's, while Sufi was resorting to anti-Semitic rhetoric.[50] When a State Supreme Court justice granted an injunction against Reid and Kemp during a picket campaign against a local shoe store, on the grounds that their activity would stimulate "racial riots and reprisals," both Harlem newspapers approved the court action.[51] Reid and Kemp retained a large following in the Garvey organizations and among Harlem crowds, but leaders of the large churches and the fraternal and civic organizations feared the raw prejudices unleashed by nationalists and the possibility of reprisals against blacks working out of Harlem.[52] Still wary of Communist intentions, the civic and church leaders were attracted by the party's proposals for protest coalitions that would link blacks to an array of white allies while applying mass pressure against discriminatory institutions.

COMMUNISTS IN THE FOREFRONT

From 1935 to 1937, the Communist party played a leading role in a wide array of Harlem protest movements. Aided by a new international line that enabled party members to proclaim their loyalty to democracy and accept the legitimacy of major black organizations, it formed alliances with a large number of Harlem organizations.[53] In addition, the vocabulary that the party used to describe its tactics—"mass action," "working-class unity," "the united front against fascism "—became common parlance among Harlem's journalists, clergymen, and civic leaders. Thus, much of Harlem's political discourse took a leftist tone.

The internal consolidation of the party following Ford's arrival in Harlem helped make the new policy successful. The party increased its black membership to over three hundred by January 1935 (seven hundred by that summer), developed a smooth-running administrative structure that enabled it to react quickly to political crises, and promoted more women to positions of party leadership.[54] Bonita Williams and Audley Moore, women with immense organizational skills and a down-home eloquence much appreciated among Harlem's poor, both rose to prominence during this period, giving the party leadership an ability to communicate comfortably with everyone in Harlem from the head of the Elks to followers of Father Divine. Though all party organizations in Harlem remained interracial as a matter of principle, units in black neighborhoods of Harlem became predominantly black, and the party increasingly dealt with local groups as one "uptown" organization to another.[55] White Communists continued to play an important role as office managers, education directors, and administrative secretaries. But James Ford, Ben Davis, and Abner Berry conducted all the important negotiation with the ministers, fraternal leaders, and Universal Negro Improvement Association (UNIA), NAACP, and Urban League officials with whom the party sought alliances, and won the respect, if not always the admiration, of those they dealt with.[56]

The party's political offensive took four principal forms: a campaign to turn the investigation following the Harlem riot into a broad indictment of discriminatory practices; the organization of mass protests against the Italian invasion of Ethiopia; the development of community support for CIO organizing drives; and the formation of the National Negro Congress.

The Harlem riot initially presented the party with a serious test of its legitimacy. Communist activists participated in the incident that sparked the outbreak, and, in the days following the riot, police officials and the Hearst press called for the party's suppression for inciting the crowds to violence.[57] However, a large number of Harlem community leaders rejected this interpretation of the riot and joined with Communists in blaming it on police misconduct and on underlying social conditions in the community.[58]

When the mayor set up a commission to investigate the riot, the Communist party developed a coordinated strategy to exonerate itself and to show the collaboration of city officials in discriminatory practices against blacks. Both black and white party leaders, supported by a team of ILD attorneys, attended every session of the commission's hearings and vigorously cross-examined city officials before the many enthusiastic Harlemites who crowded into the sessions.[59] The hearings were raucous, and several had to be cancelled when demonstrations by people in the audience got out of control.[60] By the time the hearings concluded, the party had made its case. The commission's report described the riot as "spontaneous and unpremeditated"; presented a lengthy and devastating description of the hardships suffered by Harlemites in every sphere of life; and praised Communists who attended the hearings for giving "direction to the . . . vague dissatisfaction of the people," and for "preventing these hearings from becoming purely the resentments of blacks against whites."[61]

More significantly, the party's activity at the hearings, often planned in tandem with leading ministers and Urban League and NAACP officials, led to the formation of action coalitions around housing conditions, police brutality, relief discrimination, and inadequate schools. During the hearings, several "mass trials" of city officials were held at large Harlem churches; issues were dramatized through marches and demonstrations; and delegations were sent to city departments.[62] The coalitions formed around relief discrimination and educational issues had a particularly lasting impact: blacks were appointed to advisory boards in both the home-relief bureaus and the Works Progress Administration (WPA); officials accused of racism were moved out of Harlem; and the number of black relief investigators continued to increase.[63] The Committee for Better Schools, formed after the investigation, remained a powerful organization for years, fighting for the construction of new schools, reform of the curriculum, the opening of schools out of the district for Harlem children, and the removal of racist teachers.[64] Both black and white Communists, many of them employees in the city agencies that were attacked, played a prominent role in these activities.

Mussolini's invasion of Ethiopia presented a different kind of challenge for Harlem Communists. It aroused great indignation in Harlem, which some Garveyites sought to direct into a boycott of Italian-American merchants and street vendors in the black sections of Harlem.[65] Party leaders felt that they had to seize the initiative from the nationalists in order to prevent racial warfare between black and Italian neighborhoods, and to define the Ethiopian issue as an "anti-Fascist struggle" rather than as a conflict of "black against white."[66]

To make its interpretation of the issue legitimate, the party brought leading Italian-American Communists to protest meetings in Harlem, where they stunned black audiences by giving impassioned speeches calling for the overthrow of the Mussolini government. The party also initiated a program of direct action, which included mass marches, demonstrations, picket lines at the Italian consulate, and efforts to raise money for food, arms, and medical supplies for Ethiopian troops.[67] Some nationalists demanded that such actions should be carried out by blacks alone, but the Communists successfully argued that the power of the movement would be greatly increased by the participation of white trade unions and leftist and liberal groups. The major Ethiopian protest in Harlem took place under their initiative. On August 3, 1935, the American League Against War and Fascism sponsored a protest march of twenty-five thousand people in Harlem, supported by most of the community's churches and civic organizations, which included a phalanx of several hundred Italians chanting "Down with Mussolini."[68]

Tactics such as these enabled the party to retain a position of leadership in the Ethiopian movement despite the damaging revelations of Soviet trade agreements with the Italian government.[69] In the spring of 1936 and 1937, the party organized large mass marches in behalf of Ethiopian independence, which featured anti-Fascist slogans and sizable white support. It took the lead in the formation of a medical committee for the defense of Ethiopia, which sent supplies to Ethiopian soldiers, and it established official contact with representatives of the Ethiopian government-in-exile.[70] Some Harlem nationalists continued to agitate against Italian merchants and tried to launch independent fund-raising efforts on an all-black basis, but their activities were denounced by both Harlem newspapers and by many prominent ministers and civic leaders.[71] Harlem leaders may have had doubts about Communist "sincerity," but they were deeply impressed by the energy with which white radicals and liberals rallied to the Ethiopian cause, and enthusiastically endorsed a strategy that united blacks and whites under the banner of antifascism. "When the next war is fought," Benjamin McLaurin of the Pullman Porters' union declared at one Ethiopian protest meeting, "it must be a workers war—a war of the workers, Negro and white."[72] Even some Garveyites, caught up in the enthusiasm of the protests, rejected narrowly racialist definitions of the conflict. "This is a fight of the masses against the classes," Captain A. L. King of the UNIA declared. "We black people will join you liberal whites all over the world not only to protect the rights of Negroes, but in the interests of all mankind."[73]

Labor-organizing drives in Harlem during 1935 and 1936 attracted support from a similar array of community groups. When editorial employees of the *Amsterdam News* were fired for union activity in the fall of 1935, leaders of Harlem churches and civic organizations joined trade unionists and Communists in a boycott that featured daily picket lines in front of its offices and the newsstands that sold it.[74] The management's appeal to the community to defend the paper against the inroads of "white unions" fell completely flat. Trade unionism had captured the imagination of many Harlem leaders, superseding their commitment to the development of black business. "I believe fundamentally in the cause of workers when they come in conflict with the employers," Reverend Shelton Hale Bishop of St. Phillips Church told a reporter who interviewed him on the picket line.[75] "Unionism is the only hope of all, especially Negroes," Adam Clayton Powell, Jr., declared.[76] After two months, the boycott was so successful that owners of the *Amsterdam News* had to put the paper up for sale. It was purchased by two Harlem physicians with pro-labor sympathies, who immediately began negotiations with the Newspaper Guild and returned discharged employees to their previous posts. Their first editorial in the paper's new format was entitled "Fight Fascism Now."[77]

Several union-organizing drives in the winter of 1936-1937 also received widespread community support. A Pharmacists Union and a Grocery Clerks Union both conducted successful campaigns for recognition in Harlem stores, aided by picket lines and mass meetings staged by Communists and non-Communist community leaders.[78] During an East Coast strike of a seaman's rank-and-file committee (which later became the National Maritime Union), Harlemites led by Adam Clayton Powell, Jr., and Lester Granger organized a Committee to Aid the Striking Seamen.[79] All three of these unions had both black and white Communists in their leadership, and had shown some willingness to fight racial discrimination in their industries. The only opposition they met in the community came from Ira Kemp and Arthur Reid, who had organized an all-black group called the Harlem Labor Union, which sought to place its members in Harlem stores by underbidding its AFL and CIO competitors.[80]

The convergence in strategic outlook between Communists and leaders of Harlem civic groups emerged most dramatically in the organization of the National Negro Congress.[81] Early in 1935, black Communists cautiously began sounding out allies and sympathizers about the formation of a nationwide black organization that would define mass action, trade unionism, and solidarity against fascism as its central strategic precepts.[82] John P. Davis, a close ally of the party, called a conference in Washington, D.C., to lay the basis for the congress, and it attracted a large enough and representative enough group of black leaders to proceed. A. Philip Randolph, despite his longtime antagonism to the party, agreed to serve as the first president of the new organization, and displayed no opposition to working with Communists to build it. In accordance with the Popular Front strategy, Communists remained in the background, concentrating their energies on fund-raising, publicity, and administrative work, but the non-Communist leaders who publicly represented the congress expressed views indistinguishable from those of black Communists. Lester Granger and John P. Davis, in a support meeting for the congress in Harlem, told their audience that the future of black workers lay in "mixed unions in their industries."[83] A. Philip Randolph's speech at the first congress in February 1936 called for blacks and whites to protect democratic institutions against the "hydra-headed monster of fascism." Randolph, who only three years before had opposed the Scottsboro march on Washington, called on blacks to express their grievances with greater militancy, using "parades, picketing, boycotting, mass protest, the mass distribution of propaganda, as well as legal action."[84] In 1931, such views would have been heterodox in most Harlem circles; by 1936, they were commonplace.

Throughout 1937, Communists continued to serve as a unifying force in much Harlem protest activity. Party organizers engaged in rent strikes, campaigns to improve local schools, efforts to lower meat and milk prices, and organizing drives of CIO unions. Their agitation in the relief system reached a new peak of intensity. During the spring and the summer of 1937, WPA workers' unions engineered widespread community resistance to firings on local WPA projects: work stoppages, marches, sit-down strikes at Harlem work sites and downtown offices, and a lunch-hour business stoppage that affected one thousand Harlem stores.[85] At the same time, the local chapter of the Workers Alliance organized a Harlem contingent for its Hunger March on Washington.[86] Thousands of Harlemites participated in these protests, which received enthusiastic support from Harlem ministers, social workers, and civic leaders who had worked with the party in the past.

The elan exhibited in these actions, and the substantial national gains registered by the CIO unions, strongly reinforced the belief in mass action as the key to social progress and the notion that black people had to conduct their struggle for equality in alliance with labor and the Left. "Practically all of the social and economic legislation passed during the Roosevelt administration is the outcome of sustained agitation by Radicals and Liberals," the *Amsterdam News* declared in August 1937. "The role of Negroes now is to join those groups which are agitating for social and economic justice in the United States."[87] Adam Clayton Powell, Jr., expressed similar sentiments: "Our future will be decided, not by ourselves, but by a union of all working class forces, white and black."[88]

The optimism generated by this seeming confluence between black protest and labor activism proved to be short lived. The belief in militant action remained widespread among all sections of Harlem's population, but the belief in a Negro-labor alliance—which Communists had elevated to an absolute—gradually lost much of its credibility. In New York City, CIO organizing drives ultimately disappointed those black leaders who had hoped that union activity would rapidly improve the position of blacks in the economy or eliminate job discrimination. Although most CIO unions took strong public stands against racial discrimination, they concentrated their efforts on winning union recognition for workers already employed, not on insuring unemployed workers equal access to jobs. Since the overwhelming majority of Harlemites remained unemployed or on WPA, conflicts of interest surfaced between unions and black community groups.[89] Some small CIO unions, conducting organizing drives in the Harlem community, placed the struggle to employ blacks on a coequal basis with the effort to win recognition—for example, the Pharmacists Union—but some larger CIO unions, operating in a market that did not depend upon black patronage, made the elimination of job barriers against blacks a distant priority.

The Transport Workers Union, a union led by Communists and Communist sympathizers, provided the most glaring example.[90] In 1936 and 1937, the TWU won recognition from four important utility companies in New York City (the Fifth Avenue Coach Company, the New York Omnibus Company, the Brooklyn-Manhattan Transit Company, and the Interborough Rapid Transit Company) without eliminating the open discrimination against blacks that was practiced by these companies.[91] The bus companies refused to hire blacks as drivers or as mechanics; the subway companies refused to hire them as conductors, as motormen, or as ticket agents. The TWU publicly opposed such discrimination and had initially proposed nondiscrimination clauses in contract negotiations, but it had withdrawn them at the companies' insistence.[92] Nevertheless, non-Communist Harlem organizations—and many blacks who worked as porters and cleaners in these companies—wanted to know why the union did not make elimination of job barriers to blacks the first condition of its negotiations.[93] In the fall of 1937, the NAACP tried to push the TWU leadership into more vigorous action, but it only succeeded in getting the TWU to negotiate an agreement to promote a few blacks from porters to platform agents on the IRT.[94] The unions' protests that discrimination was the companies' responsibility convinced few Harlemites, and even pro-labor Harlem columnists began to assume a more critical attitude toward the CIO. In April 1938, Adam Clayton Powell, Jr., reviewing the problems in transport, argued that henceforth blacks would have to conduct their struggle for equality on two fronts—"against the employer, and against the trade unions for admission, recognition, and advancement."[95]

The Communist party's poor handling of such criticism eroded its credibility. Party leaders publicly defended the TWU's inaction, even though other Communist-led unions had a far better record in fighting discrimination, and emphatically opposed "mass pressure" on unions to force them to respect black interests. According to Harlem Communists, critics of CIO policy were threatening the Negro-labor alliance on which black progress depended and were dividing blacks from their "natural allies."[96]

The party's actions in this dispute reflected a fundamental change in party trade-union policy that had begun to take place during the Popular Front years. Once the CIO organization offensive began, the party's national leadership took the position that no other domestic political concern, however significant, should be allowed to jeopardize the success of the CIO campaign or to interfere with smooth relations between party trade-union functionaries and top CIO officials. In 1938, the party leadership went to the extent of dissolving their shop units (secret caucuses of all Communists active in a particular union), the major form of party trade-union activity for more than ten years, to counteract suspicions that Communists aimed to dominate the CIO, and to give Communist trade-union leaders greater flexibility.[97] But even earlier, the policy had emerged as a tendency not to make demands on Communist labor leaders that might jeopardize their position of power in the union or the union's struggle for recognition. In dealing with the Transit Workers Union, where a leftist leadership maintained an uneasy hegemony over a conservative (and often racist) membership, the party simply did not push the leadership very hard to make antidiscrimination measures a primary focus of their activity.[98] A similar situation ensued in other unions where the Left was in a tenuous position or where its leaders were particularly opportunistic—for example, the Hotel and Restaurant Workers and the National Maritime unions.[99] As a consequence, the struggle against job discrimination, though still a major party priority, was sometimes sacrificed when it conflicted with the dynamics of trade-union unity and survival or with the leadership aspirations of party unionists.

Perhaps the most reprehensible single example of this new policy came in 1938, when Harlem Communists openly opposed a series of bills in the state legislature to limit the bargaining rights of unions that discriminated against blacks. The AFL had vehemently and successfully opposed an antidiscrimination rider to the Wagner Act in 1935; both it and the CIO opposed the suggestion of a state investigatory commission to add a similar clause to the State Labor Relations Act.[100] Communists, after initially supporting the legislation, quickly reversed their position to conform with that of CIO leaders, justifying their views in the most self-righteous tones.[101] In hearings on the legislation held from 1938 to 1940, both black and white Communists argued that employers fostered discrimination, that labor could be counted on to eliminate discrimination in its ranks through internal measures, and that the proposed bills could be used to delay or undermine union-organizing drives.[102] Non-Communist Harlemites were enraged by the party's position, which seemed to suggest that any advance by labor necessarily helped blacks. "We are constantly being told that employers are the 'natural' enemies

of Negroes, and that organized labor is their 'natural' friend," Roy
Wilkins wrote. "Well, let labor 'put it on the line.' Let labor give us something for which to fight and we will fight. . . . But to expect us to sympa-
thize with labor, support labor, show solidarity with labor, just for the
fun of being labeled 'progressive' is asking too much."[103]

The party's position on the Transit Workers issue and on legislative
proposals banning union discrimination, though it marked an important
break in the "united front" between Communists and Harlem activists,
did not serve to isolate the party from the mainstream of Harlem protest.
In 1938, Communists played a leading role in the formation of a major
community effort to challenge discrimination in the job market: the
Greater New York Coordinating Committee on Employment.[104] Working closely with Reverends William Lloyd Imes and Adam Clayton Powell,
Jr., the organization's major spokesmen, Communists helped develop a
strategy aimed at winning jobs for blacks, without stirring up nationalist
sentiment. The campaign focused on the public utilities, sought cooperation from organized labor, and insisted that no white workers be fired
when blacks were hired.[105] During the spring of 1938, through a campaign that featured mass picketing and efforts to disrupt company service
by tying up phone lines and paying bills in the most time-consuming
manner possible, the committee forced Con Edison and New York Telephone Company to grant a small number of jobs for blacks.[106]

It then turned its attention to 125th Street, where the Garveyite-led
Harlem Labor Union (HLU) was conducting a vigorous campaign to place
its members in stores, often at the expense of AFL or CIO unions that
had already won bargaining rights at these establishments. Some store
owners had bolted the traditional trade union to sign with the HLU, and
a number of both black and white union members had been displaced.[107]

The Coordinating Committee, eschewing a strategy of mass protest,
tried to settle the 125th Street question entirely through negotiations
at the top. In April 1938, it signed an agreement with the Harlem Chamber of Commerce, which guaranteed that one-third of all jobs in Harlem
would be given to blacks, with positions opening as white workers left or
retired. Black employees would be referred to the chamber by the Urban
League and the YMCA.[108] In return, the organizations composing the
Coordinating Committee, including churches, fraternal organizations,
and trade unions, would try to stop the picketing for jobs staged by the
Harlem Labor Union, which all parties agreed was a source of racial tension

This agreement, which the Communists strongly supported, failed completely. Both Harlem newspapers criticized it for relinquishing the community's right to protest, and the Harlem Labor Union, a nominal affiliate of the Coordinating Committee, refused to stop its picketing.[109] Throughout the summer of 1938, bitter controversy ensued between the HLU, the Coordinating Committee, and organized labor, with the HLU making considerable headway in smaller stores and in black-owned concerns. In October 1938, the major groups on the Coordinating Committee conceded that the question of jobs could not be settled by fiat. They worked out a division of labor within which the Coordinating Committee would focus its efforts on companies outside of Harlem, and the HLU would not try to organize those establishments in Harlem with AFL or CIO contacts.[110]

The 1938 jobs campaign contained more than its share of ironies. The Communists, who had done so much to popularize direct action in Harlem in the early 1930s, were now trying to suppress nationalist agitation for jobs on the grounds that it threatened black-white unity and the gains of organized labor. With mass-protest techniques now the property of all segments of the Harlem community, from the Garveyites to the black church, Communists, concerned with building a power base in the CIO and operating within the New Deal coalition, increasingly assumed a conservative role in community struggles. In the fall of 1938, several former Communists, writing in Harlem newspapers, complained that the Communist party had become a "recognized party" that had sacrificed much of its militancy to protect its relationship with the Roosevelt and the LaGuardia administrations, and that its leadership was dominated by Harlem's "upper crust" rather than by "hogmaw, blackeye peas eating race men."[111]

The party's tactical shift did not quite represent a complete reversal of its previous positions. In the winter and the spring of 1939, Communists continued to participate in a wide range of protest activity in Harlem. Both black and white Communists operating in the Coordinating Committee helped engineer a large protest movement designed to win jobs for blacks at the New York World's Fair. It featured mass picketing at the fair's Manhattan offices and at the Flushing Meadow fair ground itself.[112] Simultaneously, the Workers Alliance held sporadic protests against evictions and cutbacks in relief allotments.[113]

But in one important sphere of party work, the unemployed movement, the party's support for LaGuardia and Roosevelt had a profoundly depressing effect on its activity. As early as May 1938, Workers Alliance leader Herbert Benjamin had signalled a major shift in alliance strategy, away from mass protest and toward lobbying and election of progressive candidates. "The unemployed," Benjamin wrote, "are not likely to become involved in the type of spontaneous actions which were characteristic of previous struggles. . . . No one could long maintain leadership of the unemployed who would direct the struggle of the unemployed against progressive public officials supported by organized labor and progressive forces."[114] Throughout the remainder of 1938, alliance protests, even at Harlem relief bureaus, became increasingly infrequent.

More seriously, the alliance proved extraordinarily quiescent in the face of massive cutbacks in Harlem WPA programs in the spring of 1939, cutbacks that inspired "terror and fear" in the community. Thousands of Harlemites, particularly those in white-collar positions, lost their jobs in the works projects and were forced onto the relief rolls when they could not find employment in the private sector. Harlem newspapers claimed that "unrest among relief clients was at the highest point in years," but neither the Workers Alliance nor the project workers' unions took the initiative in organizing the kind of massive resistance—sit-ins, strikes, and mass marches—that they had sponsored two years before in response to similar cuts.[115] The alliance put much of its dwindling energies into lobbying against the cuts, but its efforts had no effect. The layoffs ensued unimpeded, and Communist unemployed organizations experienced a significant loss of credibility because of their inability to protect the relief programs they had fought so hard to create.[116]

AFTER THE PACT: COMMUNISTS ON THE DEFENSIVE

The Nazi-Soviet pact, and the Communist party's response to it, crystallized emerging dissatisfaction with the party's role in the Harlem community. Communists defined their highest priority as keeping America out of war, and injected their analysis of the European conflict as a "struggle of rival imperialisms" into every movement in which they were participating.[117] Several Harlem civic leaders who had worked closely with the party broke with it because of its attempts to impose its foreign-policy line on black protest movements. The most significant of those who broke with the party, A. Philip Randolph, resigned the presidency of the National Negro Congress in the spring of 1940 and issued a ringing denunciation of the party's efforts to control the NNC's political perspective. "The Congress cannot afford to become a part of any labor or political organization," Randolph declared, "since it may want to fight its present friends in the future."[118]

Not all prominent figures in the Harlem community parted company with the party. Adam Clayton Powell, Jr., after denouncing the Communists vigorously in the fall of 1939, quietly began working with them in the Coordinating Committee in late 1940.[119] Some ministers and fraternal leaders still maintained relationships with the party in the Better Schools Committee, in tenants' activity, and in cultural programs.[120] Communists helped effect one of the most impressive victories in the Harlem jobs movement in the spring of 1941—a bus boycott cosponsored by the Transport Workers Union, which resulted in an agreement to assure blacks 17 percent of the driver and mechanics positions on the Fifth Avenue Coach Company.[121]

The Communists had nonetheless become isolated from the single most significant form of protest activity in the Harlem community—the drive to win equal employment rights for black workers on defense industries. Former allies of the party, using rhetoric and tactics that the Communists had popularized, placed relentless pressures on the Roosevelt administration in national defense while they endorsed the pro-Allies foreign policy.

In January 1941, after months of petitioning and lobbying by NAACP and Urban League officials, A. Philip Randolph announced that he would lead ten thousand Negroes in a march on Washington unless the president issued a proclamation banning discrimination in national defense.[122] The campaign immediately won the endorsement of both Harlem newspapers and a coalition of organizations as broad as any formed during the depression. Only the Communists were excluded—at first, by their own choice, and later, on the initiative of Randolph, who declared them "a definite menace, pestilence, and nuisance, as well as a danger to the Negro people."[123]

The rhetoric of the March on Washington Committee simultaneously mirrored and diverged from the strategic perspectives that Communists had emphasized in the mid-1930s and that Randolph himself had articulated at the first National Negro Congress. In line with his earlier pronouncements, Randolph insisted on mass protest action as the black community's best weapon against discriminatory policies. "The Negro is forced to abandon the old methods of personal or group appeal to the goodwill, sympathy, or pity of his so called white friends," he wrote. "He is compelled to supplement the technique of the conference with mass action . . . to pit his mass power against the forces that seek to victimize him."[124] Randolph now insisted that blacks had to act on their own and could not subordinate their interest to the needs of any coalition or alliance with white groups. Whites were barred from participating in the march. Movement propaganda emphasized the need for blacks to act independently, although it did not reject the goal of an integrated society or the value of interracial cooperation.[125]

The dramatic success of the movement, reflected in the creation of the Fair Employment Practices Commission and in Roosevelt's proclamation banning discrimination in defense industries, reinforced certain political lessons that Harlem leaders had derived from the struggles of the depression years. First, it reaffirmed the commitment to direct action techniques—or the threat of them—as the most potent weapons at the black community's disposal. Second, it demonstrated that blacks could venture beyond their alliances with organized labor and with white radicals and liberals and still make impressive gains. Most Harlem leaders still sought such alliances, but approached them with a greater sense of their own power. Finally, it showed that a united front of black organizations could mount an effective protest without Communist participation. Not all Harlem leaders broke their ties with the party, but most now knew they could do so without doing irreparable damage to black protest activity.

The Harlem experience indicates that Communists contributed, both by positive and by negative examples, to major changes in black political attitudes and behavior. Depression-era Harlem was the scene of an unprecedented explosion of protest activity, much of it under Communist auspices, much of it independent of party control. Communists expanded the possibilities available to black leadership by demonstrating that direct action could produce results. They also helped break down deep-seated hostility to the white working class and the labor movement by providing concrete, meaningful examples of solidarity in relief struggles, in the Scottsboro movement, and in campaigns against job discrimination. Moreover, their tactical and ideological focus encouraged a large segment of black leadership to see the government rather than the private sector as the major lever for black economic progress, and to seek to influence government policy through disruption and organized protest as well as through court action and political pressure.

In view of these contributions, it is all the more unfortunate that the party proved unwilling to sustain its mass-protest orientation and its single-minded commitment to fighting discrimination in the job market, once it sought broader influence in the CIO and the New Deal. Though the party remained the most important organized force fighting discrimination practices in the unions, its actions fell far short of the expectations of black leaders who regarded the continuing marginality of the black poor—and the spectre of a permanent class of black welfare recipients—with growing dismay.[126] The increasing tactical conservatism that the party displayed in the face of the desperate plight of working-class blacks helped sow the seeds of a split between the black community and the Left, which the party's flip-flops on foreign policy, its wartime de-emphasis of black issues, and the wave of postwar repression widened into a chasm. As a cursory look at the battered landscape of urban America will tell us, we are all paying the price for that division.

CONCLUSION

For contemporary activists, the Communist experience offers few comforting lessons. The effectiveness of party work stemmed from many features that New Left organizers disdained: its discipline; its insistence on defining local issues within a national and international perspective; its ability to link strategies in the neighborhood with those in the workplace; its ability to motivate people for day- to-day political work in terms of a vision of social change (however flawed) larger than participatory democracy. Following these precepts, Communists not only inspired an extraordinary range of protest in an impoverished community, they also developed alliances between both black and white working people that were virtually unprecedented at the time, and that have rarely been duplicated since.

To imitate Communist methods mechanically, of course, would be a grave mistake. Communists failed to achieve many of their objectives because the very "internationalism" that gave them energy ultimately undermined their best work. American Communists readily sacrificed their most effective local programs when they conflicted with the requirements of Soviet policy as defined by the Comintern. Similarly, the party's discipline and political coherence, though valuable in some contexts, took a form that precluded serious criticism of party errors and that sometimes led to the dogmatic justification of policies that seemed indefensible to community residents.

Nevertheless, the party's accomplishments should sensitize us to the value of conducting community organizing within the framework of a Socialist movement that sees the neighborhood, the workplace, and the political arena as parts of a coherent whole, and that seeks to balance the claims of different oppressed groups in a principled way. The ability to coordinate different constituencies in community struggle is a powerful weapon. Perhaps the next generation of American radicals will find a way of amalgamating Socialist principles and American traditions more effectively than did their Communist forebears, and of building a movement in which organizational discipline does not occur at the expense of freedom of expression and popular participation in setting policy.

NOTES

1. See Mark Naison, "The Communist Party in Harlem in the Early Depression Years: A Case Study in the Reinterpretation of American Radicalism," *Radical History Review* 3, no. 4 (Fall 1976), and "Historical Notes on Blacks and American Communism: The Harlem Experience," *Science and Society* 42, no. 3 (Fall 1978), for material on the mobilization of white Communists for work in black communities.

2. Works that discuss the role of Communists in depression-era mass protest include: Dan T. Carter, *Scottsboro: A Tragedy of the American South* (New York: Oxford University Press, 1971); August Meier and Eliot Rudwick, *Along the Color Line: Explorations in the Black Experience* (Urbana, Ill.: University of Illinois Press, 1976); and Harvey Sitkoff, *New Deal for Blacks: The Emergence of Civil Rights as a National Issue in the Depression Decade* (New York: Oxford University Press, 1978).

3. Stanley High, "Black Omens," *Saturday Evening Post,* June 4, 1938, p. 40.

4. *New York Herald Tribune,* October 8, 1933, section 2; *New York Post,* March 21, 1935.

5. On charitable activities of Harlem churches, see *New York Age,*

December 13, 1930, and January 17, 1931. On more coordinated strategies to deal with unemployment, see *New York Amsterdam News,* April 2, 1930, and *Negro World,* February 7, 1931. Some Harlem groups tried to start a "Don't Buy Where You Can't Work" movement in the spring of 1931, modeled on a similar campaign in Chicago, but they failed to get it off the ground. The first use of direct action tactics by a non-Communist Harlem group was the picketing of stores to force them to hire black workers in 1932. This campaign, organized by Sufi Abdul Hamid, was supported by almost no other organizations, and the concept didn't "catch on" until the spring of 1934, when the Citizens League for Fair Play began picketing Blumstein's Department Store on 125th Street.

6. For details on reorganization of the party following the Sixth World Congress of the Comintern, see Naison, "The Communist Party in Harlem in the Early Depression Years."

7. *Liberator,* March 1, 1930.

8. *Liberator,* March 15, 1930.

9. I discovered fourteen recorded examples of eviction resistance in Harlem during 1930 and 1931 (as recorded in black and Communist newspapers), although one former Communist organizer in Harlem informed me that they occurred far more frequently than they were recorded in print. Interview with Theodore Bassett, Brooklyn, N.Y., August 29, 1974, personal holding.

10. For more detailed descriptions of how eviction resistance took place, see *New York Amsterdam News,* October 3, 1930, and *Daily Worker,* August 14, 1931, and September 8, 1931.

11. Mark Naison, "The Communist Party in Harlem, 1928-1936" (Ph.D. diss., Columbia University, 1976), p. 138; *Liberator,* July 1, 1933.

12. *Liberator,* November 14, 1931, and November 21, 1931.

13. For more detailed descriptions of relief bureau protest in Harlem, see Naison, "The Communist Party in Harlem," pp. 136-41. On the general strategy of relief bureau protests, see Frances Fox Piven and Richard Cloward, *Poor People's Movements: Why They Succeed, How They Fail* (New York: Pantheon, 1977), pp. 56-60. Specific actions are described in *New York Amsterdam News,* June 29, 1932; *Hunger Fighter,* September 1932. *Hunger Fighter* was a newspaper of the Unemployed Councils.

14. James W. Ford and Louis Sass, "The Development of Work in the Harlem Section," *The Communist* 14, no. 4 (April 1935): 316-17; *New York Amsterdam News,* October 22, 1938; *Daily Worker,* April 7, 1938.

15. See *Harlem Business Men's Bulletin* 1, no. 1 (March 1931), for

a good description of the Garvey movement's approach to the problem of unemployment, as well as Ralph Gothard's regular column in the *Negro World,* "It Can Be Done," which appeared from 1930 to 1932.

16. *New York Amsterdam News,* October 16, 1929; *Negro World,* February 8, 1931, March 21, 1931, April 25, 1931.

17. Perhaps the most outspoken "leftist" critic of Communist direct action tactics was W. E. B. Du Bois, who expressed his views in editorials in *The Crisis.* See W. E. B. Du Bois, "Postscript," *The Crisis* 38, no. 9 (September 1931): 313-14.

18. *New York Times,* April 25, 1931, May 17, 1931, and June 29, 1931.

19. *New York Amsterdam News,* July 2, 1931; *Interstate Tatler,* July 2, 1931.

20. *Daily Worker,* May 9, 1932, and May 17, 1932; *Interstate Tatler,* May 19, 1932.

21. Scottsboro Unity Defense Committee, press release, September 1932; *International Labor Defense Papers,* Schomburg Collection, New York City, Reel 2, c. 17.

22. Louis Sass, "Some Problems of the Harlem Section," *Party Organizer* 8, no. 3 (March 1934): 19.

23. *New York Amsterdam News,* February 24, 1932, p. 9; *Interstate Tatler,* April 28, 1932, p. 3.

24. See Naison, *The Communist Party in Harlem,* pp. 141-42, 147-51, 152-55, for a description of "united front" activities in Harlem that *preceded* the changed international line of the Comintern.

25. *Daily Worker,* April 4, 1933, and April 9, 1933.

26. *New York Amsterdam News,* April 12, 1933; *New York Times,* April 10, 1933; *Daily Worker,* April 11, 1933.

27. *New York Amsterdam News,* April 12, 1933.

28. *New York Times,* April 11, 1933.

29. *Harlem Liberator,* June 10, 1933. Virtually all party leaders I have interviewed mentioned the party's difficulties in bridging the cultural gap between working-class Harlemites and party functionaries who went through party training schools. At no time was this gap greater than in the early thirties. Interview with Abner Berry, July 5, 1977, personal holding; interview with Theodore Bassett, December 15, 1973, personal holding.

30. *Daily Worker,* April 24, 1933.

31. *New York Age,* April 22, 1933.

32. *New York Age,* May 13, 1933; "Reformist Saboteurs of the Scottsboro March," press release, *ILD Papers,* Reel 2, c. 33; *Harlem Liberator,* May 13, 1933.

33. *Harlem Liberator,* May 13, 1933; *New York Age,* May 20, 1933; Carter, *Scottsboro,* pp. 250-51.

34. *Harlem Liberator,* May 13, 1933.

35. *New York Age,* May 20, 1933.

36. *New York Times,* March 18, 1934; *New York Amsterdam News,* March 24, 1934; Report, A. L. Wirin to Hon. F. H. LaGuardia, March 26, 1934, *Fiorello H. LaGuardia Papers,* Municipal Archives, New York City, Box 2550, H # 9; Report, From the Chief Inspector to the Police Commissioner, March 26, 1934, *LaGuardia Papers,* Box 2550, H # 9.

37. Melville Weiss, "Don't Buy Where You Can't Work" (M.A. thesis, Columbia University 1941), pp. 56-57; *Harlem Liberator,* August 5, 1933, August 26, 1933.

38. MacKawain, "The League of Struggle for Negro Rights in Harlem," *The Party Organizer* 8, no. 4 (April 1934): 60; James W. Ford and Louis Sass, "Development of Work in the Harlem Section," *Communist* 14, no. 4 (April 1935): 323; Charles Krumbein, "Small Progress in New York District," *Party Organizer* 7, no. 11 (November 1933): 18.

39. *Harlem Liberator,* August 19, 1933, August 26, 1933, September 9, 1933; *New York Amsterdam News,* August 17, 1935; Harry Haywood, *The Road to Negro Liberation* (New York: Workers Library Publishers, 1934), pp. 53-54.

40. Sass, "Problems of the Harlem Section," pp. 19-20; interview with Richard B. Moore, November 14, 1973, personal holding.

41. Interview with Harry Haywood, May 16, 1973, personal holding; George Charney, *A Long Journey* (New York: Quadrangle, 1968), pp. 93-94; interview with Richard B. Moore, November 14, 1973, personal holding; *New York Amsterdam News,* February 28, 1934.

42. *New York Amsterdam News,* June 30, 1934; Benjamin J. Davis, *Communist Councilman from Harlem* (New York: International Publishers, 1969), pp. 82-100; *Daily Worker,* September 21, 1936, December 1, 1934; interview with Abner Berry, December 3, 1973, personal holding.

43. Sass, "Problems of the Harlem Section," pp. 19-20; interview with Abner Berry, July 29, 1974, personal holding; interview with Richard B. Moore, November 14, 1973, personal holding.

44. *New York Age,* May 26, 1934, and June 23, 1934; Weiss, *Don't Buy Where You Can't Work,* pp. 56-57; Wilbur Young, "Activities of Bishop Amiru, Al-Mu-Minin Sufi A. Hamid," *Federal Writers Project Papers,* Schomburg Collection, New York City, Reel 1; *New York Age,* October 1, 1932.

45. *Daily Worker,* June 9, 1934. For more detailed discussion of the

development of the party's theoretical position on this issue, see Naison, *The Communist Party in Harlem, 1928-1936,* pp. 198-205.

46. *New York Amsterdam News,* August 4, 1934; *Negro Liberator,* August 4, 1934.

47. *New York Times,* September 1, 1934; *Daily Worker,* September 7, 1934, September 8, 1934, and September 11, 1934.

48. *Negro Liberator,* September 15, 1934.

49. *26th and 28th PCTS Bulletin,* October 29, 1934, *La Guardia Papers,* Box 2550, H # 5; *New York Amsterdam News,* December 8, 1934; *Negro Liberator,* December 15, 1934; Harry Dolimer and Allan McKenzie, *The Negro Worker in the ERB* (New York: Association of Workers in Public Relief Agencies, 1937), p. 1; *Report of the Mayor's Commission on Conditions in Harlem,* reprinted in the *New York Amsterdam News,* July 18, 1936, Xerox copy in the Schomburg Collection, New York City, pp. 10-11.

50. *New York Age,* September 15, 1934, September 22, 1934, October 6, 1934, and October 27, 1934; *New York Amsterdam News,* October 6, 1934.

51. *New York Age,* November 17, 1934; *New York Amsterdam News,* October 20, 1934.

52. *New York Age,* December 8, 1934; *New York Amsterdam News,* October 13, 1934.

53. James W. Ford, "The United Front in the Field of Negro Work," *Communist* 14, no. 2 (February 1935): 169-73; Ford and Sass, "Development of Work," p. 154; George Charney, *A Long Journey* (New York: Quadrangle, 1968), p. 60; Al Richmond, *A Long View from the Left* (Boston: Houghton Mifflin, 1972), p. 254.

54. Ford and Sass, "The Development of Work," p. 323; *Daily Worker,* August 3, 1935.

55. *Negro Liberator,* July 1, 1935; interview with Audley Moore, May 3, 1974, personal holding; George Charney, *A Long Journey,* p. 102; in the two published descriptions of Harlem neighborhood branches in the *Daily Worker,* the membership is described as predominantly black, 16 out of 20 in one case, and 95 out of 100 in the other. See *Daily Worker,* September 11, 1937, and May 20, 1938.

56. *New York Amsterdam News,* September 4, 1937; Lester Granger, "Along the Party Line," *Opportunity* 17, no. 3 (March 1939): 91.

57. *New York Times,* March 21, 1935; *New York Herald Tribune,* March 26, 1935; *New York American,* March 20, 1935; *New York Evening Journal,* March 23, 1935.

58. *New York Times,* March 21, 1935; *New York Herald Tribune,* March 21, 1934; *New York Amsterdam News,* March 30, 1935.

59. Harlem Section, International Labor Defense, to Chairman, Mayor's Committee to Investigate Harlem Conditions, March 25, 1935, *LaGuardia Papers,* Box 667; *Report of the Mayor's Commission on Conditions in Harlem,* p. 5; *New York Amsterdam News,* April 6, 1935; interview with Abner Berry, July 29, 1974, New York City, personal holding.

60. *New York Age,* May 4, 1935.

61. *Report of the Mayor's Commission on Conditions in Harlem,* p. 3; *New York Times,* August 10, 1935.

62. *Negro Liberator,* June 1, 1935, June 15, 1935, and July 1, 1935; leaflet "Protest Terror at Mayor's Committee Hearings," *LaGuardia Papers,* Box 667.

63. *New York Amsterdam News,* October 5, 1935, and March 14, 1936; *New York Age,* September 28, 1935, and October 26, 1935; *New York Times,* November 14, 1935; Dolimer and McKenzie, *The Negro Worker,* pp. 5-9.

64. *New York Amsterdam News,* March 14, 1936, and December 21, 1940.

65. *New York Amsterdam News,* April 27, 1935; *Negro Liberator,* July 1, 1935; leaflet "Defend Ethiopia, Don't Buy Italian Merchandise, Buy from NEGROES," *Universal Negro Improvement Association Papers,* Schomburg Collection, New York City, Reel 4, Box 11.

66. Interview with Abner Berry, December 3, 1973, New York City, personal holding; *Daily Worker,* March 25, 1935.

67. *Daily Worker,* February 13, 1935, and February 15, 1935; James W. Ford, "For Defense of Ethiopia," *Negro Worker* 5, no. 5 (May 1935): 5-6; *Negro Liberator,* July 1, 1935.

68. *New York Times,* August 4, 1935; *New York Amsterdam News,* August 10, , 1935; *New York Age,* August 10, 1935; *Baltimore Afro-American,* August 10, 1935.

69. *New York Times,* September 8, 1935; *New York Age,* October 5, 1935; "Soviet Russia Aids Italy," *The Crisis* 42, no. 10 (October 1935): 305.

70. *New York Amsterdam News,* September 28, 1935; *Daily Worker,* October 4, 1935; James W. Ford, "The Negro People and the Farmer-Labor Party," *Communist* 14, no. 12 (December 1935): 1137; James W. Ford, *The Communists and the Struggle for Negro Liberation* (New York: Workers Library Publishers, 1936), pp. 61-62; *New York Amsterdam News,* April 3, 1937.

71. *New York Amsterdam News,* October 5, 1935; *New York Times,* October 4, 1935, p. 6; *New York Age,* October 12, 1935.

72. *New York Age,* October 5, 1935.

73. Ibid.

74. *Daily Worker,* October 17, 1935; *New York Age,* October 19, 1935, and October 26, 1935; Loren Miller, "Labor Trouble in Harlem," *New Masses* 17 (October 22, 1935): 20.

75. *New York Age,* November 23, 1935.

76. Ibid.

77. *New York Amsterdam News,* January 25, 1936.

78. Interview with Leon Davis, November 23, 1976, New York City, personal holding; interview with Abner Berry, July 5, 1977, New York City, personal holding; *Daily Worker,* November 20, 1936, December 10, 1936, and June 4, 1937; *New York Age,* December 5, 1936; *New York Amsterdam News,* November 21, 1936, January 30, 1937, and February 18, 1939.

79. *New York Amsterdam News,* November 14, 1936, and November 28, 1936; *Daily Worker,* January 12, 1937, January 14, 1937, and February 4, 1937.

80. Weiss, "Don't Buy," pp. 86-89.

81. John Hope Franklin, *From Slavery to Freedom,* 3d ed. (New York: Alfred Knopf, 1966), p. 398.

82. *Negro Liberator,* February 15, 1935, and March 15, 1935; *Daily Worker,* May 23, 1935. Although most historians have attributed the idea for the congress to John P. Davis, Abner Berry, the section organizer for the Communist party in Harlem during the middle and late 1930s, claims that the idea of the congress originated among Harlem Communists, and that the party designated Davis, who had an office in Washington, D.C., to push the movement nationally. There is some good circumstantial evidence for this view. Harlem Communists began referring to the need for a congress in January 1935, and raised the issue regularly in party publications from that point on. This was well before the Washington Conference, called by Davis's Joint Committee on National Recovery, which developed specific plans for the congress. Interview with Abner Berry, December 3, 1973, personal holding.

83. *New York Amsterdam News,* June 1, 1935.

84. *Official Proceedings of the National Negro Congress, February 14, 15, 16, 1936* (Washington, D.C.: National Negro Congress, 1936), p. 11.

85. *New York Amsterdam News,* May 29, 1937, June 26, 1937, and

July 24, 1937; *New York Age,* June 19, 1937, July 24, 1937; *Daily Worker,* May 28, 1937, June 14, 1937, June 15, 1937.

86. *Daily Worker,* January 28, 1937, June 11, 1937, June 19, 1937, and August 16, 1937; *New York Amsterdam News,* October 29, 1938.

87. *New York Amsterdam News,* August 14, 1937.

88. *New York Amsterdam News,* July 14, 1937.

89. Unemployment rates in Harlem remained astronomically high in the late years of the depression. In 1939, the *Amsterdam News* claimed that "eighty percent of the population of Harlem was on direct or work relief," and black spokesmen periodically expressed their fear that the urban black population would become "permanent parasites" unless their position in the private sector improved. *New York Amsterdam News,* January 21, 1939, and December 30, 1939.

90. James J. McGinley, S.J., *Labor Relations in the New York Rapid Transit System, 1901-1944* (New York: Kings Crown Press, 1949), p. 317; interview with Theodore Bassett, November 2, 1973, New York City, personal holding; L. H. Whittemore, *The Man Who Ran the Subways: The Story of Mike Quill* (New York: Holt, Rinehart and Winston, 1968), pp. 16-30.

91. *New York Amsterdam News,* October 30, 1937, April 30, 1938, and December 23, 1939.

92. New York State Temporary Commission on the Urban Colored Population, *Public Hearings* (Albany, 1938), vol. 8, pp. 1423-1425. Copies of the hearings are available at the Schomburg Collection in New York.

93. *New York Age,* November 5, 1938, April 22, 1939, December 2, 1939; *New York Amsterdam News,* March 21, 1938, April 15, 1939, April 22, 1939.

94. *New York Age,* October 23, 1937, September 3, 1938, and February 25, 1939.

95. *New York Amsterdam News,* April 30, 1939.

96. *Daily Worker,* March 23, 1938, and March 26, 1940.

97. On the dissolution of shop units, see Bert Cochran, *Labor and Communism, the Conflict that Shaped American Unions* (Princeton: Princeton University Press, 1977), pp. 135-36; Joseph Starobin, *American Communism in Crisis* (Cambridge: Harvard University Press, 1972), p. 39.

98. Interviews with Abner Berry, September 5, 1977, and February 4, 1978, personal holdings; *New York Amsterdam News,* March 30, 1940; Louis Sass, "Harlem Concentration on Transport," *The Party Organizer*

9, no. 3 (March 1935): 23-25. The TWU had great difficulty in getting
its membership, which was overwhelmingly Irish, to support a vigorous
campaign against racial discrimination in the industry, and they were
very cautious about publicizing their commitment to equal opportunity
in employment. From 1937 to 1941, when the TWU leader spoke several
times in Harlem about the union's willingness to end discrimination, the
TWU paper, *The Transport Bulletin*, failed to report on any of Quill's
appearances before black audiences, or to mention the union's commitment to ending the exclusion of blacks from the higher-paying jobs in
the transport industry.

99. At the state convention of the Communist party of New York
State in 1938, there were numerous complaints that the party was losing
credibility in black communities because of the failure of comrades in
union leadership to wage an effective fight against discrimination. See
*Proceedings, 10th Convention, Communist Party of New York State,
May 20-23, 1938* (New York: International Publishers, 1938), pp. 35,
151. According to Abner Berry, one of the major culprits was the leftist
leadership of the Hotel and Restaurant Workers Union, which failed to
lead an effective fight for the upgrading of black workers in the food-
service industry. Interview with Abner Berry, February 4, 1978, personal
holding. The National Maritime Union, where the Left played a major role
in the leadership, found it did not have the power to completely eliminate
separate black and white hiring halls in its industry. Ferdinand Smith, "Protecting the Negro Seaman," *Opportunity* 18, no. 4 (April 1940): 112-14.

100. On AFL opposition to an antidiscrimination clause in the Wagner
Act, see Raymond Wolters, *Negroes and the Great Depression* (Westport,
Conn.: Greenwood Press, 1970), pp. 183-187, and Herbert Hill, *Black
Labor and the American Legal System* (Washington, D.C.: Bureau of
National Affairs, 1977), pp. 102-106. On trade-union opposition to state
legislation banning discrimination by unions, see *Daily Worker,* Decem-
ber 16, 1937, and *New York Amsterdam News,* May 27, 1939.

101. For statements by Communists initially supporting state legislation banning discrimination by unions, see *Daily Worker,* December 17,
1937; *New York Age,* December 25, 1937; New York State Temporary
Commission, *Public Hearings,* vol. 8, pp. 1612-1618. The first signs of
the party's retreat from this position can be found in a speech by James
Ford in *Daily Worker,* December 21, 1937.

102. *New York Amsterdam News,* May 27, 1939, and July 1, 1939;
Daily Worker, March 6, 1939, May 7, 1939, May 14, 1939, May 17, 1939.

103. *New York Amsterdam News,* March 14, 1941.

104. Interview with Abner Berry, July 5, 1977, personal holding; Weiss, "Don't Buy," pp. 95-96; *Daily Worker*, August 14, 1938; *New York Amsterdam News*, February 26, 1938.

105. *Daily Worker*, February 17, 1938; *Proceedings, 10th Convention, Communist Party of New York State*, pp. 103-104.

106. Adam Clayton Powell, Jr., *Marching Blacks* (New York: Dial Press, 1945), p. 103; interview with Abner Berry, July 5, 1977, personal holding; *New York Amsterdam News*, April 2, 1938, May 7, 1938; *Daily Worker*, March 4, 1938, May 1, 1938, and May 23, 1938.

107. *New York Age*, April 9, 1938, April 23, 1938, April 30, 1938, and September 3, 1938.

108. Weiss, "Don't Buy," pp. 99-102.

109. Ibid., pp. 103-105; *New York Amsterdam News*, August 13, 1938, and October 22, 1938; *New York Age*, August 13, 1938.

110. *New York Age*, November 5, 1938; *New York Amsterdam News*, November 12, 1938.

111. *New York Amsterdam News*, October 22, 1938, and October 29, 1938.

112. *New York Amsterdam News*, April 8, 1939, and May 6, 1939.

113. *Daily Worker*, March 29, 1939, May 5, 1939; *New York Amsterdam News*, June 24, 1939, August 5, 1939.

114. H. B. [Herbert Benjamin?], "Unemployment—An Old Struggle under New Conditions," *Communist* 17, no. 5 (May 1938): 426.

115. *New York Amsterdam News*, April 8, 1939, and April 22, 1939.

116. *New York Amsterdam News*, September 2, 1939. One commentator stated: "Communism made a bid for the Negro with promises of abundant home relief, but their promises failed and since they could not offer Russia or Siberia, Garveyism has taken the lead again."

117. *Daily Worker*, October 5, 1939, and June 6, 1940.

118. *New York Amsterdam News*, May 11, 1940.

119. *New York Amsterdam News*, November 11, 1939, November 16, 1940, and November 23, 1940.

120. *Daily Worker*, October 5, 1939, and September 15, 1940; *New York Amsterdam News*, December 21, 1940.

121. Powell, *Marching Blacks*, p. 102; Meier and Rudwick, *Along the Color Line*, p. 329; *Daily Worker*, April 22, 1941 and April 27, 1941; *New York Amsterdam News*, March 22, 1941 and April 26, 1941.

122. *New York Age*, January 23, 1941.

123. *New York Amsterdam News*, June 21, 1941.

124. *New York Age*, June 14, 1941.

125. August Meier, Elliot Rudwick, and Francis Broderick, *Black Protest Thought in the Twentieth Century,* 2d ed. (New York: Bobbs Merrill, 1971), pp. 220-24.

126. In 1939, black leaders were beginning to become quite concerned that blacks would become a class of "permanent parasites" dependent upon the relief system for sustenance. See *New York Amsterdam News,* January 21, 1939, May 6, 1939, February 17, 1940.

Tenant Organization and Housing Reform in New York City: The Citywide Tenants' Council, 1936-1943

JOSEPH A. SPENCER

During the past decade, tenants in an increasing number of American cities have joined together in grass-roots organizations devoted to housing reform. Such organizations pressure landlords and government officials to maintain rent levels, and to improve housing and neighborhood conditions in the face of growing deterioration and a short supply of decent urban housing. Efforts to achieve these goals, and the leaders of such endeavors, have received considerable attention from both scholars and the news media. Historians, however, have generally neglected earlier periods of tenant activism. Several have examined specific examples of tenant protest as aspects of other movements, most notably as organizations of the unemployed during the early years of the depression.[1] Others, such as Roy Lubove and Richard O. Davies, have focused directly on housing, yet have emphasized the impact of government or middle-

---

Note: A portion of the research for this paper was done as part of the Tenant Movement Study under grant no. 1-R01-MH23814 from the Metropolitan Studies Division of the National Institutes of Mental Health. It was funded through the Center for Policy Research, Inc., New York City. Ronald Lawson, Principal Investigator.

An earlier version of this paper was presented at the Annual Meeting of the Organization of American Historians, New York City, April 15, 1978.

and upper-class reformers.[2] Thus, despite a generation of "history from the bottom up," there remains virtually no published work on the history of organized tenant activity.

This lack of scholarship is doubly puzzling. Though shelter is among the most basic human needs, a shortage of decent, affordable housing has been one of this nation's most serious and persistent urban problems. Many American cities have rich histories of tenant protest. New York City, for example, has experienced several major periods of activism since the turn of the century. And tenant organizations have played a role in the development of every significant housing program instituted in the city since World War I.

Between 1936 and 1943, a small group of committed organizers formed the Citywide Tenants' Council (CWTC), New York's first permanent coalition of neighborhood tenant groups. With limited resources and personnel, they succeeded in establishing a stable movement capable of assisting individual families at the grass-roots level and presenting a tenant perspective on long-standing housing problems and remedies such as public housing and urban redevelopment. An examination of this movement, as it functioned at both the local and citywide levels, provides valuable insights into both the history of tenant activism and the evolution of urban housing problems and programs. In addition, an appreciation of the council's successes and failures adds to our understanding of the choices that confront the leaders of present-day grass-roots movements.

New York's prewar housing problems inspired a range of reform programs. Upon assuming office in January 1934, the fusion administration of Mayor Fiorello LaGuardia faced major housing challenges. The city had seventeen square miles of slums. Half of its multifamily buildings were "old law" tenements, grossly inadequate structures built prior to the passage of the Tenement House Law of 1901. In Manhattan, more than a quarter of all apartments lacked hot water and/or central heating; and poor maintenance added to such structural deficiencies. In Albany, a pliant legislature had granted repeated moratoria on major provisions of the 1929 Multiple Dwelling Law. Uninterrupted Tammany rule from 1917 through 1933 had made code enforcement a distant memory: the number of Tenement House Department citations remained low although few buildings complied fully with the law.[3]

Mayor LaGuardia and Tenement House Commissioner Langdon Post, an experienced reformer, attacked the housing problem with a vigorous, two-part policy, advocating a substantial federal public housing program and campaigning for strict code enforcement to protect those living in substandard tenements. Post believed that an improved housing situation depended on success in both efforts. Code enforcement would encourage the repair of many buildings, but it would also hasten the boarding up or demolition of the most deteriorated and least economically viable tenements.[4] This policy would create a major housing shortage unless a comparable number of low-rent units were constructed to offset the loss. As the situation actually developed, however, Post was able to mount a widespread, coercive code-enforcement program well before public housing became a significant reality.

During 1934 and 1935, thousands of families responded to financial reverses by "doubling up"—that is, moving in with friends or relatives to save rent money. This trend pushed the vacancy rate to nearly 20 percent, thus keeping rents low and creating a supply of alternative apartments for those forced to leave condemned buildings. In the first three years of his tenure, Post used long-neglected powers of his office to vacate over fifteen hundred tenements deemed unfit for human habitation. An administration committed to housing reform forced the owners of thousands of other buildings into compliance with the law.[5]

By late 1936, however, Post was finding it increasingly difficult to use coercive enforcement measures. Demolition of buildings for major public-works projects, voluntary abandonment by some owners, and city "vacate" orders removed thousands of low-rent apartments from the market. At the same time, improved economic conditions caused a rise in the marriage rate and the "undoubling" of families, thereby increasing demand. Thus the city's vacancy rate fell precipitously in late 1936, from 8 percent to 4 percent in just six months. During the following year, it shrank by half once again. With large-scale public housing still on the horizon, it became exceedingly difficult to resettle tenants displaced as a result of code enforcement.[6]

Realtors and bank officials, who controlled thousands of buildings through foreclosure, quickly appreciated the situation and turned it to their advantage. In December 1936, when Post announced his firm intention to enforce new code provisions that called for sanitary improvements and fire retarding (including criminal liability for owners in fire-related deaths), five savings banks holding title to over four hundred tenements on the Lower East Side responded with threats to vacate and board up their properties rather than pay the cost of fire retarding. Although such threats were largely a bluff, LaGuardia feared the political impact of wholesale evictions and decided to compromise. At his urging, the legislature authorized the city to grant a six-month exemption from enforcement to those owners who agreed, in writing, either to comply with the codes or to vacate their buildings in an orderly manner. Despite Post's insistence that it was not just another moratorium, such legislation represented a tacit admission that the city could no longer press for unconditional enforcement of the Multiple Dwelling Law. The owners of only 5 percent of the city's noncomplying tenements signed six-month exemption agreements. Most owners adopted a wait-and-see attitude and eventually ignored the new code requirements. The administration was never again able to compel compliance because the housing market was not sufficiently flexible to allow use of the only weapon that had proved effective—the vacate order.[7]

When federal public-housing funds arrived, they were inadequate: by 1941, the New York City Housing Authority had only 10,233 units open for tenancy. Inadequate funding, coupled with the inability to compel the improvement of old-law tenements, placed LaGuardia in a difficult position. Faced with limited options, the mayor turned increasingly toward the private sector. After a bitter dispute, he replaced Post with Alfred Rheinstein, a builder with close ties to banking and realty groups. From 1938 on, the administration emphasized positive inducements to code compliance, such as tax exemptions for residential property improvements and government-subsidized, low-interest rehabilitation loans.

The chief instrument of this new orientation was the Mayor's Committee on Property Improvement (MCPI), appointed in early 1938. Composed almost entirely of savings bank officials and realtors, the MCPI served as a clearinghouse, or expediter, of building improvements. Radio and printed advertising informed property owners of the committee's existence, and invited them into one of the MCPI's eight local offices, which assisted them in applying for FHA, RFC, and private loans, as well as for tax exemption on the resulting repairs. Finally, in 1940, in cooperation with the city's major savings banks, the committee established a $35,000,000 loan fund, which permitted the fire retarding of thousands of tenements.[8]

As a means of encouraging code compliance, these incentives succeeded well, but their impact did not always benefit low-income tenants entirely. Both tax exemption and low-interest loans were available for any improvement, not just for code-compliance repairs made in old-law tenements. Furthermore, there was no limitation on rent increases in rehabilitated buildings. Not surprisingly, many owners substantially upgraded their properties with elevators, steam heat, new kitchens, and other improvements, and then sought considerable rent increases. The net result, therefore, was a decrease in the supply of low-rent apartments.[9]

While the merits of subsidized rehabilitation were being debated, a new remedy appeared. Urban redevelopment, in which tax incentives and broad condemnation powers were granted to private builders who carried out approved, large-scale slum-clearance projects, had widespread appeal: realtors saw it as an alternative to public housing; tenement owners viewed it as a means for disposing of unprofitable holdings; and insurance companies and others with large amounts of capital hoped that they would gain from it a sound investment opportunity. Above all, for a mayor seeking dramatic housing reform, urban redevelopment offered the chance to clear whole blocks of slums and blight with one stroke. As many housing reformers and tenant leaders quickly pointed out, however, redevelopment offered much less to slum residents—namely, eviction and the replacement of their deteriorated yet affordable apartments with middle- and upper-income units beyond their means. Despite such objections, New York State pioneered in urban redevelopment with the first enabling legislation in the early 1940s and with the first completed project, Metropolitan Life Insurance Company's Stuyvesant Town, completed in 1945.[10]

Thus, code enforcement, public housing, subsidized rehabilitation, and urban redevelopment represented the principal approaches to New York's housing problems in the years preceding World War II. Yet, there was little planned progression from one approach to the other. As the effectiveness of the city's coercive code-enforcement measures diminished, various proponents advanced the merits of their favorite remedy. It was within this context that the tenant movement fought to represent the interests of rent-paying families.

THE CITYWIDE TENANTS' COUNCIL: FOUNDING, STRUCTURE, AND PROGRAM

In early 1936, New York City lacked a true tenant movement; only a few isolated local organizations were active. The powerful Consolidated

Tenants' League of Harlem (CTLH), then in its third year, was building a solid base among Manhattan's black tenants. The Tenants' Protective League (TPL) of the northeast Bronx, the only permanent organization to emerge from the ad-hoc antieviction riots of the early thirties, was slowly disintegrating.[11] A third group, the Knickerbocker Village Tenants' Association (KVTA), represented residents in a large, subsidized middle-income complex on the Lower East Side. The vast majority of the city's one and a half million rent-paying families had nowhere to turn when confronted with a housing problem.

In March 1936, however, a strike by Local 32B of the Building Employees Union provided the spark for a revival of tenant activism. A group of trade unionists living at Knickerbocker Village joined with the KVTA in forming a committee to aid the project's striking maintenance workers. The committee found many allies among tenants who were already antagonistic toward management. Over one hundred village residents walked the picket lines, fed strikers, and convinced local merchants to grant discounts to union members. The daily newspapers made much of this tenant-labor solidarity, and, in the first few days of the strike, they published accounts of similar activity throughout the city. Heinz Norden, a writer active in the KVTA, eventually visited the city's active tenant organizations in an effort to coordinate strike support. A hastily formed citywide committee organized rallies and raised funds until the maintenance workers achieved victory after two weeks on the picket lines.[12]

Following the settlement of the strike, however, the committee members decided to remain active and form a permanent, citywide, direct-membership tenant organization. In late March, representatives from the CTLH, KVTA, TPL, the Lower East Side Public Housing Conference,[13] and a dozen individual buildings met and established the Citywide Tenants' League (CWTL). During the following weeks, they chose an executive committee (with Norden as acting chairperson), signed up five hundred members, secured office space, and began to formulate a legislative program. Within a few months, however, the leaders found that their following had evaporated: a "mass meeting" called in the summer of 1936 attracted only fifty persons.[14]

The leaders, few of whom had had any prior organizational experience, found that they had made several tactical mistakes. The first concerned constituency. Except for the CTLH, support for the new group had come mostly from middle-class professionals. Such tenants did not usually have acute housing problems, and most, therefore, ceased to participate. But, while they were losing interest, an increasing number of poor slum tenants were appearing at the Citywide League's office with immediate problems—rent increases, collapsing ceilings, and eviction notices. If a potential for mass membership existed, it was among such tenants.[15]

In addition, it was clear that a direct-membership, citywide approach was impractical. First, one centralized organization could not properly respond to specialized local needs. Second, and most important, the recruitment of individual tenants would place the new league in direct competition with established local organizations such as the Consolidated Tenants' League. Therefore, the executive committee decided to restructure the group as the Citywide Tenants' Council (CWTC) to serve as a federation of local grass-roots leagues. The neighborhood units would organize members around local issues and needs, while the council, composed of representatives from the affiliates, would coordinate activities, develop policy, and supervise lobbying.[16]

Although the federated structure may have been ideal, it could not be implemented immediately. The KVTA and the CTLH were the city's only strong local organizations. In reality, the early council was little more than a nucleus of a dozen young left-wing activists—from New Deal Democrats to Communists—who were interested in housing reform. In most cases, they had to build locals from the bottom up. During its early years, CWTC's founders each spent several nights per week publicizing the council at union, civic, and fraternal meetings, and responding to appeals for help from tenants in areas that lacked a local affiliate. In their work, tenant organizers sought to use personal contact with individual tenants as a means of establishing neighborhood groups. In the typical case, CWTC organizers provided advice and legal aid when necessary, but they insisted that the tenants form a house committee and perform the bulk of the work—obtaining building records from the Tenement House Department, negotiating with the landlord, picketing, and administering a rent strike, if necessary.[17] Tenants were told to publicize their own cause in the neighborhood. This was especially encouraged during rent strikes, when the house committee and the CWTC organizer first used leaflets and street meetings to gain local support, and then mounted postcard, telephone, and picketing campaigns against the building owner. Such publicity often inspired tenants in

nearby buildings to initiate similar action, particularly if they had the
same landlord.[18]

Once a neighborhood had been awakened to the possibilities of tenant
activism, the council often found several individuals, frequently housewives or unemployed persons, willing to staff a permanent local organization. Next, CWTC representatives and the new recruits appealed to
nearby settlement houses, unions, Workers' Alliance branches, and other
organizations for assistance such as additional volunteers, office and
meeting space, and mimeograph facilities. Thereafter, council leaders
made every attempt to make the new local group a vital community force.
They used parades, street-corner rallies, leaflets dealing with local housing
problems, and joint conferences with other groups to publicize their
activities. Once the new affiliate was well established, it could handle
appeals for help without requiring the intervention of the council.[19]

Obviously, this ideal pattern did not always develop. Sometimes, local
residents were unwilling or unable to assume a leadership role, or such an
attempt would falter after a few months, and the organizing process
would have to be repeated. But these tactics did work in a number of
neighborhoods, most notably in Chelsea and in Greenwich Village in
Manhattan, and in the Williamsburg, Boro Park, and downtown sections
of Brooklyn. The council gained affiliates in other ways as well. The
South Bronx Tenants' League grew out of CWTC's intervention on behalf
of families displaced by construction of an approach ramp to the Triborough Bridge. A direct, concentrated effort by the council and the
Lower East Side Public Housing Conference produced the East Side
Tenants Union (ESTU). In 1937, Lenox Hill Neighborhood House established the Yorkville Tenants' League in response to appeals from over
three hundred area residents, and the new group soon joined Citywide.
Tenants from the East New York and the Brownsville sections of Brooklyn formed the Brooklyn Rentpayers in mid-1936, yet remained unaware of CWTC's activities until leaders of both groups appeared at the
same City Hall hearing some months later. The Brooklyn Rentpayers
immediately affiliated and became a mainstay of the council. The most
unique case involved the West Side of Manhattan. Citywide leaders felt
that the area from 34th to 59th streets needed a tenant organization yet
lacked the coalition of local groups so helpful in sustaining tenant
activism in its early stages. Therefore, CWTC first helped to organize the
West Side Federation and then established a tenant union with its aid.[20]

As the work of organizing progressed through the late 1930s and early 1940s, the Citywide Tenants' Council came to resemble more closely than before the structure its founders envisioned. A significant number of locals took root and handled a large share of the day-to-day work, enabling the council to devote more of its effort to lobbying, fund-raising, and coordinating local activities. By 1940, the CWTC represented nearly two dozen affiliates, with a combined membership in excess of twenty thousand.

Yet such "paper-strength" figures were misleading. Although the council did indeed become a strong and effective organization, it never succeeded fully in overcoming several serious problems that limited its accomplishments. One major problem stemmed from its origins. Despite the seeding of several solid grass-roots affiliates, CWTC remained an organization built mostly from the top down, never really deriving its power from a citywide network of strong locals. Rather, throughout its history, the major impetus came from ten to twenty young men and women who devoted all of their spare time to the movement. Many of them, such as Norden of KVTA, Jules Seitz of the ESTU, Henry Berg of the Bronx Tenants' League, and Donelan Phillips of CTLH, not only held top positions in the council, but they were also key leaders in an affiliate. Although there was no truly "typical" CWTC activist, some fairly common characteristics stand out. Most were in their mid-twenties, college educated, and either unemployed or working on a WPA or other New Deal project. Many had been, or were, involved in the Workers' Alliance, the Communist party, the American Labor party, or some other left-wing group. The majority originally became involved in tenant organizing because of a housing problem of their own or a friend's. In one sense, the tenant movement received a "depression dividend," a core of talented, young people committed to reform who had few other opportunities to keep their skills sharp. Some of the best examples were the council's volunteer lawyers; many were struggling young members of the National Lawyers Guild who served tenants without a fee, partly out of dedication to the cause, but also in the hope that such contacts would provide non-housing-related cases and the basis of a viable, if meager, practice.[21]

Organizationally, the council's strength rested on a small number of affiliates that did develop into strong, grass-roots groups. The most successful were the ESTU, Consolidated Tenants' League, Chelsea Tenants' League, Brooklyn Rentpayers, and Bronx Tenants' League. These locals built considerable strength by combining a small core of experienced, permanent activists with a constantly shifting pool of volunteers (often recruited following a dispute with their own landlords) and several young lawyers. For popular support, the locals relied on a varied base composed of the organizations' own members, the Workers' Alliance, and other local groups, and of neighbors who could be counted on for picketing and demonstrating. These locals were the mainstays of the council in that they dealt with problems in their own areas and regularly contributed dues, delegates, and demonstrators to CWTC.[22]

Beyond these locals, the council experienced mixed success. It had difficulty organizing outside of older, working-class neighborhoods with seriously deteriorated housing.[23] Thus, Staten Island never had a functioning affiliate. Queens had but one, the short-lived Flushing Tenants' League. Nor were results in working-class neighborhoods in the Bronx, Brooklyn, and Manhattan always encouraging. The council organized some locals that remained active for several months and then ceased to function. Other areas sustained activity for years under the aegis of several successive groups. In many ways, these weak locals drained the council's limited resources; they often failed to send delegates to meetings and to pay dues, while continually requiring legal aid and organizational assistance. Nevertheless, CWTC tried to sustain the feeble groups and never refused appeals for help. It does appear, however, that by the early 1940s, Citywide leaders were redirecting some of their efforts away from weaker areas, and devoting increasing energies to a new Interproject Council composed of affiliates organized in recently built public-housing projects.[24]

In addition, CWTC's membership fluctuated considerably. Although the council tried to keep membership figures current, and often cited impressive totals in communications with public officials, the leaders recognized the impossibility of accurately determining actual membership. This was largely due to a high rate of turnover: many members dropped out once their own problems had been solved, and other families facing a rent increase or eviction replaced them. Another source of uncertainty was the varying criteria that individual locals used to determine membership. Consolidated Tenants' League, for instance, claimed the greatest strength (about five thousand), yet it routinely listed members who had ceased active participation. The Chelsea Tenants' League, on the other hand, seldom claimed more than one hundred dues-paying members, yet it served as one of the most effective affiliates. In truth, few CWTC officials concerned themselves with formal membership. They felt that the strength of the organization was determined by its broad support among tenants and allied neighborhood organizations. As Heinz Norden observed in a recent interview:

> We were always asked, "How many members do you have?" Well, who was a member? One who paid twenty cents, or came to a meeting, or one whom you helped? It was impossible to establish the membership in those terms. . . . We felt then, and I feel today, that the demands often made upon us—"whom do you represent, how big is your membership?—were a snare and a delusion put forward in bad faith to discredit what was a vigorous and necessary movement. Essential was that when it came to real demonstration and action, the movement was able to mobilize sizable groups—to march, to demonstrate, to appear at mass meetings.[25]

CWTC's inability to build strong affiliates in all neighborhoods and its need to rely on other organizations for numerical support were due largely to a lack of resources. Tenants unable to pay a three-dollar rent increase could seldom afford tenant organization dues, though only fifteen or twenty cents a month. Therefore, during its first several years, the council had to raise funds through parties, concerts, and dances. Eventually, Norden formed the Committee to Aid Tenant Organization, supported by such figures as Eleanor Roosevelt, journalist Max Lerner, and attorney Charles Abrams, and it succeeded in collecting several hundred dollars per year. But such amounts were still insufficient. Partial records show, for example, that the organization's income for the period January 1938 through March 1940 totalled only $1,552, necessitating reliance on donated facilities and volunteers, who gave as much time as possible after fulfilling job and family responsibilities. Consolidated Tenants' League was the only affiliate that managed to hire full-time workers.[26] From 1938 through the early 1940s, the CWTC paid one of its members fifteen dollars per week as an executive secretary. This was the extent of the movement's paid staff. It was even more difficult to find money for other necessities; CWTC newsletters occasionally appealed to the locals for immediate donations lest the office's electricity and phone service be suspended.[27]

The council's lack of resources hindered its growth as initiator of local tenant organizations and as coordinator of citywide activities, and forced it to function on two levels. If one considers the eight or ten strongest locals and their representatives on the council's executive committee, CWTC performed as originally intended. Yet, its leaders never freed themselves from a second, service-oriented role: devoting precious time and resources to helping individual tenants and sustaining weak locals. Every former council activist interviewed by the author insisted that the potential for a much larger movement existed but that inadequate staff and facilities prevented its realization. Such difficulties notwithstanding, the council did succeed in building an effective network with strong grass-roots groups in many neighborhoods, in assisting tenants throughout the city, and in developing leaders who defended the rights of all low-income families.[28]

In truly representing its constituents, the council remained at arm's length from the old-line housing-reform movement. While recognizing the substantial contributions of groups such as the Welfare Council, the Charity Organization Society, and United Neighborhood Houses, CWTC leaders felt that such organizations viewed the tenant as "an abstraction" and went too far in maintaining an impartial stance. Council activists, on the other hand, viewed housing issues strictly from the tenant's perspective. Although they accepted the need for compromise, activists saw the movement's role in the bargaining process as "stirring things up" and applying "unremitting pressure" for pro-tenant measures. In doing so, they confronted the core of the city's housing problem: the private sector's failure to provide decent, affordable accommodations for low-income families. The council answered with a broad program calling for substantial public-housing construction, rent control and strict code enforcement for existing dwellings, and safeguards against unjust eviction.[29]

Despite Mayor LaGuardia's and Commissioner Post's commitment to housing reform, the tenant movement often disagreed with the fusion administration. The first major break came in December 1936, when the CWTC bitterly opposed the mayor's compromise on fire retarding. Tenant leaders blamed the unprofitability of many tenements on decades of speculation and overcapitalization, and argued that low-income families should not have to choose between firetraps and higher rents as a consequence. Yet, CWTC received little support from the city after 1936. Thereafter, when council affiliates removed major code violations with little or slight increases in rent, they did so primarily with rent strikes and with the mobilization of neighborhood pressure against landlords and government officials.

The council also lobbied actively in Albany and succeeded in defeating a series of realtor-inspired bills to weaken the Multiple Dwelling Law. Efforts to enact a rent-control statute proved less fruitful, despite Citywide's lawyers formulating model legislation under which the New York City Housing Authority could impose rent control in specific districts whenever the vacancy rate dropped below 5 percent. This plan reflected the realization that, while the average vacancy rate throughout the city might remain relatively high, a shortage of apartments in particular neighborhoods might lead to escalating rents. This was especially true in Harlem, due to segregation, but it also applied in the Lower East Side, in Yorkville, and in parts of Brooklyn.[30]

Although such a measure never passed, CWTC did procure the enactment of a significant related law in early 1938. The Minkoff Act effectively prohibited rent increases in old-law tenements that did not comply fully with the housing codes. Citywide lobbyists had skillfully portrayed the Minkoff bill as a code-compliance measure. But, in practice, it served as a tenement rent-control act, since over 90 percent of such buildings continued to have major violations.[31]

The Citywide Tenants' Council and the LaGuardia administration cooperated most successfully in pressing for public housing. The charter groups of CWTC—CTLH, KVTA, and the Lower East Side Public Housing Conference—had strongly supported public housing and had stepped up their demands once the council was organized. In January 1937, Citywide representatives attended the National Public Housing Conference convention in Washington, D.C., and urged a ten-year, ten-million-unit federal housing plan. Subsequently, the council worked with LaGuardia, Post, and other advocates of public housing in lobbying for the Federal Housing Act of 1937. One year later, New York tenant leaders strongly supported the public-housing amendment to the New York State Constitution. Following its passage, they protested the legislature's failure to appropriate the full $300 million that had been authorized. On a third level, the council supported LaGuardia's successful efforts to initiate a small-scale, municipal, low-rent housing program.[32]

Yet, even on the subject of public housing, LaGuardia and the council eventually split, principally because the mayor dismissed Post and endorsed subsidized rehabilitation and urban redevelopment as slum-clearance measures. For council members, public housing was the only legitimate remedy. They hoped these projects would be the centerpieces of "neighborhood rehabilitation," in which families on the site would be temporarily rehoused nearby and then given preference in selecting the new affordable apartments. So long as the projects produced a net gain of apartments, this process could be repeated several times until a significant percentage of the neighborhood's slum buildings were replaced. Obviously such a program required massive amounts of federal funding: Post once estimated the cost for New York City alone at nearly $3 billion. With available funds well below that figure, CWTC representatives resisted all attempts to divert any money to alternative programs. They opposed subsidized rehabilitation primarily because improving scattered properties in a potential slum-clearance area raised the eventual cost of purchasing land for such a project. Similarly, tenant leaders had strong reservations about urban redevelopment. While accepting the need for private investment in housing, they saw redevelopment as a program for the middle class rather than as a substitute for public housing. Accordingly, CWTC resisted attempts to shunt public housing to the outer boroughs and to save choice, Lower Manhattan parcels for private slum-clearance efforts.[33]

In defending public housing, the tenant movement had only limited success. The City Housing Authority did construct projects in several neighborhoods represented by council affiliates, but the restricted scope of the public program precluded a broad attack on slum conditions. And, as noted earlier, government at all levels continued to encourage alternative programs, particularly subsidized rehabilitation.

While pressing for adoption of major government programs, the movement nevertheless continued to defend individual tenant's rights. In hundreds of cases, council lawyers successfully used Section 1436A of the Civil Practices Act, which gave judges discretionary power to grant a six-month stay of eviction in disposses cases if the tenant was unable to find a comparable apartment at a similar rent. CWTC leaders also sought to expand the law to protect tenants for whom a forced move would affect "proximity to work, traditional ties or possible loss of voting rights." Although their efforts were unsuccessful, they represented a significant attempt to place the essence of neighborhood into laws protecting tenants from eviction.[34]

A far more extreme eviction threat resulted from the proliferation of New Deal highways, bridges, and tunnels. Then, as in the 1950s and 1960s, public construction projects and policies altered neighborhoods and violated tenants' rights. Citywide's involvement with this issue began in the fall of 1936, when construction of the South Bronx approach to the Triborough Bridge required the demolition of seven square blocks containing eleven hundred apartments. When the news reached the affected tenants, most sought accommodations in the surrounding area. Some succeeded, but soon vacancies disappeared and rents increased. Meanwhile, the city acquired title to the condemned buildings and soon stopped providing services; in some buildings, remaining tenants had to furnish their own heat by buying coal or by burning the woodwork. With little advance warning, the city announced the start of demolition—just two weeks before Christmas.

The Citywide Tenants' Council, the Port Morris Community Council, and the South Bronx Merchants' Association quickly organized the tenants and demanded orderly and fair resettlement. They held several mass meetings to pressure local legislators. They picketed City Hall. Their Medical Committee documented cases of pneumonia resulting from the suspension of services. Ultimately, the six hundred remaining families won several major concessions from the city, including the delay of demolition until the spring; restoration of building services; emergency food, clothing, and medical care; assistance in finding new apartments; and payment of moving expenses by the Emergency Relief Bureau.[35]

During the late 1930s, the council increasingly protested evictions caused by government construction projects. One former tenant leader recalls that CWTC had a "permanent picket line" around Robert Moses's office because of the frequency with which he evicted tenants. In such cases, CWTC fought for tenants' rights to proper notice, moving expenses, and resettlement in the same neighborhood. Movement leaders met with success on the first two demands, but displaced tenants often had to move to other areas.[36]

THE EAST SIDE TENANTS' UNION: TENANT ACTIVISM AT THE NEIGHBORHOOD LEVEL

In New York City's long war against slum housing, the Lower East Side served as the major battleground; no other area suffered from such deteriorated conditions. The typical tenement in the section was built prior to 1900 and, certainly by the 1930s, was unprofitable, poorly maintained, and loaded with code violations. Throughout the decade, the Lower East Side had the highest foreclosure and tax delinquency rates in the city. During the early depression years, the area had a vacancy rate of approximately 35 percent, the highest in the city.[37]

Yet, one characteristic of the Lower East Side countered the impression such figures gave: it was a viable and vital collection of neighborhoods. Although, during the 1920s and early 1930s, thousands of families left to seek better housing in the outer boroughs, others endured Lower Manhattan's inadequate tenements rather than break long-established social and economic ties or forego the area's rich cultural and associational life. This attachment was clearly noted in a survey of a typical block conducted by the Henry Street Settlement in 1935. Despite relatively frequent moves from one apartment to another, 77 percent of the families had lived in the neighborhood for ten years or more. Most interestingly, more than half expressed unwillingness to move to newly constructed garden apartments in other boroughs even if the apartments were affordable and well served by public transportation. The majority cited neighborhood ties and/or proximity to work as their reasons for wanting to stay. This survey, and other similar studies, illustrated the stability and positive aspects of the Lower East Side during the prewar period.[38]

The Lower East Side, however, was not an idyllic community, and all of its residents were not there by choice; it also served as a neighborhood of last resort for poor families who could only afford its deteriorated, cold-water, walk-up apartments. Indeed, as the city began to experience an apartment shortage in the late 1930s, many families moved back into the area, and those already there clung desperately to their flats.[39]

It was this dual role, as both a neighborhood of choice and a "safety valve" during housing crises, that led the CWTC to sponsor its first local tenant organization on the Lower East Side. In effect, the effort represented a pilot project, an opportunity to test organizational techniques in a section that greatly needed housing reform. The area was also rich in potential allies: the Lower East Side Public Housing Conference was a charter member of the CWTC, and the Lower East Side Federation, a coalition of over a hundred local groups, was eager to cooperate. In early November 1936, representatives of these three organizations formed the Joint Committee for Tenant Organization (JCTO). Just two weeks later, after a door-to-door canvass by volunteers from the Workers' Alliance and the Unemployed Council, the JCTO announced the birth of the East Side Tenants' Union (ESTU). Within a few days, the ESTU was firmly established, with limited funds, in an office on lower Second Avenue (donated by the Church of All Nations), a half dozen organizers and office workers, a volunteer legal staff, and long lines of tenants seeking help.[40]

The new tenant organization received an added boost just one month later, when the city's savings banks confronted Tenement House Commissioner Post with their determination to vacate over four hundred buildings rather than comply with the new fire-retarding and sanitation provisions of the Multiple Dwelling Law. In effect, over ten thousand Lower East Side tenants became hostages in the resulting power play. As hundreds of families received the first series of eviction notices, effective at the end of December 1936, they turned to the ESTU as the only organization that could help them. Tenant leaders opposed all attempts by the banks and other holders of realty to win a new moratorium or a relaxation of code enforcement. At hastily scheduled City Hall hearings, CWTC and ESTU representatives insisted that no police be used to evict tenants, that the city pay the moving expenses and any resulting rent increases for families forced to vacate, and, lastly, that the city provide emergency services in tenanted buildings abandoned by their owners. Meanwhile, members of ESTU picketed both LaGuardia's office and the local branches of the savings banks with signs reading "Bankers Say Move. We Say Where?," "We Will Not Be Driven from Firetrap to Firetrap," and "Santa Brought Us Evictions."[41]

The hard-line stand of tenant leaders reflected their belief that the crisis was artificial and that the savings banks would relent if the mayor held firm and backed the CWTC's program. East Side Tenants' Union lawyers had examined the eviction notices given to hundreds of its member families, and found most of them unenforceable due to improper delivery, failure to provide thirty days' notice, misspelled names, and other errors. These faulty documents would prevent court action until February or March 1937. Those families receiving proper notices could apply for a six-month stay of eviction under Section 1436A. After assessing the situation, the lawyers separated their cases into several major categories, and then mimeographed standardized court papers, allowing one attorney to handle dozens of cases at once. Therefore, although tenant leaders demanded that the city accept responsibility for possible evictees, they were actually confident that no mass evictions need occur, and that Post could safely call the bankers' bluff.[42]

The ESTU did not get a chance to prove its mettle, however, as LaGuardia and Post compromised. The city implemented the six-month exemption program and thus lost the initiative in the battle for code enforcement. Having once demonstrated their ability to intimidate the LaGuardia administration, and with the vacancy rate declining steadily, bankers and realtors no longer feared coercive code-enforcement measures.

The resulting inability of the Tenement House Department to enforce code compliance represented a major challenge to the tenant movement. While the CWTC lobbied in Albany to prevent further weakening of the codes, the local affiliates continued the day-to-day effort to maintain low-income families in reasonably safe quarters at affordable rents. In this task the ESTU was the most effective organization. Though it consistently had a formal membership of about one thousand, its real strength came from a nucleus of skilled organizers and lawyers and from broad neighborhood support.

In fighting to improve buildings, to keep rents down, and to prevent evictions, ESTU organizers had few legal weapons at their disposal. They relied, therefore, on extralegal tactics, especially the rent strike. A fairly typical example developed in November 1937, after the owner of four tenements on East Eleventh Street demanded a two-dollar rent increase while refusing to provide improved maintenance. With the help of the ESTU, fifty-five families (about three-fourths of those affected) joined together, elected a house committee, and decided to resist. After visiting the Tenement House Department and obtaining the violations records of their buildings, the committee offered to negotiate a settlement calling for a smaller increase in return for repairs. When the owner refused to compromise, the tenants voted to strike. They signed a trustee agreement under which all participants paid their rent into a joint account that could be turned over to the landlord only upon successful completion of the strike or by a three-fourth's vote of the strikers. After the landlord again refused to negotiate, ESTU representatives began to mobilize neighborhood support through several street rallies. Soon picket lines marched in front of the buildings and the landlord's neighborhood office. When he responded with eviction notices against five of the strikers, ESTU picketed his home.

One week later, when the eviction cases came to trial, the ESTU's lawyer argued that the existence of the trustees account demonstrated the strikers' willingness to pay rent if the landlord removed all code violations. As often happened, the judge refused to evict any tenants, and suggested that both parties meet to settle their differences. Faced with the court's refusal to oust the strikers, the landlord had little choice. He quickly rescinded his request for a rent increase and agreed to perform needed repairs.[43]

Rent strikes and court proceedings were not always necessary. Some landlords compromised immediately. Others relented when pickets and street-corner speakers held them up to public scorn. On the other hand, not all actions were successful; the least successful actions often involved savings banks and other institutional owners less vulnerable to neighborhood pressure. In such instances, tenant lawyers used Section 1436A and other defenses to keep families in their apartments at the old rent for as long as possible.[44]

What is important about such examples is the range of tactics used by the ESTU: citation of Tenement House Department records to put landlords on the defensive; use of trustee accounts to demonstrate the strikers' good faith; reliance on legal technicalities to have eviction cases dismissed or to have the impact of unsuccessful actions softened; appeals to judges to choose equity over the letter of the law; and, above all, mobilization of neighborhood support to pressure landlords and to aid striking families.

Popular pressure was not used exclusively against landlords. The ESTU always had thirty or forty spectators in court during eviction cases. As one former organizer recalled: "The judges lived on the East Side and were elected from those districts. They certainly didn't want their neighbors to look down upon them. Times were hard and they were expected to show mercy."[45] The city bureaucracy was also a target: the ESTU moved against the Emergency Relief Bureau when its direct rent payments to landlords effectively prevented assisted families from joining rent strikes. Picketing the bureau's offices soon won a concession: relief officials agreed to suspend rent payments to landlords who were the subjects of a rent strike. Ultimately, this victory benefited all CWTC locals.[46]

It is impossible to estimate the total number of buildings organized by the ESTU since few records survive; but certainly the number was substantial. A partial listing for the month of November 1937 indicates successful actions (not necessarily rent strikes) in twelve buildings housing

189 families. Furthermore, the level of activity increased substantially following passage of the Minkoff Act in March 1938. By allowing tenants to refuse rent increases in old-law tenements with code violations, the law effectively legalized the rent strike. This newly bestowed legitimacy, widely publicized in an ESTU pamphlet, *Calling All Tenants,* emboldened many slumdwellers to organize and to confront their landlords. During the last few years of the decade, ESTU handled approximately a half dozen "Minkoff cases" per week.[47]

The ESTU also achieved a major victory over "firetrap landlords" during these years. The struggle began early on the morning of March 4, 1937, when fire swept through two tenements at 137-139 Suffolk Street, killing three tenants. The tragedy was particularly galling to ESTU leaders since many of the residents were members, and it had been pressing the titleholder, the Central Savings Bank, to fire retard the buildings. Worst of all, bank officials were immune from criminal liability because the properties had recently been covered by a six-month exemption agreement. The tenant organization did what it could to aid the victims, including leading a sit-in at Emergency Relief Bureau headquarters that gained extra benefits for the burned out families. But ESTU leaders also decided that something had to be done to prevent landlords from escaping responsibility for future fires. The union picketed the offices of the Central Savings Bank with signs reading "Three Burned Beyond Recognition" and "How Many More Must Die?" Several hundred members demonstrated at City Hall, demanding an end to the exemption program. Lastly, the ESTU held a public funeral for the three tenants; as the cortege passed the gutted ruins, six hundred marchers swore "that these dead shall not have died in vain."

In the aftermath of the tragedy, tenant leaders missed few opportunities to keep the issue before the public. For example, the ESTU helped form a small, amateur theater group that performed a specially written and produced play, "The Kingdom of 137," throughout Manhattan. For another year, however, repeated attempts to gain prosecution of landlords after tenement fires were fruitless. In several cases, six-month exemption agreements again prevented action. In others, a tangled pattern of ownership made it difficult to fix legal responsibility.

Then, in June 1938, fiery tragedy again struck the Lower East Side as two persons died in an East Houston Street blaze. The ESTU had a twenty-four-hour rally under way at the site before the embers were cold.

When union officials learned that the building had been neither fire retarded nor covered by exemption, they mounted a campaign for prosecution. This time, they left nothing to chance: ESTU lawyers carried out their own investigation of the building's violations and ownership, and eventually, they submitted a detailed report to Manhattan District Attorney Thomas Dewey. In September 1938, nearly two years after the criminal liability statute took effect, the first landlord was indicted for manslaughter. In March 1940, again with pressure from CWTC and its affiliates, a landlord received a jail sentence in another similar case. It was such prosecutions, which the city had been unable or unwilling to pursue, that prompted increasing compliance with the fire-retarding provisions of the Multiple Dwelling Law in the early 1940s.[48]

Although the ESTU concerned itself primarily with the question of rents and conditions in old-law tenements, it also supported CWTC's campaign against upgrading and urban redevelopment. Indeed, upgrading was a particular problem on the Lower East Side, where Joseph Platzker of the East Side Chamber of Commerce, aided by the Mayor's Committee on Property Improvement, led a vigorous campaign for the rehabilitation of tenements. As early as the summer of 1937, he reported a "boom" in remodeling, noting:

> While some owners are only removing violations, the majority are making extensive modernizations. This wholesale tenement repair work is also wiping out gradually thousands of outmoded suites which formerly housed the lowest income class.

In subsequent reports throughout the early 1940s, he documented the upgrading of hundreds of buildings.[49]

Such improvements caught organized tenants on the wrong side of the Minkoff Act, which provided no legal limits on rents once an owner removed code violations. As the ESTU's pamphlet *Calling All Tenants* advised members, the only defense against large increases in rehabilitated buildings was organization, the threat of a rent strike, and the rallying of neighborhood support. These were the same tactics used against noncomplying buildings prior to passage of the Minkoff Act. But, in cases involving rehabilitation, ESTU experienced much less success. The owner who wanted a substantial rent increase in return for extensive improvements could not be portrayed in the same terms as the slumlord, regardless of the impact such increases might have on his tenants. Municipal Court judges were more reluctant to support strikes against landlords who upgraded, especially once the mayor began to encourage such rehabilitation.[50]

While aiding tenants affected by upgrading, ESTU leaders began to see redevelopment as an equally dangerous threat to their dreams of public housing. In recruiting banker and realtor support for his Committee on Property Improvement, LaGuardia had encouraged the redevelopment of Lower Manhattan, especially the construction of luxury apartments along the newly completed East River Drive. This proposal coincided with a growing belief among realtors that inner-city property, adjacent to major business centers, was too valuable to use for public housing. Eventually, several local banks and insurance companies requested that the FHA prepare a confidential evaluation of the prospects for upper- and/or middle-income residential redevelopment of the Lower East Side. The final report, written by the noted urban geographer Homer Hoyt, indicated that there was a market for a middle-income complex if it were built as an "entirely independent community" with low density, its own educational, cultural, and shopping facilities, and a private bus line to carry the residents "through the long, unattractive approach of the blighted area with a minimum of inconvenience."[51] In sum, powerful financial interests wanted an enclave devoid of contact with the neighborhood, with rents beyond the means of area families.

ESTU members experienced some success in agitating against erection of such projects. During early 1938, the East Side Chamber of Commerce asked the City Planning Commission to revise the land-use and height designations of virtually the entire Lower East Side, resulting in a considerable increase in the area zoned for residential purposes. In part, this was a reasonable request that would have brought the zoning maps into compliance with actual land usage. But it also would have opened the way for redevelopment and boosted land values. The ESTU, Knickerbocker Village Tenants' Association (KVTA), and the Lower East Side Public Housing Conference united to resist the proposed zoning change, fearing that any increase in land values would prevent construction of public housing. They held a United Community Conference and subsequent rallies to develop support. In March 1938, representatives of the organizations testified against the proposals at City Planning Commission hearings. When proponents of the plan cited Knickerbocker Village as an example of redevelopment's potential benefit to the area, members of the KVTA protested. They reminded the commission that few of the former residents of the Knickerbocker site had been able to afford apartments in the new buildings; in fact, displacement of tenants from the site had added to the congestion of the surrounding area.[52]

Community opposition ultimately proved effective. The Planning Commission postponed decision for nearly a year and then adopted a compromise. While the area zoned for residential use was increased, the planners designated virtually the entire Lower East Side for buildings of six stories or less, thus reducing the area's appeal for large-scale developers.[53]

Agitation for public housing by the ESTU and other local groups produced a more positive result: Vladeck Houses and Lillian Wald Houses. Tenants did much of the grass-roots work in this effort, leading tours of completed low-rent projects in other boroughs, organizing an annual Public Housing Week, and collecting signed petitions demanding preference for the Lower East Side in Housing Authority site selection. Victory came in 1940 with the completion of Vladeck Houses, a joint federal-municipal project with more than seventeen hundred apartments, and with the purchase of land for a second project, Lillian Wald Houses, which was completed only after World War II.[54]

While the Vladeck Houses project was under construction, ESTU leaders served as a liaison between the Housing Authority and area residents, especially those displaced from the project site. ESTU leaders carefully publicized application procedures and requirements, and interceded with the authority to place as many families as possible in the new project. Eventually, 40 percent of the former site tenants, and many additional residents of nearby tenements, were accepted for tenancy, a rather high rate of success compared to other projects.[55]

Construction of this one public-housing project, though important, did not produce a major impact on the Lower East Side. And, with the diversion of public-housing funds to defense housing after 1940, there was little hope of additional building. The ESTU, nevertheless, remained active, organizing tenants and leading rent strikes into the early 1940s.

Yet, ultimately, the ESTU and the CWTC did not survive the dislocations of World War II. Indeed, events in 1943 served as a paradoxical last chapter to the prewar tenant movement. The movement achieved a major, long-sought victory with the imposition of wartime rent controls; but it also suffered a serious defeat when the state legislature enacted a revised

Urban Redevelopment Act. The new law, passed at the urging of Robert Moses and the Metropolitan Life Insurance Company, exempted redevelopment corporations from responsibility for resettling families evicted from the building site.[56] The implications for the future were clear. The postwar period brought new housing crises, new tenant movements, and recurring struggles over urban renewal and neighborhood preservation.

CONCLUSION

Though envisioned as a broad-based coalition of local tenant organizations from dozens of neighborhoods, the CWTC never grew beyond a nucleus of eight or ten powerful, effective grass-roots groups and a shifting coterie of weaker local bodies led by a handful of activists who did their best to represent all tenants, but particularly low-income tenants living in substandard dwellings. Ultimately, both the successes and the failures of the movement stemmed from this condition.

Not surprisingly, the movement was most effective at the local level. In neighborhoods like the Lower East Side, a small number of skilled, young activists forged a viable tenant organization from the work of volunteers, donated facilities, contributions from allied groups, and broad popular support. The actual day-to-day accomplishments of CWTC's affiliates—preventing rent increases and evictions, removing code violations—while difficult to document and impossible to quantify, represent the most important contribution of the movement.

Unfortunately, the council's leaders were less successful in achieving influence at the level of policy formation. Although CWTC could often mobilize large numbers of demonstrators, and succeeded in portraying vividly the needs and desires of slum tenants, it never developed strength equal to that of organized realtors and bankers or, for that matter, equal to that of older, philanthropic housing organizations such as the Charity Organization Society. The council's lack of money and staff proved an insurmountable hindrance when lobbying in Albany and at City Hall. Indeed, it is remarkable that Citywide did achieve some major victories, especially the Minkoff Act.

The CWTC was but one of many New York housing-reform organizations during the late 1930s and early 1940s; yet, it was the most successful in gaining improved housing conditions for poor families. And it was the only organization that truly spoke for and, more importantly, helped poor families to speak for themselves. This unique commitment enabled council representatives to perceive accurately that subsidized rehabilitation, urban redevelopment, and other emerging governmental strategies destroyed neighborhoods. That their warnings were not heeded is unfortunate, for the history of post-World War II housing and neighborhood deterioration in New York City has largely been the fulfillment of their predictions: an inflexible rent-control program; the absence of effective code enforcement; and upgrading, urban renewal, and public-works programs that have displaced low- and moderate-income families from previously viable neighborhoods.

NOTES

1. Mark Naison, "The Communist Party in Harlem, 1928-1936" (Ph.D. diss., Columbia University, 1975); Roy Rosenzweig, "Organizing the Unemployed: The Early Years of the Great Depression, 1929-1933," *Radical America* 10 (July-August 1976); Frances Fox Piven and Richard A. Cloward, *Poor People's Movements* (New York: Pantheon, 1977), Chapter 2.

2. Roy Lubove, *The Progressives and the Slums* (Pittsburgh: University of Pittsburgh Press, 1962); Richard O. Davies, *Housing Reform During the Truman Administration* (Columbia, Missouri: University of Missouri Press, 1966).

3. New York City, *Sixteenth and Final Report of the Tenement House Department* (1937), pp. 1-20; New York City Housing Authority, *Real Property Inventory, City of New York* (1934), Manhattan, 18A-18B. The 1929 Multiple Dwelling Law was passed at the urging of both builders and housing reformers. It set higher safety, ventilation, and sanitary standards than did the 1901 Tenement House Act, and applied such standards to apartment hotels, lodging and rooming houses, and residential clubs, as well as to tenements. In addition, it revised construction requirements to allow use of newly developed materials and construction techniques. See Joseph McGoldrick et al., *Building Regulation in New York City* (New York: The Commonwealth Fund, 1944), pp. 86-89.

4. The boarding up of old-law tenements should not be confused with today's abandonment problem. In many cases, owners vacated apartments yet continued to rent ground-floor "taxpayer" stores, and thus kept title to their properties.

5. New York City Housing Authority, *Report to His Honor, Mayor Fiorello H. LaGuardia . . . January 25, 1937*, pp. 30-50; New York City Housing Authority, *The Failure of Housing Regulation* (New York: 1936), pp. 12-17; McGoldrick et al., *Building Regulation in New York City*.

6. By the end of 1936, the Housing Authority had only one facility in operation—First Houses. Although historically noteworthy as the nation's first low-rent public-housing project, it contained only 122 apartments and served more as a symbol than a remedy. Vacancy figures from a speech by Charles Abrams, published in Welfare Council of New York, *Rent Control: Four Opinions* (New York: 1937), pp. 2-4.

7. *New York Times,* December 9, 1936, p. 29, and December 18, 1936, p. 21; *Sixteenth and Final Report of the Tenement House Department* (1937), pp. 18-20; interview with Jules Seitz, former executive secretary, East Side Tenants Union, and organizer, Citywide Tenants' Council, March 20, 1978. The number of buildings actually vacated under the Tenement House Department Order fell steadily, from 853 in 1936 to 94 in 1940. Source: McGoldrick et al., *Building Regulation,* pp. 439-40.

8. *New York Times,* April 4, 1938, p. 35; June 22, 1938, p. 25; September 25, 1938, section XI, p. 1; February 25, 1940, p. 16; January 20, 1941, p. 10.

9. See, for example, *New York Times,* December 28, 1937, p. 40; March 2, 1941, section XI, p. 1.

10. For the development of federal public-housing and urban-redevelopment policies, see Mark Gelfand, *A Nation of Cities* (New York: Oxford University Press, 1975), Chapters 4 and 6. Most works on the impact of urban redevelopment and renewal and on public-works construction focus on the post-World War II period. Perhaps most influential is Jane Jacobs, *The Death and Life of Great American Cities* (New York: Random House, 1961). For New York, see J. Clarence Davies III, *Neighborhood Groups and Urban Renewal* (New York: Columbia University Press, 1966), and Robert Caro, *The Power Broker* (New York: Alfred Knopf, 1974).

11. In New York City during the early years of the depression, organizations of the unemployed, most notably the Communist-led Unemployed Councils, forcefully prevented hundreds of evictions and forced dozens of landlords to reduce rents. Yet, for a variety of reasons, such activity did not produce an organized tenant movement: internecine warfare between Communists and Socialists frightened some potential adherents; Communists used aid to the unemployed as a means of recruiting for their own party; and, most leaders of the unemployed, not only the Communists, wished to keep the movement oriented toward a

variety of relief issues and thus avoided emphasis on any one issue. See note 1 above.

12. *Knickerbocker News* (a semiweekly paper published by the Knickerbocker Village Tenants' Association), February 22, 1936, March 7, 1936, and March 21, 1936; Heinz Norden, "History of the Citywide Tenants' Council" (unpublished manuscript in possession of the author), pp. 9-10.

13. The Lower East Side Public Housing Conference was a federation of settlement houses, mothers' clubs, and other neighborhood groups formed in 1933 to lobby for public housing.

14. Norden, "History of CWTC," p. 10.

15. Ibid.; author's interview with Heinz Norden, former chairperson of Citywide Tenants' Council, June 4, 1976.

16. Ibid.

17. During the 1930s and 1940s, the rent strike had no legal legitimacy and exposed tenants to eviction for nonpayment of rent. But, in many cases, municipal judges refused to evict striking tenants who had genuine grievances.

18. Interviews with Donald Schoolman, former organizer, CWTC, February 12, 1976, and with James Berger, former chairperson, CWTC Education Committee, February 26, 1976. Also Norden, "History of CWTC," pp. 18-21.

19. Citywide Tenants' Council Papers (hereafter, cited as CWTC Papers), in possession of author, folder entitled "Memos, Leaflets, Minutes."

20. Norden, "History of CWTC," pp. 25, 50. Citywide played a role in the formation of other neighborhood federations, including the Lower West Side Congress, the Chelsea Conference for Action, the Yorkville Civic Federation, and the Bronx Legislative Conference—all outgrowths of attempts to revive the Community Council movement in the late 1930s.

21. Interviews with Heinz Norden, Jules Seitz, Donald Schoolman, James Berger, and Leonard Wacker, former counsel, East Side Tenants' Union, February 11, 1976.

22. Interview with Donald Schoolman; CWTC Papers, "Memos, Leaflets, Minutes," and "Bulletins."

23. Ibid. There was one exception to this trend. The council had successful affiliates in several of Manhattan's middle-class apartment complexes—the aforementioned Knickerbocker Village, as well as in London Terrace and Tudor City.

24. Interview with Heinz Norden.

25. Ibid.

26. The Consolidated Tenants' League had been founded in 1934, and

was well established by the time it joined CWTC in 1936. It charged higher fees and dues than did other affiliates, using such income to maintain a paid office and legal staff.

27. CWTC Papers, "Memos, Leaflets, Minutes," and "Committee to Aid Tenant Organization"; interviews with Donald Schoolman, Jules Seitz, and Heinz Norden.

28. Interviews with James Berger; Henry Berg, former chairperson, Bronx County Tenants' League of the Sixth Assembly District, February 18, 1976; Donelan Phillips, president, Consolidated Tenants' League, March 28, 1975; Heinz Norden; Jules Seitz; and Donald Schoolman.

29. Interview with Heinz Norden; Norden, "History of CWTC," pp. 46-51.

30. *Public Hearings of the New York State Temporary Commission on the Condition of the Urban Colored Population,* vol. 7 (n.p. 1937), pp. 1245-55; *The Tenant* (monthly newsletter of the CWTC), March 1940. The Consolidated Tenants' League was particularly insistent on this type of rent-control statute. Post-World War I rent-control laws had been repealed in 1929, when the citywide vacancy rate reached 7 percent, even though Harlem continued to face a housing shortage.

31. William Rudell, "Concerted Rent Withholding on the New York City Housing Front," unpublished paper, Yale Law School, Property Law Division, 1965, pp. 72-74; interviews with Leonard Wacker, Heinz Norden, Jules Seitz, and Donald Schoolman.

32. *New York Times,* January 25, 1937, p. 6, and January 27, 1937, p. 19; CWTC Papers, "Bulletins"; CWTC *Housing Newsletter* (a semi-weekly published during the 1940 legislative session), vol. 1, nos. 1-9, passim; interviews with Heinz Norden and Jules Seitz.

33. Interview with Jules Seitz; CWTC, *Housing Newsletter,* vol. 1, nos. 5-7, passim.

34. Rudell, "Concerted Rent Withholding," p. 36; CWTC Papers, undated 1938 memo.

35. The *New York Times* and other major dailies ignored the incident, but complete coverage can be found in the *Bronx Home News* and the *Daily Worker* for December 1936 and January 1937.

36. Interview with Jules Seitz. For 1938 alone, the city's Vacancy Listing Bureau estimated that thirty-eight thousand persons had been displaced by bridge, tunnel, highway, and school construction; see *New York Times,* March 23, 1939, p. 25.

37. Citizen's Housing Council, *Ailing City Areas* (New York: 1941), pp. 7-8, 14-16; *Real Property Inventory* (Manhattan), pp. 2a-4b.

38. Henry Street Settlement, *What Some Slum Dwellers Want in*

Housing (n.p: 1935), passim. The survey block, bounded by East Broadway, Henry, Montgomery, and Clinton streets, contained 219 families. See also Fred L. Lavanburg Foundation and Hamilton House, *What Happened to 386 Families Who Were Compelled to Vacate Their Slum Dwellings to Make Way for a Large Housing Project* (New York: 1933), and Community Service Society, *The Rehousing Needs of the Families on the Stuyvesant Town Site* (New York: 1945).

39. Interview with Jules Seitz; speech by Charles Abrams in Welfare Council, *Rent Control: Four Opinions,* pp. 1-5. A similar situation developed during the post-World War I housing crisis. Thousands of Lower East Side tenements, vacated prior to the war, were reoccupied by desperate families.

40. Norden, "History of CWTC," p. 10; interview with Jules Seitz.

41. *Daily Worker,* December 16, 1936, p. 1, December 19, 1936, p. 1, December 24, 1936, p. 5, December 29, 1936, p. 1, December 31, 1936, p. 1.

42. Interviews with Jules Seitz and Leonard Wacker.

43. *Daily Worker,* November 16, 1937, p. 3, November 23, 1937, p. 5, November 27, 1937, p. 4.

44. Interview with Jules Seitz.

45. Ibid.

46. Ibid.

47. CWTC Papers, list of actions for November 1937, in folder "Bulletins"; interview with Leonard Wacker.

48. Details of fires and ESTU efforts to gain prosecutions from Norden, "History of CWTC," pp. 23-24; *Daily Worker,* March 5, 1937, p. 5; *New York Times,* November 21, 1940, p. 31, January 29, 1941, p. 19. In early 1940, Commissioner of Housing and Buildings William Wilson stated that successful prosecution of firetrap landlords had inspired a wave of code compliance. See *New York Times,* March 22, 1940, p. 21.

49. Platzker quote from *New York Times,* August 1, 1937, section XII, p. 4. See also ibid., December 28, 1937, p. 40; September 25, 1938, section XI, p. 10, December 7, 1941, section XII, p. 3.

50. Citywide Tenants' Council, *Calling All Tenants* (n.p: n.d.), p. 8; interviews with Jules Seitz, Leonard Wacker, and Heinz Norden.

51. *New York Times,* November 25, 1937, p. 29; Homer Hoyt and L. Durward Badgley, *The Housing Demand of Workers in Manhattan* (New York: The Corlears Hook Group, 1939), pp. 33-35, 62.

52. *Knickerbocker News,* March 11, 1938; *Daily Worker,* March 17, 1938, p. 3; New York City, *Minutes of the City Planning Commission of the City of New York for 1938* (n.p: n.d.), p. 150.

53. *New York Times,* January 26, 1939, p. 1; New York City, *Minutes of the City Planning Commission of the City of New York for 1939* (n.p: n.d.), pp. 35-44.

54. *Knickerbocker News,* April 8, 1938; CWTC Papers, "Memos, Leaflets, Minutes," passim; *New York Times,* July 15, 1938, p. 19.

55. *Knickerbocker News,* November 18, 1940; New York City Housing Authority, *Seventh Annual Report* (1940), p. 3, and table 16; New York City Housing Authority, *Eighth Annual Report* (1941), p. 9.

56. Gelfand, *A Nation of Cities,* pp. 129 ff; Arthur Simon, *Stuyvesant Town USA* (New York: New York University Press, 1970), Chapter 2.

The Citizens' Council
in New Orleans:
Organized Resistance to
Social Change in a Deep South City

During the first decade of federally mandated public-school desegregation,
no organization contributed more to the mood of white southern intran-
sigence than did the Citizens' Council. A movement of die-hard white
supremacists dedicated to "states' rights and racial integrity," the council
generally enjoyed its greatest successes in the somnolent, isolated county
seats of the rural South, where all of life seemed to move to the rhythms
of cotton, segregation, and the past. Its birthplace and great stronghold
was Mississippi, from which it spread rapidly to every southern state by
the late 1950s. Its influence was most notable in the plantation counties,
the sections of the old Confederacy known variously to southerners as
delta, low country, tidewater, and black belt. Rarely an effective force
in the region's cities, the council's urban successes were confined primarily
to Birmingham, Jackson, Memphis, Montgomery, and New Orleans.[1]

Of these, New Orleans alone is difficult to explain. Birmingham,
known to its black inhabitants as the "Johannesburg of the South,"
practiced a policy of apartheid that was brutally oppressive even by the
standards of the Deep South. Jackson, Memphis, and Montgomery, whatever their other differences, were all essentially commercial centers of the
cotton South, provincial, steeped in southern tradition, and closely allied
to black-belt oligarchies. But New Orleans, as its citizens invariably noted,
was different. A cosmopolitan and urbane port city notable for its ethnic
and religious pluralism, its exotic "Latin" flavor, its elegant restaurants
and genteel dissipation, the Crescent City was, if nothing else, unique

among southern cities. Often viewed in a region of hard-shelled Baptists and bone-dry Protestants as the "scarlet witch" of Dixie, permissive, Catholic New Orleans—"the city care forgot," the city redolent with memories of absinth houses, Storyville, voodoo, and octoroon balls—was an unlikely habitat for the South's largest Citizens' Council.

In retrospect, in the backwash of its school desegregation disorders of 1960-1961, it is easy to believe that New Orleans's reputation for racial moderation was greatly exaggerated. But at the time, indeed as late as 1959, most observers expected that New Orleans would lead the way to peaceful racial accommodation in the lower South. Although Jim Crow institutions were the rule, the races lived in apparent harmony, with perhaps less residential segregation than in virtually any other American city. As was common in the French Catholic parishes of South Louisiana, Orleans Parish Negroes (37 percent of the total population) voted in substantial numbers (17 percent of the electorate in 1960). During the later fifties, they won additional rights long denied to blacks in the lower South. Under the benign and efficient leadership of Mayor DeLesseps S. Morrison, the city added a few "token" blacks to its police force, and peacefully complied with federal court orders to end racial segregation in public transportation, public libraries, municipal recreational facilities, and the professional programs of Louisiana State University of New Orleans. These were substantial achievements by regional standards. In them, progressive New Orleanians found evidence, as one liberal clergyman said, that "if the experiment [of school desegregation] can work out anywhere in the South, it should work out here."[2] It did work out in New Orleans, but only after a year of almost unrelieved crisis in which the direction of events was more nearly controlled by the rabid segregationists of the Citizens' Council than by the city's traditional elites.

ORIGINS OF THE NEW ORLEANS RESISTANCE MOVEMENT

Not by coincidence, the organized resistance movement and the threat of school desegregation came to New Orleans at approximately the same time. Although an NAACP suit had been pending against Orleans Parish public schools since September 1952, Federal Judge J. Skelly Wright's desegregation order did not come until February 1956.[3] Earlier that same month, Archbishop Joseph Francis Rummel announced the imminent desegregation of parochial schools in the Archdiocese of New Orleans.[4] The council's response to these developments was a public meeting at the New Orleans Municipal Auditorium on March 20, featuring an hour-long Dixieland jazz concert and anti-Supreme Court speeches by Roy V. Harris and State Attorney General Eugene Cook, Georgia's roving ambassadors of segregation. Some six thousand to eight thousand white citizens attended, many of whom waved miniature Confederate flags. The rally launched a parish-wide house-to-house membership drive to enlist fifty thousand members.[5]

Until that time, March 1956, council organizers in New Orleans, and indeed throughout Louisiana, had enjoyed only modest success. Although founded in Mississippi in July 1954, the Council movement did not appear in Louisiana until April 1955, when three officers of the state legislature's official "watch-dog committee," the Joint Legislative Committee to Maintain Segregation, organized the Citizens' Council of Homer in black-belt Claiborne Parish. Six months later, in September, a second organization, the Greater New Orleans Citizens' Council, was formed with the help of Mississippi council leaders; by January 1956, it had affiliated chapters in eight communities in Orleans and its surrounding parishes—Jefferson, Plaquemines, and St. Bernard. By that date, at least four other similar but unrelated segregation organizations—the Knights of the White Christians, the Society for the Preservation of State Government and Racial Integrity, the Crescent City White League, and the Federation for Constitutional Government—had appeared in the city. None managed to recruit a significant following, however, and all were rapidly eclipsed and absorbed by the Greater New Orleans Citizens' Council (GNOCC).[6]

The vitality of the GNOCC owed much to the quality of its leadership. Affirming that it was an "open," "nonsecret" organization dedicated to "legal" and "nonviolent" forms of resistance, it had an impressive list of leaders, including a number of locally prominent Catholic lay people. Louis B. Porterie, a lawyer, founder, and early council official, was the son of Gaston Porterie, former state attorney general and federal judge. Dr. Emmett Lee Irwin, perennial president of the GNOCC until his death in 1962, was past president of the Louisiana Medical Association and former head of the Department of Surgery at Louisiana State University Medical School. Jackson Ricau, the organization's first executive director, was a graduate of Loyola University of the South and a former editor of its alumni association's monthly publication. A public-school teacher who resigned his position to accept full-time council employment, Ricau was also a founder, board member, and executive secretary of the Association of Catholic Laymen, organized in March 1956 to oppose parochial-school integration. Emile A. Wagner, Jr., another Loyola graduate active in council circles, was an attorney, a member of the Orleans Parish School Board, president of a downtown savings and loan company, and an official of the Association of Catholic Laymen.[7]

The most influential spokesman for the movement in the area, however, was Judge Leander H. Perez, powerful boss of St. Bernard and Plaquemines parishes and a dominant force behind the scenes in the state legislature. Although never a council officer, Perez was the movement's chief patron and a founder and charter member of both the GNOCC and the Association of Citizens' Councils of Louisiana. By all accounts, Perez was a lion among southern white supremacists.[8] To be sure, Perez was neither a resident of New Orleans nor a power in its internal politics, and none of the other council leaders came from the "first families" of a relatively closed city where one's social standing was inherited rather than achieved. All of them, particularly Perez, were masters of racial idioms that the city's polished aristocracy deemed "coarse." They did not represent what might be called the "power elite." But they were, nevertheless, successful, respectable men, not to be confused with the "rabble" often associated with the more militant varieties of racism.

The larger, statewide Council movement, the Association of Citizens' Councils of Louisiana (ACCL), was also led by men of power and stature. Although Louisiana's movement attracted fewer members (probably never more than fifty thousand) than did either Mississippi's or Alabama's, in no other state did the council have its officials more strategically placed. In fact, the officers of the ACCL and the official Joint Legislative Committee to Maintain Segregation so overlapped that the actions of one were scarcely distinguishable from those of the other— a fact that greatly complicated the efforts of New Orleans moderates to steer a course independent from the rural extremists who dominated the state legislature. State Senator William M. (Willie) Rainach of Claiborne Parish, whose sartorial trappings usually included a Confederate-flag necktie, served as both president of the ACCL and chairman of the Joint

Legislative Committee. State Representative John S. Garrett, also of rural Claiborne Parish, was committee spokesman in the lower house and Rainach's successor as council president in 1959. William M. Shaw, general counsel for the committee, was executive secretary of the state council organization. Other state officials, including Attorney General Jack P. F. Gremillion, Secretary of State Wade O. Martin, and State Superintendent of Education Shelby M. Jackson, conspicuously supported the movement. Governor Earl K. Long (1956-1960), a moderate who privately deplored racial extremism, muted his public criticism in deference to the council's political clout. His successor, Governor Jimmie Davis (1960-1964), was elected with council support and, in grateful acknowledgment, worked closely with its leaders to block school desegregation in New Orleans.[9]

Until the news of the public-school (seventy-eight thousand pupils) and parochial-school (seventy-five thousand pupils) desegregation orders in early 1956, the movement's presence in the New Orleans area was hardly noticed. Orleans Parish councilors counterpetitioned the parish school board when local integrationists urged immediate desegregation in September 1955; a month later, Plaquemines Parish councilors protested the appointment of a black priest to a church at Jesuit Bend.[10] But not until the orders by Judge Wright and Archbishop Rummel in March 1956 did council organizers enjoy appreciable success. Then, following the mass meeting in Municipal Auditorium, the organization began a citywide membership drive. "We're organizing in a ward-by-ward, precinct-by-precinct, block-by-block manner just as a political organization might," Gentilly council spokesman L. P. Davis reported. Although reliable membership figures are not available, it seems certain that this canvass brought a host of new members. In New Orleans, as in Jackson, Mississippi, and other cities where councilors launched citywide, door-to-door drives, organizers used effective tactics. Emphasizing that the NAACP was "Communist-led," and sometimes inquiring, "Are you for us or against us?" they found hundreds of citizens willing to sign the roster and pay membership dues of $5.00. That a high percentage of these new members ever actively participated in council affairs, or even occasionally attended council meetings, is problematical. In fact, the canvass was more nearly a segregationist census than a membership drive. As one council leader put it, "we . . . make it clear that joining our organization is just like casting a vote for segregation."[11] Apparently, many white New Orleanians were unready at this date to vote openly against segregation. Only days after the drive began, the membership chairman reported it to be a "booming success": "I believe we will by far exceed our goal of fifty thousand members. In fact, I think we will top one hundred thousand very shortly."[12] Because council rolls were kept secret—lest patriotic citizens, it was often said, suffer integrationist harassment—questions about the organization's size, and particularly about the characteristics of its membership, cannot be satisfactorily answered. But most informed observers believed that, even at peak strength, its members numbered fewer than twenty-five thousand, most of them from the working class. Even so, this was an inordinately large community action organization. As even Mississippi council officials acknowledged, the GNOCC was the largest Citizens' Council anywhere. In fact, at least half of all Louisiana councilors were to be found in the New Orleans area.[13]

Whatever the council's actual size, a huge and active membership was not really vital to its work. Councils everywhere functioned as pressure groups. Like their counterparts throughout the South, GNOCC leaders became the self-appointed guardians of the status quo, the enforcers of southern racial orthodoxy. Their intent was to sustain a racial drumfire that would keep the "horrors of integration" (presumably, intermarriage, venereal disease, rape, runaway crime) foremost on the public mind. Most whites, they correctly reasoned, feared social change. The council's task, then, was to mobilize the white community's overwhelmingly segregationist sentiment, to force the great mass of whites to close ranks against the "aliens" (the NAACP, the federal courts, even latter-day "scalawags" and "pseudo-southerners") who threatened "our southern way of life." Whatever their validity, the large membership figures council leaders quoted had sufficient credibility to impress City Hall, and to intimidate moderate civic and business leaders who might otherwise have bowed to the inevitability of at least token compliance with federal law.

It mattered little, in moments of acute public anxiety, whether the thousands (usually characterized by observers as middle-aged persons of the upper lower class) who attended council rallies to enjoy a concert and hear colorful, spread-eagle oratory were actually card-carrying members. It was enough that they came to join in the prayers for segregation and the singing of "Dixie." Waving their small, plastic Confederate flags and angry placards, and fervently crying "never" in the litany of defiance, they were the embodiments of white anxiety. As long as the hope of successful resistance survived, their cause and the Citizens' Council's were one.

Nor was financial support a problem. At peak strength, the organization commanded several hundred thousand dollars in dues alone. And wealthy donors, including Leander Perez and B. H. J. Balter, the prominent realtor in whose downtown office building the GNOCC kept its headquarters, provided whatever additional resources it required.[14] During the tense period of school desegregation, a local television station provided "public service" time for the council's Sunday evening "Segregation News Roundup" telecasts.[15] And the city's two major dailies, both published by the conservative Times-Picayune Publishing Company, provided ample and uncritical coverage of council events. On occasion, the *Times-Picayune* even obligingly inserted council meeting announcements in news columns covering the integration controversy.[16]

THE COUNCIL VERSUS THE ARCHBISHOP

As it developed, the first test of council strength centered on parochial rather than on public schools. The Orleans Parish School Board, pledging to use "every legal and honorable means of maintaining segregation," appealed Judge Wright's ruling of March 1956. Action on the case was delayed four additional years, during which time most white New Orleanians seemed to believe that the crisis of public-school desegregation had passed. Archbishop Rummel's order, however, was a different matter. Nearly eighty years old in 1956, Rummel had a long and well-deserved reputation for racial liberalism. In 1949, he had inveighed against segregated religious processions and had removed "white" and "colored" signs from church pews. In 1953, he reminded parishioners that "there will be no segregation in the kingdom of heaven," and directed an end to all discriminatory church practices. In 1956, he applauded Judge Wright's public-school order, declared segregation to be "morally wrong and sinful," and called for the gradual desegregation of Catholic elementary schools.[17]

Not remarkably, given the authoritarian structure of the church, his liberal views found ready reflection in the hierarchy of the Archdiocese of New Orleans. But many lay Catholics, and indeed not a few parish priests, proved less responsive. Led by two founders of the GNOCC,

segregationists formed the Association of Catholic Laymen, an organization limited to "persons of the Caucasian race who profess the faith of
the Holy Catholic Church." They picketed Rummel's rectory, appealed
for the intercession of Pope Pius XII, and urged fellow communicants to
withhold contributions to the church. This protest, however, was short
lived. Following a tense audience with the archbishop, the laymen
quietly disbanded under threat of excommunication.[18]

The council's approach proved more effective. In a predominantly
Catholic city (some 60 percent), the organization was careful to note
that it opposed, not Holy Mother Church, but the policies of a liberal
archbishop. Even its most vicious attacks on Rummel's character and
patriotism were offered in "the name of God's justice and with Christian
charity for all." On May 17, 1956, the second anniversary of the *Brown*
decision, councilors sponsored a parade down Canal Street followed by
a massive open-air protest meeting in Pelican Stadium, where speakers
denounced the NAACP, the Urban League, the Supreme Court, and the
aged prelate. At every mention of the archbishop's name, reporters
noted, a crowd of from four thousand to six thousand people booed.
Afterward, in the early morning hours of May 18, an eight-foot cross
was set ablaze in front of the archbishop's residence. The council was
blamed for this act by the Commission of Human Rights of the Catholic
Committee of the South, a liberal church agency, which denounced the
rally as "anti-American, anti-Southern, anti-Catholic, and irreligious."
These "untrue and libelous accusations" were denied. As proof, Dr.
Emmett Irwin, chairman of the GNOCC, noted that the meeting was
begun with the Lord's Prayer and was occasioned by the singing of both
"Dixie" and "The Star-Spangled Banner." As for the fiery cross: "The
Citizens' Council does not do this kind of thing."[19]

Throughout the spring and the summer, the organization attacked an
ever-widening circle of Catholic leaders as "Communist dupes." In August,
it identified the archbishop himself as an accomplice, although perhaps
unwitting, of "world Communism." Rummel's grade-a-year desegregation
plan was "surreptitious infiltration" designed to "condition the minds of
Catholic parents in truly Communist fashion." An anonymous and crudely
printed handbill circulated at council gatherings invited Catholic church-
goers into "Arch Bishop Rummel's Black Melting Pot," where the only
alternatives were "Murder—and—Rape or Ex-communication."[20]

In the face of this attack, the archbishop retreated. Perhaps he feared a flight from integrated parochial schools to lily-white public schools. Perhaps he became convinced that he was too far in front to lead, that he had gone beyond the demands even of the city's conservative black leadership. For whatever reasons, he issued a pastoral letter in the summer of 1956 acknowledging, "We are not now ready to introduce integration." Desegregation of the archdiocese's sixty thousand white and twelve thousand black students would be delayed until September 1957. But that date, too, came and went without implementation of the archbishop's order. In July 1959, Rummel again announced that Catholic schools would be integrated. He set no date, but promised the change would come "definitely not later than when the public schools are integrated." Subsequently, a confidential letter to all pastors in the archdiocese disclosed a tentative date of November 21, 1960, one week following the entrance of the first black students to white public schools. But a copy of this letter fell into Citizens' Council hands, and was published. This development, and a serious fall that broke the aged prelate's hip, brought further delay. Not until September 1962 was his wish for biracial parochial classrooms carried out. By that date, council leaders Perez and Ricau, having persisted in their obstructionist tactics despite the archbishop's "paternal admonition," were excommunicated.[21]

The collapse of effective church leadership in the school desegregation controversy was a critical development and a major victory for the organized extremists. Elsewhere (in San Antonio, Texas; Raleigh, North Carolina; St. Louis, Missouri), change had come first to Catholic schools.[22] But in this Catholic city, the South's largest Catholic diocese, the home of roughly half of all southern Catholics, the segregationists forced a half decade of delay. In so doing, they deprived beleaguered public-school officials of the moral example of the church. Embarrassed by its own failures, the hierarchy could only watch helplessly from the wings as the tragedy of the city's public-school crisis unfolded. For the moment, the council had not only helped to block interracial private education, it had also stilled a voice for moderation.

COUNCIL PROBLEMS: APATHY AND DIVISION

Ironically, delays in the desegregation of both public and private schools proved a mixed blessing for council organizers. Once the immedi-

ate threat had passed, the intensity of white interest in council affairs
quickly waned. Although membership soared in 1956, it apparently began to sag in 1957. By 1958, council officials complained that popular
support was "very low" despite recent court orders ending city-bus
segregation and overturning discriminatory New Orleans pupil-placement
laws. At one sparsely attended public rally in July 1958, Cullen E. Vetter,
Gentilly council chairman, inquired, "What's the matter with you white
people? Aren't you interested in the preservation of the white race?"[23]
Elsewhere in Louisiana, the problem was even worse; by the spring of
1960, the Association of Citizens' Councils of Louisiana seemed about
to collapse. Time and events would prove, however, that popular interest
was not dead but dormant. In every southern state and locality, organized
resistance groups experienced periods of both feverish growth and public
lack of interest: peak periods came in times of acute racial unrest, when white
perceptions of the imminence of desegregation was greatest; slumps coincided with periods of relative racial calm.[24] In New Orleans, the period
from the autumn of 1957 until the summer of 1960 was the calm before
the storm. Once public-school desegregation again became an immediate
threat, council activities increased sharply.

Meanwhile, public apathy was perhaps the least of the organization's
problems. During the autumn of 1958, its depleted ranks were divided
when a faction, led by Executive Secretary Jackson Ricau and Joseph E.
Viguerie—charter members of the GNOCC—and one of five incorporators
of the state association, withdrew from the Greater New Orleans organization to form the South Louisiana Citizens' Council (SLCC). Although
ostensibly founded "to meet a growing need for expansion of the Citizens' Council movement in the area," the emergence of a splinter group
was the first public indication of a growing cleavage within council ranks.
While it was not fully apparent for more than a year, at the heart of this
rift lay essentially the same vexatious issues that had troubled councilors
in several other states. Representing the more "respectable" wing of the
New Orleans-area movement, the Ricau-Viguerie faction feared the increasingly strident anti-Semitism of such GNOCC stalwarts as Leander
Perez. Jew baiting, they believed, not only risked unfavorable association
with the Ku Klux Klan, but it muddied the waters. The problem at hand
was caused, not necessarily by Jews, but by liberals of every faith who
advocated race mixing. All whites, they argued, should join in the struggle.

Doubtless they agreed with the pragmatic council spokesman from a neighboring state who reminded his followers not to be overzealous: "We can't fight everybody." For reasons that were both tactical and philosophical, then, the new South Louisiana Council, like the status-conscious, regionwide Citizens' Councils of America with which it was affiliated, attempted to confine its intolerance to the color line and thereby win the support of the "better class" of segregationists.[25]

The Greater New Orleans group was less discriminating. Reflecting the dominance and personal values of Perez, its spokesmen were given to the most extravagant conspiracy theories, which invariably linked Jews, Communists, and the NAACP—the "unseen web"—in a "worldwide scheme" to overthrow "white civilization." "The most dangerous people in this country today," Perez believed, "are the Zionist Jews." More than any other element in the city, he said, Jews were plotting to "destroy" New Orleans schools. In order to educate the public to the "Jewish menace," the GNOCC sponsored the "Voice of Truth," a telephone-recording project that, among other things, warned that "some Jews—not all—but some are in favor of complete integration. . . . Why do some Jews want the Negroes and the Gentile to mix? Can it be that a segment of our Jewish brethren want to destroy the Gentile?" On at least one occasion, Perez even casually suggested a boycott of Jewish businesses until such time as the "Jew merchant and Jewish people in our midst . . . stand up and be counted" in the segregation struggle.[26]

For the most part, the divergent paths of the two New Orleans-area councils escaped popular notice. Having divided quietly, without either fanfare or public rancor, the rival organizations worked in apparent harmony during the school crisis of 1960-1961. Privately, such comparatively restrained segregationists as Ricau and Viguerie may have questioned the utility of Perez's searing diatribes. But, in the interest of resistance movement unity, and in recognition of the Plaquemines County boss's enormous prestige in archconservative circles, they did not criticize him openly. The SLCC's pretensions to greater respectability aside, both groups were usually seen as one by the press and the public. Of the two, however, the GNOCC was larger and noisier. At peak strength in 1960, the SLCC claimed (probably with some exaggeration) only two thousand members, though for its official newsletter, *The Citizens' Report,* it boasted sixty thousand subscribers.[27]

GROWING EXTREMIST DOMINANCE

Whatever their organizational problems, the extremists soon emerged as the dominant force in the city. In large measure, their success came by default. Although *Bush* v. *New Orleans,* the case filed by a Negro plaintiff against the city's racially separate schools, had been pending since September 1952, the city was caught unprepared when court-ordered public-school desegregation finally came in November 1960. The School Board, having bought four additional years when it appealed Judge Wright's first order, made no preparation for compliance. Even after it was ordered to present a plan for desegregation by March 1, 1960, the board procrastinated. That date passed, and the deadline was extended until May 16. Ultimately, the exasperated federal justice had to draft a plan of his own. On May 25, Wright ordered Orleans Parish public schools to begin desegregation with the first grade in September 1960. The board's initial response was to invoke the shade of John C. Calhoun. Of the board's five members, only Emile Wagner was a hard-liner, who preferred to close the schools rather than to desegregate them. Even so, the four moderates, including board president Lloyd Rittiner, a former councilor, voted to ask Governor Davis to implement a state statute permitting the "interposition" of Louisiana's "sovereignty" between New Orleans schools and federal law.[28]

The reaction from other quarters was no more constructive. As one City Hall official acknowledged in 1957, "New Orleans is trying to tiptoe around the segregation issue, hoping it will go away."[29] When it did not, the city's traditional leaders simply ignored it. "Most community leaders are trying to look the other way," commented the news editor for WDSU-TV, the local NBC affiliate, in May 1960. "Few people want to talk about it."[30] Having learned nothing from the tragic experience of Little Rock, where federal troops were used to enforce a court order, New Orleans leaders believed that their public schools would never be desegregated. Adrift in an "atmosphere of unreality," the city suffered, as a study sponsored by the United States Office of Education concluded, from "a lack of leadership": "The mayor said that what happened in the schools was not his concern; the city's elite said the school issue was too controversial; . . . the newspapers did not discuss the issue and the public in general acted as though nothing of importance was taking place."[31]

In short, a reluctant, unimaginative, and isolated School Board was left
to its own meager devices.

The dimensions of the city's problems were perhaps best reflected
by a School Board poll of May 1960, when parents of public-school
children were asked to indicate whether they preferred that their schools
be integrated or closed. The intent was to show that, given the choice
between no public schools at all and schools that were operated in compliance with federal law, New Orleans would accept desegregation.
Moderates found the results to be shocking: more than 80 percent of
nearly fifteen thousand white respondents voted to close the schools.[32]
Later, in mid-crisis, when school closure became a real possibility, white
sentiment softened appreciably. The city's leadership, however, contributed
little to this promising development. Its two major dailies gave the desegregation issue scant coverage. Soon after the poll, a *Times-Picayune*
editorial admitted that "closing of the schools would be a tragedy"—but
so, too, was integration. "Whether public education can survive forced
integration in a community like ours, with a large Negro population
and ingrained customs, remains to be seen." The decision, the paper said,
must be left to the people. At the eleventh hour (August 26), both the
Times-Picayune and the *States-Item* urged editorially that the schools be
kept open. In its columns, however, the *Times-Picayune* still identified
School Board moderates as the "four surrender members." As the State
Advisory Committee to the Civil Rights Commission aptly put it, the
city's major newspapers ultimately supported the School Board, but they
did so "belatedly, reluctantly, vaguely, and timorously."[33]

The city's "first families," its dominant professional and business community, which comprised what has been characterized as a "traditionalist,"
"nonmodernizing," "relatively closed elite," also remained aloof. Opposed
to the "vulgar boosterism" of such nouveaux riches cities of the South
as Houston and Atlanta, valuing "good breeding" and ancient family ties
even more than wealth, this proud aristocracy betrayed no concern that
a repetition of the Little Rock disorders could damage the city's image
and retard its growth.[34]

Similarly, Mayor DeLesseps S. Morrison, despite a carefully nurtured
image as a progressive reformer, elected not to involve his office in the
unfolding crisis. At no point did he support either the federal desegregation order or the School Board's reluctant decision to obey it. When his

one belated attempt to garner support quietly for orderly compliance among civic leaders failed, he shrugged: "I'll be damned if I'm going to stick my neck out." In all fairness, the position of this complex and ambitious man during New Orleans's period of anguish defies brief analysis. A lame-duck magistrate who could not succeed himself, the four-term mayor aspired to both state and national office. In 1955-1956 and 1959-1960, he ran unsuccessfully in the Democratic gubernatorial primaries. Some said he wanted a seat in the United States Senate. He clearly sought a cabinet or a diplomatic post in the Kennedy administration. Friends believed he would be president. To succeed in Louisiana, he needed the credentials of a white supremacist; his hopes for success in the larger arena required a record of enlightened moderation. Not able to be both, he pursued, as his biographer has written, "an evasive middle road in the integration controversy that sought to please everyone, but ultimately satisfied no one."[35] To Leander Perez and his followers in the Citizens' Council, "Chep" Morrison was a "weasel, snake-head," a hypocrite integrationist.[36] He was in fact, by instinct and habit, a moderate and a conciliator. But he was nonetheless a segregationist who, despite his urban polish and his old New Orleans family ties, shared the dominant racial values of the rural black belt where he was born. Given the context and the potency of race in Louisiana politics, it seems unremarkable that a politician as shrewd as Morrison should shrink from controversy. Yet he, more than any other single individual, was responsible for the collapse of reason and authority in New Orleans.

In less troubled times, the Morrison administration had quietly cultivated black support. Although the mayor's political organization, the lily-white Crescent City Democratic Association, was closed to Negroes, it nonetheless maintained relatively close ties with the city's conservative black leadership and with such black organizations as the Orleans Parish Progressive Voters' League, the Consumers' League of Greater New Orleans, and the Crescent City Independent Voters' League. Although they were aware of Morrison's racial views, New Orleans's black ministers and black business leaders could remember less sympathetic and less moderate mayors and, thus, generally supported his administration. The dividends for this allegiance were few, but so, too, were the practical alternatives. A numerical minority in an atmosphere unremittingly hostile to their political objectives, blacks were never in a position to bargain effectively with city officials. But, until school desegregation became imminent, their more moderate leaders at least had contacts in City Hall. Once the crisis developed, however, Morrison quickly severed even these tenuous links with the black community.

Smarting from segregationist charges that he was "soft" on race and the "NAACP favorite," the mayor was particularly chary of any contact with the city's more militant civil rights organizations. Indeed, he proudly told white audiences that "I've been sued by the NAACP more often than any other official in the state." He missed few opportunities to identify both the NAACP and the Congress of Racial Equality (CORE) as "extremist groups," and to equate them with the "hot heads" of the Citizens' Council. Although the equation was absurd, the civil rights groups had helped to precipitate the crisis. And once it unfolded, they kept the pressure on—petitioning a federal court for swift implementation of the school desegregation order, demanding that city officials appoint a race-relations committee to smooth the way for social change, and staging the city's first sit-in at a segregated downtown lunch counter. Virtually alone among formal community organizations, the NAACP and CORE demanded not only compliance with Judge Wright's ruling, but an end to segregation throughout the city.[37] If they stood at the opposite extreme from the Citizens' Council, it was only because the spectrum was slanted so heavily in favor of the status quo.

Although isolated from city government and overwhelmingly opposed by the majority of the community, blacks who sought social change were not totally alone. For even in this climate of fear and timidity, progressive white citizens did organize to promote public acceptance of federal school law. Such groups were few in number, however, and their impact on white opinion was small. Save Our Schools (SOS), for example, an organization of whites who advocated peaceful compliance with court-ordered desegregation, was formed quietly in 1959. Composed primarily of social workers, educators, and professional people, a high percentage of whom were Jews, liberal Catholics, and newcomers to the city—and none of whom could be considered members of the power elite—SOS chose not to operate openly until after the parents' poll. Even then, it carefully skirted the integration question, claiming it sought only to keep the schools open. Nevertheless, it was quickly isolated by the Citizens' Council as "a group of known liberals and integrationists," "outside agitators," and "pro-Communists." So effective were these charges that a self-styled "parents' committee," the Committee for Public Education

(CPE), though it pursued the same objectives, refused open alliance with SOS. Organized in the summer of 1960, the less controversial CPE established close ties with the moderate members of the School Board and, by its very existence, served in time to embolden other moderate elements in the community.

Significantly, neither SOS nor CPE attracted more than a few dozen activists; even CPE, easily the more respectable of the two, could never attract more than a few hundred concerned citizens to its public forums.[38] Somewhat earlier, other progressive groups, including interfaith organizations sponsored by Jewish and Catholic clergymen, functioned furtively, only to collapse under allegations that they were sanctuaries for integrationists. A Catholic Interracial Council, which folded early in the parochial-school controversy, did not reemerge until after the worst of the public-school disorders had passed. Most telling of all, in June 1960, when the embattled School Board stood alone, the citywide Parents-Teachers Association passed and then rescinded a resolution in support of open (even if desegregated) schools.[39] Other blows to the open-schools movement came from State Superintendent Shelby Jackson, a council supporter, who endorsed a system of state-financed "private" segregation academies, and from the Louisiana School Boards Association, which erased from membership its own president, Matthew Sutherland of the Orleans Parish School Board, and his three fellow moderates.[40]

TRIUMPH OF EXTREMISM

There was, then, in this city of some 630,000 people, no individual, element, institution, or organization able or willing to compete in the public arena with the Citizens' Council. On November 14 four frightened black girls entered two white elementary schools in the impoverished Ninth Ward. The *Times-Picayune* urged citizens to choose only lawful means of protest on this "Dreadful Day."[41] As word spread, the white parents of students at Frantz and McDonogh No. 19, the schools secretly "targeted" by the School Board for desegregation, rushed to take their children home. Crowds gathered near the two schools to chant racial epithets and sing "Glory, Glory Segregation" (to the tune of the "Battle Hymn of the Republic"). City officials, though they had denied use of the facility earlier that year to the

NAACP, scheduled Municipal Auditorium to the Citizens' Council for a mass meeting the following evening. On November 15, five thousand people came to hear council orators call for a march on the School Board building and on City Hall. "This is total war," Willie Rainach said. "We must use every weapon at our command," including "scorched-earth tactics" and "civil disobedience." Perez assailed the Communists and the Jews. "Don't wait for your daughter to be raped by these Congolese," he urged. "Don't wait until the burr-heads are forced into your schools. Do something about it now." It was, some witnesses believed, "a gathering straight out of Nazi Germany."[42]

The following morning, a mob estimated at from one thousand to three thousand people, most of them truant teen-agers, marched on the civic-center complex. Some swept through City Hall, others moved on the Board of Education building, where mounted police and high-pressure fire hoses were used to turn them back. Once dispersed, they roamed through the business district, carrying crudely lettered placards and throwing debris at integrated city buses and cars carrying Negroes. Angry whites also massed at Frantz and McDonogh schools, where council leaders had urged "a few peaceful demonstrations." Sporadic disturbances continued until school recessed on Friday for Thanksgiving vacation.[43]

The holiday brought a week of respite, but, when school reconvened, the council's campaign of disruption continued. Shifting from mob action to a boycott of the integrated facilities, the organization stationed "observers" at all entrances to discourage parents from bringing their children. Pre-desegregation enrollment reached 1,038, but, by the end of the first week, daily attendance at the two schools fell to six: three black children at McDonough; one black and two whites at Frantz. Except for a few days in January 1961, when one family crossed the council's picket line, the white boycott at McDonogh was total for the remainder of the school year. That family's fate was an example for all the others: the father lost his job and, unable to find another, moved his family out of the city. At Frantz, the boycott was never quite complete, though there, too, several white families who had defied the daily mob were hounded out of town.[44]

To enforce the walkout, a shrill band of women, most of them the wives of working-class and unemployed whites, surrounded the schools each day to intimidate the children as they crossed the picket line. According to one SOS observer, they were "the howling harridans," "screamers [who] shouted obscenities (Nigger-Jew bitch, dirty Jew, and others too filthy to record) and then raced home to telephone the returning families and their escorts with threats of arson, acid-throwing, kidnapping, beatings, and murder."[45] John Steinbeck, then on the last leg of his "travels with Charlie," found their slurs "bestial and filthy and degenerate."[46] Psychologist Robert Coles noted the mob's impact on one black six-year-old who lived in terror from the mob's daily threats on her life: "You little nigger, we'll get you and kill you"; "We're going to poison you until you choke to death."[47] Councilors augmented the mob's work by circulating lists containing descriptions of the automobiles and phone numbers of the dozen SOS volunteers who escorted white children to Frantz. Through School Board member Emile Wagner, it sought (and, in February 1961, obtained) a court order to force parish school administrators to release the names and addresses of attending white students. Harassment, economic pressures, and, in some cases, violence resulted. As hostilities toward nonboycotters mounted, the safe passage of pupils became a question of major concern. Following a series of threatening incidents, including a two-mile chase and an attempt by a truck to ram one of the escort vehicles, federal marshals began accompanying the children of both races to Frantz.[48]

The success of the boycott owed much to official nonfeasance and to School Board mistakes. From the outset, the mayor insisted that "the New Orleans police department has not and is not enforcing the federal court order. . . ." Its duties, he said, were limited to keeping the peace. Even here, it was a feckless effort. Permitting all but the most flagrant disturbances, the police allowed the jeering crowd verbally and physically to abuse the nonboycotters. Some arrests were made, but charges were nearly always dropped. Elsewhere in the city, when civil rights groups attempted sit-ins in downtown department stores, police firmly dispersed crowds and arrested demonstrators. But the "cheerleaders," as they were called, enjoyed unimpeded access to the streets immediately surrounding the schools. Reporters and cameramen who came to cover the disturbances were invariably directed to move on. Although expressing concern about the city's image, the mayor did not urge obedience to the law of the land. At first, he blamed the trouble on the Citizens' Council; then, he accused "outsiders." Eventually, he taxed the out-of-state press. The city, he often said, was doing all it could to maintain order. The following year, after Morrison's resignation to accept an ambassadorial post, another mayor directed police to prevent demonstrations in school areas. The disturbances stopped, and the council soon abandoned efforts to reimpose the boycott.[49]

The School Board's decision to begin the process of change in the Ninth Ward also helped the radical segregationists. By choosing only two schools in a single, politically neglected, low-income ward located on the borders of a parish dominated by Perez, the board inadvertantly played into council hands. Although at least two PTAs in affluent districts actually petitioned the board for Negro students, officials chose schools attended by some of the city's most disadvantaged white children, where, it was said, blacks could more effectively compete. The decision could not have been worse. Of all the predominantly white wards in the city, the Ninth, as the State Committee on Civil Rights concluded, was the least prepared for social change. Inhabited by "extremely poor and racially prejudiced whites," many of whom lived in ramshackle housing projects, the neighborhood, the committee observed, "was ripe for dissidence."[50] Parents there deeply resented the black intruders, believing their schools were selected because they were poor and powerless. The Citizens' Council, abetted at every turn by Perez lieutenants, effectively tapped these race and class antagonisms. Moreover, with both schools located in a single hostile neighborhood, the extremists found it easy to focus white opposition. Close proximity to St. Bernard Parish meant that parents could honor the council boycott without great sacrifice. At Perez's invitation, some six hundred children attended "his" public schools. Others went to a hastily improvised Citizens' Council school in an abandoned St. Bernard warehouse. In both cases, parish taxpayers paid the bills, and were later reimbursed by the state legislature.[51]

Perez's obliging hand was also active in Baton Rouge, where he was often called the "third house" of the state legislature. Since 1954, Perez and such key council figures as State Senator Rainach and State Representative Garrett had served as the architects of official defiance in Louisiana. To Governor Long, who completed his second full term in 1959, the militant segregationists in the legislature were "grass eaters," busily doing that which the courts would only undo.[52] But Perez and his council stalwarts enjoyed the confidence of the lawmakers. The portly, cigar-chewing boss of the deep delta was regarded as a brilliant lawyer, a master of constitutional law. Ensconced in a hotel suite near the state capital, he drafted the race measures that the Joint Committee steered to enactment in session after session. Sometimes, these measures were kept secret by legislative floor leaders almost until the time of enactment. Where racial matters were concerned, Louisiana's lawmakers were not given to lengthy debate. Sometimes, critics noted, they voted on measures they had neither discussed nor read. All told, during the first decade after the *Brown* ruling, they enacted 131 segregation laws—more than twice the number enacted by any other state. The great bulk of these measures came in 1960-1961, when Governor Davis set a state record by calling five special legislative sessions to block school desegregation in New Orleans.[53]

At a GNOCC rally in September 1960, State Representative Garrett, Rainach's successor as state council president, promised New Orleans councilors that the legislature would pass "whatever measures are necessary."[54] The strategy, according to State Attorney General Germillion, another council advocate, was to "legislate and litigate"—to draft a body of "massive resistance" laws so voluminous that the federal courts would be overwhelmed by the sheer bulk of it.[55] Before old measures could be struck down, new measures would be enacted. To a limited degree, the strategy worked. The governor briefly assumed control of the schools. The legislature fired Orleans Parish School Superintendent James Redmond, replaced the four "traitorous" moderates on the School Board, impounded school funds, and, for months, withheld the paychecks of teachers at the Frantz and McDonogh schools. Such measures created temporary chaos but were soon overturned. Federal District Judge Wright was unwavering in his resolve to uphold the *Brown* and the *Bush* rulings. Supported by the Fifth Circuit Court of Appeals, he set aside laws, over-ruled state administrative orders, and, at one point, enjoined 755 state and local officials—including the governor and every state legislator—from interfering with the operation of the two elementary schools. Effectively countering official acts of defiance, the court issued wholesale declarations of unconstitutionality against entire groups of Louisiana segregation law.[56] Yet, though it could strike down obstructionist law, the federal judiciary could not totally efface the damage inflicted by a governor and a legislature willing (as Governor Davis said) to take the "last step before secession." By allying themselves with the city's extremists, state officials helped to legitimize council actions and to isolate further the city's timorous community of moderates.[57]

The hour of the extremists, however, soon passed. With business in sharp decline, the city's carefree reputation badly tarnished, and rumors circulating that Mardi Gras would be cancelled, long-quiescent moderates began to stir.[58] Throughout the months immediately preceding desegregation, SOS and CPE struggled to create community support for open schools. But not until the School Board election of November 8 did their lonely effort begin to succeed. Running against a field of three segregationists, including a Citizens' Council candidate, the moderate incumbent, Matthew Sutherland, won the endorsement of ninety-eight business, professional, and religious leaders, and enough votes (55.6 percent) to be reelected. To be sure, the *Times-Picayune* assured voters that Sutherland was "an ardent opponent of forced integration." Yet, his reelection was generally regarded as a turning point in the crisis and the first clear sign of public support of open schools.[59] Other signs quickly followed. Within days, the *Times-Picayune* again reminded its readers that "closing of the public schools would be worse than the damage . . . of forced integration."[60] In early December, forty-six prominent Protestant, Catholic, and Jewish clergymen joined in a public plea for an end to "this period of unrest." Soon thereafter, the Junior Chamber of Commerce did the same, and, on December 14, a group of 105 business and professional leaders, in an "appeal to reason," called for an end to "threats, defamation, and resistance," in a six-column advertisement in the *Times-Picayune.* During the same month, more than three hundred Tulane University faculty members signed a public statement endorsing the position of the businessmen, while nearly two hundred public-school teachers issued a similar statement of their own.[61]

Councilors fought back to quiet this rising chorus of moderation. In mid-December, they sponsored another mass rally in Municipal Auditorium. Following a round of inspirational speeches, a troupe of young children, some in blackface, exchanged biracial kisses for the crowd. It was, a GNOCC spokesman said, "a little demonstration of what integration means." Although it was responsive, the crowd (estimated at from one thousand to twenty-five hundred) was smaller than usual. Following the rally, there was talk of an economic boycott against moderate business firms, and some newly exposed moderates received harassing telephone calls.[62] But the council's grip on popular interest was failing. Although the school boycott remained in effect until the end of the academic year, the appeal of the extreme racists began to weaken soon after the community's civic and business leadership asserted itself.

The following September, when four additional schools admitted eight more Negroes, all was peaceful: the governor and the legislature were silent; even Emile Wagner appeared at council gatherings to urge segregationists to accept an accomplished fact. After a brief and futile effort to reimpose the boycott, councilors turned their interests elsewhere.[63] Earlier, the organization's leaders had been instrumental in organizing the New Orleans Educational Foundation, which operated the Ninth Ward Private School, and the White Educational Association, which assisted in the foundation of some two dozen so-called private-school cooperatives. Now it turned to a scheme to organize tuition-free private schools supported by state grant-in-aid funds. In time, though both the legislature and the state superintendent of education were willing, the courts also closed this avenue to segregation. Meanwhile, parochial schools desegregated in September 1962, and Tulane University did the same a few months later.[64]

The council's fall from popular grace was fairly rapid. Boycott-wary business leaders, to be sure, watched it nervously for a year or so. As late as September 1962, the Chamber of Commerce believed that the organization was still "a force to be reckoned with."[65] Yet, the school boycott was its last convincing show of strength. With at least token compliance a reality, its followers began to dwindle, and its resources began to shrink. After 1961, its public meetings rarely attracted large crowds, and those who came, observers reported, were now older and "seedier" than before.[66] The newspapers that once followed its every public statement were soon all but closed even to its paid advertising.[67] From time to time, it captured popular attention, as in 1962, when it sponsored "reverse freedom rides" to send black indigents to northern cities and "reverse sit-ins" at integrated lunch counters.[68] In 1965, it organized a campaign to put a picture of Martin Luther King at a "Communist training school" on six hundred billboards.[69] It sought the recall of Senator Russell Long and the defeat of Representative Hale Boggs, crusaded against welfare payments for illegitimate children, and warned public officials not to sign federal nondiscrimination agreements.[70]

These, however, were the empty gestures of a conservative community organization that had tried and failed to turn the tide of human rights. With a bitterness born of defeat, the organization continued for years to inveigh against irresolute public officials and business leaders who had "betrayed" the white race and had "surrendered" to "federal tyranny." The white community, the segregationists professed to believe, preferred to fight on under the council's standard of "states' rights and racial integrity," to close the schools, to preserve "our way of life" at any cost. Desegregation came, they said, not because whites accepted it as inevitable, but because their leaders were self-serving "quislings" more interested in their personal welfare than in the survival of their race.[71]

A more detached reading of the school crisis suggests other conclusions. To be sure, the organization had enjoyed some notable successes. Its extravagant claims notwithstanding, not every New Orleans segregationist enrolled in the council's army. Despite citywide, door-to-door recruitment, its peak membership probably never exceeded 25,000, and most certainly never approximated a representative cross-section of the city's population. Still, this predominantly working-class movement was the largest single pressure group in the community, and a potent bulwark of white supremacy. Well led and well financed, it, more than any other element, influenced the course of events during the desegregation controversy. Capitalizing on latent but pervasive white hostility to Negro rights, the council intimidated racial moderates, discredited constructive solutions, and, for a time, disrupted the essential processes of orderly adjustment.

These successes, however, came largely by default. As the city drifted toward its worst crisis since the Civil War, the power elite—its old money and proud first families, its press and public officials, its clergy, and its civic and business spokesmen—chose not to lead. In so doing, it left a popularly elected School Board vulnerable to white supremacist pressures, and created a vacuum into which rushed the Citizens' Council. The short-run cost of this neglect was near anarchy. Yet, in an age of civil rights, even the grossest civic derelection could not ensure the white supremacists a long-run victory. A movement dedicated to "total segregation" could hardly remain vital in a changing social order. Inevitably, once it became clear that desegregation could not be avoided, that neither a demagogic governor, a reactionary legislature, nor an obstreperous conservative protest movement could indefinitely deny a federal court order, the city's appetite for civil disobedience and its tolerance for public disorder vanished. Not by coincidence, the return of reason to New Orleans was marked by the decline of the Citizens' Council.

NOTES

1. The history of the Southwide Council movement is detailed in Neil R. McMillen, *The Citizens' Council: Organized Resistance to the Second Reconstruction, 1954-1964* (Urbana: University of Illinois, 1971).

2. Father Francis H. Fichter, S.J., quoted in Louisa Dalcher, "A Time of Worry in 'The City Care Forgot'," *Reporter* 14 (March 8, 1956): 19. Contemporary optimistic appraisals of race relations in New Orleans include: Helen Fuller, "New Orleans Knows Better," *New Republic* 140 (February 16, 1959): 14-17; Alfred Maund, "New New Orleans: A Chance for Decency," *Nation* (February 11, 1956): 128. Scholarly and somewhat more sober assessments of the black condition in New Orleans can be found in Edward Haas, *DeLesseps S. Morrison and the Image of Reform: New Orleans Politics, 1946-1961* (Baton Rouge: Louisiana State University Press, 1974); Joseph B. Parker, *The Morrison Era: Reform Politics in New Orleans* (Gretna, La.: Pelican Publishing, 1974); and Allen Rosenzweig, "The Influence of Class and Race on Political Behavior in New Orleans: 1960-1967" (unpublished master's thesis, Oklahoma University, 1967).

3. *Bush* v. *New Orleans,* 138 F. Supp. 337, 342 (1956).

4. "The Archbishop's Way," *Time* 67 (March 5, 1956): 80; "The Archbishop Stands Firm," *Newsweek* 47 (March 5, 1956): 51.

5. *Birmingham News,* March 21, 1956; New Orleans *Times-Picayune,* March 22, 1956; *Southern School News,* April 1956, p. 14.

6. For council organization in Louisiana, generally, see McMillen, *The Citizens' Council,* pp. 59-72. The most useful guide to council organizational techniques is Citizens' Councils of America, "White Book of Citizens' Council Organization" (unpublished volume, rev. ed., Jackson, Miss., 1965), a semisecret manual for council leaders.

7. *Southern School News,* October, 1955, p. 11; *Times-Picayune,* January 13, 1956; Southern Regional Council, *Special Report: Pro-Segregation Groups in the South,* November 19, 1956; *Councilor Newsletter,* November 1957.

8. On Perez's role in the organized resistance movement, see, especially, Glen Jeansonne, *Leander Perez, Boss of the Delta* (Baton Rouge: Louisiana State University Press, 1977).

9. McMillen, *The Citizens' Council,* pp. 62, 287-88, 318-19.

10. *The Citizens' Council,* December 1955; *Times-Picayune,* September 14, 27, November 9, 1955; *Southern School News,* October 1955, p. 11; *Charlotte* (North Carolina) *News,* November 10, 1955.

11. *Times-Picayune,* January 27, March 14, 22, 1956; *Birmingham News,* March 21, 1956.

12. Charles C. Bogan, quoted in *Times-Picayune,* March 22, 1956.

13. In 1958, Dr. Irwin told newsmen that the council had thirty thousand members in the Greater New Orleans area. *Times-Picayune,* May 13, 1958. See also *New York Times,* November 27, 1960; Southern Regional Council, *Pro-Segregation Groups,* pp. 6-7; *The Citizens' Council,* April 1957 and January 1958.

14. Southern Regional Council, *Pro-Segregation Groups,* p. 6; Jeansonne, *Perez,* pp. 235-36.

15. Fuller, "New Orleans Knows Better," p. 15.

16. See, for example, *Times-Picayune,* May 17, 1960.

17. Quoted in Morton Inger, *Politics and Reality in an American City: The New Orleans School Crisis of 1960* (New York: Center for Urban Education, 1969), pp. 17, 22-23; Haas, *Morrison,* p. 254; Jeansonne, *Perez,* pp. 263-64.

18. Jackson Ricau, *The Tragic Truth About the Catholic Race-Mixing Program in New Orleans* (Jackson, Miss.: Citizens' Councils of America, n.d.), pp. 3 ff; James Graham Cook, *The Segregationists* (New York: Appleton-Century-Crofts, 1957), pp. 235-37; "Appeal to Rome," *Commonweal* 67 (August 23, 1957): 58-59; "Rome and New Orleans," *America* 104 (August 24, 1957): 418.

19. *Southern School News,* July 1956; *Times-Picayune,* May 17, 25, August 30, 1956; *Montgomery Advertiser,* May 25, 1956.

20. *Times-Picayune,* August 30, 1956; *Jackson Daily News,* June 15, 1956; handbill, Miscellaneous Files, Southern Education Reporting Service, Nashville, Tenn. (SERS is now defunct; its collection is available through *Facts on Film,* 164 rolls, 1958-1972).

21. Anthony Lewis and *The New York Times, Portrait of a Decade: The Second American Revolution* (New York: Random House, 1964), p. 156; Inger, *Politics and Reality,* pp. 22-23; *Southern School News,* April and May 1962; *Baton Rouge State Times,* March 29, 1962; *Washington Post,* April 7, 1962; Jackson Ricau, "The Revealing Story of My Excommunication," *The Citizen* 6 (April 1962): 4-8.

22. Nicholas Gorman, "An Exchange of Views," *Commonweal* 74 (April 28, 1961): 127; Robert L. Crain, *The Politics of School De-*

segregation: Comparative Studies of Community Structure and Policy-Making (Chicago: Aldine Publishing, 1968), p. 250; Inger, *Politics and Reality,* pp. 23-24.

23. Quoted in *Southern School News,* September 1958.

24. McMillen, *The Citizens' Council,* pp. 28, 152, 361-62.

25. By 1960, the Ricau faction claimed two thousand members. "News from the Local Councils," *The Citizens' Council,* November 1958, February and July 1960; author's interviews with Louis W. Hollis and Medford Evans, Citizens' Councils of America officials, May 26, 1967; McMillen, *The Citizens' Council,* pp. 22-23, 50, 53, 55n, 70-71.

26. On the anti-Semitism of Perez and other GNOCC spokesmen, see the several memoranda from the New Orleans agents of the Anti-Defamation League, Southern Office, Atlanta, Georgia (ADL policy forbids more specific attribution); Reese Cleghorn, "The Segs," *Esquire* 61 (January 1964): 72; Jeansonne, *Perez,* passim; *Times-Picayune,* August 30, September 2, 1960; *Baton Rouge State-Times,* February 15, 1964. The more sedate public expressions of the Ricau faction find reflection in the SLCC's newsletter, *The Citizens' Report, 1959-1961,* and in the publication of the Association of Citizens' Councils of Louisiana, *The Councilor Newsletter, 1960* (copies of both in author's possession). A later organization, officially called the Citizens' Council of Louisiana, published *The Councilor, 1966-1968* (a tabloid boasting a readership of "254,000 in 50 States and 8 nations"), which echoed the strident anti-Semitism and conspiracy theories of its close ally, the GNOCC.

27. *The Citizens' Council,* February 1960; *Times-Picayune,* March 1, 1961.

28. See, especially, Louisiana State Advisory Committee to the U.S. Commission on Civil Rights, *The New Orleans School Crisis* (Washington, D.C.: Government Printing Office, 1961), pp. 3-20; and Crain, *School Desegregation,* pp. 244 ff.

29. Scott Wilson, quoted in Haas, *Morrison,* p. 255.

30. Quoted in *New York Times,* May 8, 1960.

31. Inger, *Politics and Reality,* p. 5.

32. Louisiana State Advisory Committee, *School Crisis,* pp. 6-7; *New York Times,* May 8, 1960.

33. Louisiana State Advisory Committee, *School Crisis,* p. 35. See also *Times-Picayune,* June 26, November 11, 1960; *New Orleans States-Item,* November 11, 1960.

34. See, especially, Crain, *School Desegregation,* pp. 237 ff; Inger, *Politics and Reality,* pp. 25-26, 76-90.

35. Haas, *Morrison,* p. 274; but see also Parker, *Morrison,* pp. 117-22. Morrison's gubernatorial campaigns are also considered in William C. Havard, Rudolph Heberle, and Perry H. Howard, *The Louisiana Elections of 1960* (Baton Rouge: Louisiana State University Press, 1963), pp. 34-54; Glen Jeansonne, "Racism and Longism in Louisiana: The 1959-1960 Gubernatorial Elections," *Louisiana History* 11 (Summer 1970): 259-70; Rosenzweig, "Influence of Class and Race," pp. 199 ff.

36. Quoted in Haas, *Morrison,* p. 270.

37. Rosenzweig, "Influence of Class and Race"; David W. Friedricks, "The Role of the Negro Ministers in Politics in New Orleans" (unpublished Ph.D. thesis, Tulane University, 1967), pp. 40-41; Parker, *Morrison,* pp. 86-88; Haas, *Morrison,* pp. 248, 249-52, 258, 260.

38. *Times-Picayune,* August 17, 18, November 13, 1960; Louisiana State Advisory Committee, *School Crisis,* pp. 6-7, 40-42; Warren Breed, "The Emergence of Pluralistic Public Opinion in a Community Crisis," in *Applied Sociology,* ed. Alvin W. Gouldner and S. M. Miller (New York: Free Press, 1965), pp. 131-32, 134-36, 142-43; Inger, *Politics and Reality,* pp. 28-29.

39. Mathew Ahmann, "Catholics and Race," *Commonweal* 73 (December 2, 1960): 248; Crain, *School Desegregation,* p. 254.

40. *Times-Picayune,* December 16, 1960; Inger, *Politics and Reality,* p. 63.

41. Editorial, *Times-Picayune,* November 15, 1960.

42. *Times-Picayune,* November 16, 1960; *Southern School News,* December 1960; George Sherman, "The Nightmare Comes to New Orleans," *Reporter* 23 (December 8, 1960): 24-26; James Lawrence, "Scandal of New Orleans," *Commonweal* 73 (February 3, 1961): 476; Louisiana State Advisory Committee, *School Crisis,* p. 14.

43. *Times-Picayune,* November 17, 1960; *Southern School News,* December 1960; "D-Day in New Orleans," *Time* 76 (November 28, 1960): 19; "Louisiana Nightmare," *Newsweek* 56 (November 28, 1960): 19-20.

44. See council advertisement, *Times-Picayune,* November 14, 1960. See also *Times-Picayune,* November 29, 1960; *New York Times,* November 17, 1960.

45. Betty Wisdom, "Letter from a New Orleans Mother," *Nation* 193 (November 4, 1961): 353. See also Douglas Cater, "The Lessons of William Frantz and McDonogh 19," *Reporter* 24 (February 16, 1961): 36-37.

46. John Steinbeck, *Travels with Charley in Search of America* (New York: Viking Press, 1961), pp. 227-28.

47. Robert Coles, *Children of Crisis* (Boston: Little, Brown, 1967), p. 78.

48. *Times-Picayune,* November 23, 30, December 3, 10, 1960; *New York Times,* November 29, 1960; Louisiana State Advisory Committee, *New Orleans School Crisis,* pp. 16-17.

49. *Times-Picayune,* November 17, 1960; Haas, *Morrison,* pp. 249-82.

50. Louisiana State Advisory Committee, *School Crisis,* pp. 14, 25.

51. Jeansonne, *Perez,* p. 261; Haas, *Morrison,* pp. 267, 275-76; Inger, *Politics and Reality,* pp. 34-39, 58n; Crain, *School Desegregation,* pp. 258-64.

52. Jeansonne, *Perez,* p. 234.

53. Earleen Mary McCarrick, "Louisiana's Official Resistance to Desegregation" (unpublished Ph.D. dissertation, Vanderbilt University, 1964), pp. 153 ff; Edward L. Pinney and Robert S. Friedman, *Political Leadership and the School Desegregation Crisis in Louisiana,* Eagleton Institute Case Studies in Practical Politics (New Brunswick, N.J.: Rutgers University Press, 1962), pp. 7-24; J. W. Peltason, *Fifty-Eight Lonely Men: Southern Federal Judges and School Desegregation* (New York: Harcourt, Brace and World, 1961), pp. 224-43; *Southern School News,* December 1960; *Times-Picayune,* December 12, 16, 1960.

54. *Times Picayune,* September 13, 1960.

55. State Advisory Committee, *School Crisis,* p. 50.

56. Peltason, *Fifty-Eight Lonely Men,* pp. 224-43; *Southern School News,* December 1960; Inger, *Politics and Reality,* pp. 53-56; Pinney and Friedman, *Political Leadership,* pp. 8-10, 12.

57. *Southern School News,* December 1960.

58. *New York Times,* November 28, December 6, 1960; *Times-Picayune,* December 14, 1960; Louisiana State Advisory Committee, *School Crisis,* pp. 23-25; Haas, *Morrison,* pp. 278-279.

59. *Times-Picayune,* November 1, 2, 4, 5, 7, 1960; Louisiana State Advisory Committee, *School Crisis,* pp. 188, 190; *Southern School News,* December 1960.

60. *Times-Picayune,* November 12, 1960.

61. *New York Times,* December 4, 9, 14, 1960; *Times-Picayune,* December 14, 1960; Louisiana State Advisory Committee, *School Crisis,* pp. 18-19.

62. *Southern School News,* January 1961; *Times-Picayune,* December 16, 1960; Louisiana State Advisory Committee to the U.S. Commission on Civil Rights, *The 50 States Report* (Washington, D.C.: Government Printing Office, 1961), p. 195.

63. See council advertisement, "The Boycott: Your Key to Freedom," *Times-Picayune,* September 15, 1961; *Southern School News,* October 1961.

64. *Times-Picayune,* July 14, August 17, 20, 1960, and January 31, 1961; *Louisville Courier-Journal,* February 12, 1963; *Wall Street Journal,* April 6, 1962; Louisiana State Advisory Committee, *School Crisis,* pp. 8, 10.

65. *New York Times,* September 13, 1962; *Baltimore Afro-American,* September 22, 1962.

66. Interoffice memoranda, 1961-1962, Southern Office, Anti-Defamation League.

67. Jeansonne, *Perez,* pp. 240-41.

68. McMillen, *The Citizens' Council,* pp. 230-31; *Baton Rouge State-Times,* September 14, 15, 1962.

69. *Augusta* (Georgia) *Courier,* May 10, 1962.

70. *Southern School News,* March and April 1965; *Baton Rouge State-Times,* February 1, March 19, June 16, 1965.

71. The post-desegregation views of New Orleans-area council spokesmen are revealed in Ricau, *Tragic Truth; The Citizens' Report, 1961; The Councilor, 1966-1968;* Jeansonne, *Perez,* pp. 271 ff.

Environmental Constraints on Neighborhood Mobilization for Institutional Change: San Francisco's Mission Coalition Organization, 1970-1974

STEPHEN R. WEISSMAN

INTRODUCTION

In the late 1960s, federal antipoverty programs often mandated the participation of the poor.[1] While the new, "post-categorical" generation of social programs attempts to decentralize power to local elected officials, Congress has insisted upon a modified dose of citizen participation.[2] For example, the Comprehensive Employment and Training Act (CETA)

Note: This study was supported by a National Science Foundation Research Applied to National Needs grant to Stanford University. In addition to Community Development Study materials cited in footnotes, the author benefited from the assistance of several individuals: in particular, Steven A. Waldhorn first suggested the need for a typology of urban inner-city organizations, and provided some valuable initial concepts; Nancy Weissman collected program output data and interviewed businessmen and agency personnel; Lynne Zucker helped draft a questionnaire for corporate personnel officials and participated in some interviews; Robert Rosenbloom shared several of his interviews with community activists.

An earlier version of this piece first appeared in the *Western Political Quarterly*, March 1978, as Stephen Weissman, "The Limits of Citizen Participation: Lessons From San Francisco's Model Cities Program," in vol. 31, no. 1, pp. 32-47.

of 1973 vests contractual authority for manpower training in units of local government, but requires "appropriate arrangements with community-based organizations serving the poverty community, and other special target groups, for their participation in the planning of programs." Local planning councils are expected to include "representatives of the client community and of community-based organizations." And federal discretionary funds may be used to support some of the older manpower programs where community organizations have won a share of the turf.[3] A similar thrust is visible in the Housing and Community Development Act of 1974.[4] Outside of the government, the late Saul Alinsky's Industrial Areas Foundation, Imamu Baraka's Congress of Afrikan People, and the Ford Foundation have launched reform-minded citizens' groups in dozens of poor neighborhoods.[5] Yet, we have surprisingly little knowledge of the impact of community-based organizations on public and private policies. As one political scientist has written,

> Important questions such as "What policy changes resulted from the emphasis on citizen participation in the Model Cities and Community Action Programs" are especially difficult to answer. We lack evidence as to what policy changes resulted from the entire program much less a specific aspect of the undertaking.[6]

The available social-science literature shows that independent neighborhood organizations had limited influence on citywide antipoverty programs, but it fails to spell out what these community groups actually accomplished. Much of the research was undertaken in the early stages of new programs. It distinguished between two contrasting paradigms of citizen participation: community representation in service delivery (to obtain improved social services for the poor so they can function more effectively); and community mobilization for political power (to modify certain public and private institutional practices that help to perpetuate poverty). This dichotomy was elaborated in terms of how different community organizations defined social problems and selected courses of action. Absent, though, were systematic analyses of either strategy's effects on the allocation of resources to poor neighborhoods.[7] While examples of community benefits have often been cited—an urban-renewal plan defeated, a highway rerouted, a modification of police tactics, a changed public-housing site, increased garbage collection and street-cleaning activities, for instance—"the cause of such changes and their extent are impossible to document."[8]

A good deal of attention has been devoted as well to the *process* of citizen participation and to the individual gains reaped therefrom. Such subjects as the employment policies of citizen organizations,[9] the political socialization (or desocialization!) of citizen representatives,[10] and their utilization of channels of communication to government officials[11] have been explored in increasingly sophisticated ways. One cannot say the same for the product of community participation (be it services or power mobilization) and the attendant individual or collective gains against neighborhood problems such as subemployment, educational failure, and poor housing and community facilities.[12]

In order to gain a greater understanding of the impact of citizen participation on urban problems, an exploratory study was made of a major community mobilization effort in San Francisco, California, during the early 1970s. The Mission Coalition Organization (MCO) was fashioned after the principles of Saul Alinsky, whose approach to neighborhood political mobilization has been the most influential and durable method to date. MCO, in particular, gained a reputation as one of the most innovative and successful community organizations in the United States. The research focused on MCO's most active and original component, its Employment Committee, and was guided by two general sets of concerns. First, what was a militant, mobilization-minded community organization receiving federal aid able to accomplish over time with regard to poor people's employment problems in the private economy? And what environmental constraints limited these results? The case at hand avoided some of the major problems in analyzing the impacts of social programs.[13] For instance, most of the other community groups adopting mobilization strategies were unable to mount substantial programs. Either their organizing was cut off by federal officials before it resulted in sustained activity,[14] or fledgling action programs were vitiated by threatened local politicians and bureaucrats.[15] An advantage of focusing on employment is that the results, such as job numbers, types, and retention rates, can be seen fairly quickly and easily; whereas, in other issue areas such as education and community development, the payoffs are usually delayed and harder to measure.[16] The use of comparative data from a service-oriented, community-based manpower program makes possible a more precise estimate of the impact of mobilization tactics on private employment decisions. An understanding of corporate and agency reactions is furthered by the existence of a compelling theoretical literature on labor markets and interorganizational relations, and by the relatively limited time span that makes unperceived intervening variables less likely.

It will be shown that the results of the Alinsky-type manpower program were largely shaped by such general forces as the political economy of urban labor markets and the urban interorganizational environment, which also influenced the very character of community organization. This case study points to the continuing constraints on neighborhood mobilization strategies, and charts some directions for reform.

THE POLITICAL ECONOMY OF THE LABOR
MARKET IN THE MISSION DISTRICT

The locus of the study is the Inner Mission, a distinct San Francisco neighborhood of approximately fifty thousand residents. A historically white, working-class community, the Mission's ethnic composition had changed radically in the last thirty years. While 36 percent of the population remained "Anglo" (older, white ethnic groups), 45 percent was now "Latino" (Mexicans and other Latin Americans); 9 percent, Oriental; 5 percent, black; and 5 percent, "other" (mainly Filipinos, Samoans, and American Indians). By the most realistic standard of urban poverty, the Bureau of Labor Statistics' lower-level budget for San Francisco, the neighborhood was in serious economic distress. In 1970, approximately 45 percent of all families, and 50 percent of Latino families, fell below the BLS minimums (for example, $7,686 for a family of four). The male unemployment rate was 10.5 percent; 11.3 percent for Latino males.[17]

Much of this poverty and unemployment stemmed from the kinds of jobs held by increasing numbers of Mission residents. The preponderance of full-time, full-year service workers and female clericals earned under $6,000 per year, as did most female operatives and a surprisingly large minority of male craftsmen. These occupations also had high area rates of part-time or irregular employment. Like many other big cities, San Francisco had a growing number of low-paying, dead-end, often short-term "secondary" jobs, particularly in the service and clerical fields. Nonprofessional jobs with the opposite qualities—the good operative and craft positions that were traditional vehicles for working-class mobility—were stable or declining in number. Highly credentialed professional, technical, and managerial jobs were increasing rapidly, but there were no serious labor-supply problems that might have occasioned a re-examination of qualifications for these jobs. Thus, the changing structure of the urban economy was associated with labor market-related poverty.[18]

Why did so many Mission residents have inferior jobs? An increasingly influential, if loosely organized, body of economic theory posits the existence of a "dual labor market," with separate sectors for good "primary" jobs and bad "secondary" jobs. Although economists argue about the degree of segmentation, and systematic empirical research on the subject is only now getting under way, it is widely recognized that certain institutional devices favored by employers and labor organizations ensure that the poorest, most recently arrived, least powerful workers bear the brunt of rising secondary employment, regardless of their individual productivity. Among these devices are racial discrimination, irrelevant licensing and credentialing requirements, and "statistical discrimination," where employers, in search of cheap screening, hire "on the basis of a few readily (hence, inexpensively) assessed traits such as race, demeanor, accent, educational attainment, test scores, and the like." Such traits "tend to be statistically correlated with job performance but not necessarily (and probably not causally) related to it."[19] In addition, the recruitment and socialization of a new group of workers may be more expensive for the company.[20] These established procedures, when directed at minority groups, have been labeled "institutional racism." They do not preclude, of course, the contribution of real "human capital" deficiencies to labor market-related urban poverty, although these may be rooted in the unstable character of certain jobs and other forms of institutional discrimination (as in educational, housing, health care, and income-maintenance systems). But studies by Ivar Berg, Bennett Harrison, and Eliot Liebow suggest that a great part of the problem lies in "false credentialism" and forms of discrimination.[21]

AN ORGANIZED COMMUNITY RESPONSE:
MCO AND ITS EMPLOYMENT COMMITTEE

Beginning in 1970, a newly formed Mission citizens' group launched a direct attack upon these practices.[22] MCO was largely inspired by local followers of Saul Alinsky, especially young Protestant ministers with awakened social consciences and declining inner-city congregations and veteran grass-roots organizers from the Mission component of the federal antipoverty program. These activists tapped a community network of social, political, and neighborhood improvement groups that had joined together a few years earlier to defeat a city urban-renewal plan that failed to guarantee community control of the redevelopment process. The Alinskyites' efforts drew added impetus from a widespread feeling among Mission Latinos that they were falling behind other, black-dominated neighborhoods in the competition for federal Great Society benefits, and from the mayor's inclination to reward his Mission supporters by channeling federal Model Cities funds through this single community organization with substantial neighborhood legitimacy.

Like other Alinsky-type groups, MCO attempted to build a strong community organization by "rubbing raw" the neighborhood's specific grievances against outside institutions. This took the form of "conflict tactics," generally dramatic protests followed by hard-nosed negotiations. (The group's initial financial supporters—churches, foundations, and the National Science Foundation—did not interfere with its militant strategy.) Following the Alinsky approach of an inclusive umbrella organization for maximum community legitimacy, MCO encompassed both established, community-based service agencies and upstart groups with more of a mobilizing thrust. Alinsky believed that even the more established service providers have a stake in the enhancement of community political power, for this is one route to larger allocations of government service dollars to existing agencies. Yet, although MCO's pragmatic Alinskyite leadership unified the organization behind its "dual agenda" of community mobilization for institutional change and new service programs for the Mission, there was a latent tension between the organization's major objectives—one that would become increasingly overt after MCO managed to obtain federal Model Cities service funds.

MCO's "issues committees," especially Employment, Housing, and Community Maintenance, were the major instruments of its mobilization strategy. Of these, it was the Employment Committee that developed the most thoroughgoing program for institutional change, the most militant and creative approach, and the greatest mass following. The Employment Committee proposed to obtain large numbers of "previously unavailable" jobs for unemployed and underemployed Mission residents. Its approach was not to offer an array of orientation, educational, and training services to enhance worker qualifications (for these techniques were judged, fairly accurately, to be of limited effectiveness), but rather to pressure large employers to disregard arbitrary qualifications in their Mission hiring. The pressure was exerted by seventy to one hundred and fifty volunteers who attended the committee's weekly meetings and who formed a pool of trained picketers, demonstrators, sitters-in, and negotiators. These participants were actually developing jobs for themselves through a point system that related job distribution to attendance at meetings and "actions." In this way, the committee created a direct tie-in between participation and individual benefit, a relationship that was often absent in other community mobilization organizations, to their great detriment.[23] In its first year, the committee placed well over one hundred of its members.

In line with the mayor's preference, MCO effectively controlled neighborhood planning for Model Cities. At the heart of the Mission Manpower Plan was the voluntary Employment Committee and its politics of confrontation. In addition, three neighborhood agencies were funded to provide auxiliary services: a new Mission Hiring Hall (record-keeping and job referral), *Arriba Juntos* ("Up Together"—follow-up and referral for social services), and Mission English Language Center (training for severely language-handicapped immigrants). In the latter two cases, the priorities of established service agencies—to obtain resources for their own programs—were met. But under the Manpower Plan, the agency service operations were clearly subordinate to the militant job-development activities of the Employment Committee.

What did a community political mobilization strategy accomplish with regard to the labor-market problems of the Mission poor, and how did it compare with the alternative strategy of community representation in service delivery? Table 2 presents data on results for beneficiaries of the two main federally financed manpower programs in the Mission during roughly comparable periods: the Alinsky-type, MCO Model Cities effort from September 1, 1971, to January 19, 1973; and the community-based but service-oriented Federal Concentrated Employment Program (CEP) from November 1, 1971, to October 31, 1972.[24] (Sponsored by the local antipoverty program, CEP was citywide, but it used job developers from neighborhood agencies to approach employers. They offered not the politics of confrontation, but subsidized education, training, and work experience to those who would hire their clients.)

In many ways, the Model Cities results were broadly similar to those

Table 2

Selected Output of Two Federal Manpower Programs
in the Mission District

	MODEL CITIES 9/1/71-1/19/73	CONCENTRATED EMPLOYMENT PROGRAM 11/1/71-10/31/72
Total Mission Job Placements	206	93
Yearly Placement Rate	154	93

Placements by Census Occupation Group

Clerical-sales	73%	68%
Craftsman-foreman	20%	5%
Operative	3%	8%
Service	3%	12%
Laborer and other	0%	7%
Median Monthly Salary	$521	$450
Mean Monthly Salary	$519	$483
On Job 6 months	83%	81% est.*
Median Education	12.5 yrs.	12.0 yrs.
Mean Education	11.5 yrs.	11.3 yrs.

Previous Job by Census Occupation Group

Clerical-sales	40%	32%
Craftsman-foreman	7%	5%
Operative	12%	11%
Service	15%	27%

Table 2 *continued*

	MODEL CITIES *9/1/71-1/19/73*	CONCENTRATED EMPLOYMENT PROGRAM *11/1/71-10/31/72*
Previous Job by Census *Occupation Group*		
Laborer and other	9%	4%
Not listed	18%	20%
Previous Mean Salary**	$417	$312

*Unlike Model Cities, CEP job-retention data are for three months and do not include work during training. However, nearly 90 percent of CEP placements worked full-time equivalents of over two months before placement. Hence, the CEP three-month retention rate is used as an estimate for six months, to be more comparable to Model Cities data.

**25 percent of Model Cities and 26 percent of CEP placements not listing previous salaries are excluded from computation of mean.

of CEP. Model Cities obtained only a tiny fraction of the jobs needed by poor Mission residents (154 per year). Furthermore, these were typically "secondary" positions in the middle and upper ranges of urban poverty (median monthly income was $521, and the mean was $519; only one-fifth of the jobs paid more than $600). Classified by occupation, nearly three-quarters of the jobs were clerical or sales, all but one-tenth of these falling in such low-status categories as junior clerk, file clerk, mail clerk, typist, teller, keypunch operator, proof machine operator, sorter, and grocery checker. Menial service (messenger, janitor, delivery boy) and unstable operative work (ice-cream packer, wrapper) accounted for 6 percent of total placements. Only one-fifth, consisting of framemen and installers for the telephone company, were subsumed under the more desirable heading, craftsman-foreman.

Model Cities also resembled CEP in the types of individuals served.

These included a high proportion of relatively well-educated poor (median years of schooling was 12.5, and the mean was 11.5), of persons in age groups desirable to employers (72 percent were between 22 and 44; median age was 25.5, and the mean was 27.4), and of labor market veterans with experience in occupations similar to those in which they were destined to be placed (40 percent listed previous jobs in clerical and sales, 7 percent in crafts; however, 15 percent were service workers, 12 percent were operatives, and 9 percent were laborers, from jobs that were generally less remunerative than clerical work; finally, 18 percent were either new entrants to the labor force or failed to list previous occupations). Among the three-quarters giving previous wages, the mean was $417, not all that far below the mean of $519 for subsequent Model Cities placements.

On the other hand, Model Cities surpassed CEP in the number of jobs obtained (154 to 93 per year), as well as in their quality (more clerical-sales and craftsman-foreman positions, less service and laborer jobs) and compensation (median monthly income of $521 versus $450). It also served clients with somewhat higher educational levels and better-quality previous employment.

LABOR MARKET CONSTRAINTS

Although, as we shall see in detail later, the Model Cities Program was unusual in opening up a number of previously unavailable jobs to the "underqualified" poor, the data just described reveal substantial limitations on program success. In order to clarify the nature and operation of these constraints—which affected CEP and other manpower programs as well—interviews were conducted with knowledgeable personnel officials in five companies that contributed 90 percent of the jobs obtained by the Employment Committee (Pacific Telephone and Telegraph, or PTT, Safeway Stores, Crocker National and Wells Fargo banks, and Standard Oil of California).

All the officials observed that minority hiring had increased rapidly since the mid-1960s. For example, PTT's California-wide figures showed 12.5 percent minority hires in 1966, 25 percent in 1968-1970, and 30.4 percent in the first nine months of 1971. Standard Oil's San Francisco headquarters and Crocker National Bank in San Francisco reported that the minority proportion of their labor forces (of nonprofessionals) had reached 36 percent and 34.5 percent, respectively, in 1972. Everywhere, the percentage of Latino employees rose with a special celerity. PTT more than doubled its Spanish-surnamed hires from 5.6 percent in 1968 to 11.6 percent in 1971.

The company representatives attributed the change in minority hiring largely to rioting and to other manifestations of protest as they affected "corporate consciences," and to growing federal pressures to meet Affirmative Action goals.[25] For instance, Crocker was said to have hired 176 blacks as an immediate result of the Hunter's Point riot of 1967, and a vice-president of the firm observed that pressure from its federal Affirmative Action officer preceded the 1972 decision to expand its Latino training program. According to a PTT vice-president, he and a colleague from Crocker headed up an Industry Manpower Action Committee (IMAC), which started some Latino-oriented training programs "to take the heat off business." The first commitments were hastened by a surprise Latino demonstration at a conference organized by IMAC.[26] In 1971, several Latino organizations complained to the California Public Utilities Commission that PTT did not provide bilingual services for Spanish-speaking customers and thus failed to meet its legal obligation to furnish "full and adequate service." Although the complaint was eventually dismissed, it generated a considerable amount of unfavorable publicity for the utility and delayed a requested rate increase. Only a few months later, the company announced a new program to hire one thousand Spanish-speaking monolinguals by 1976.[27] In order to meet federal Affirmative Action goals that specified minority employment ratios at parity with their representation in the labor force, PTT subsequently set a minimum hiring quota of 20 percent Spanish-surnamed employees per year.

To get needed minority workers, and to stay on the right side of evolving federal standards for job discrimination, the companies modified some job qualifications.[28] Even the banks would now hire ex-convicts, provided they had no felony convictions. PTT and Crocker lowered slightly the test scores required for employment, admitting that high marks at least were not essential for satisfactory job performance. Standard Oil and PTT gave added weight to other elements of the "applicant profile" such as job stability, background, and motivation. (Yet, it should be remembered that these characteristics could also be the basis for "statistical discrimination," preventing workers from ever reaching their full potentials.) Individuals who may have initially fallen below standard but who had upgraded themselves through the panoply of federal "manpower services" such as orientation, education, and work experience were also hired. Finally, to a very limited extent, the companies participated directly in manpower programs for the "underqualified," committing themselves to train and to hire those who could not make the grade. The recruitment of minorities was increasingly pursued through agencies located in their neighborhoods. The most important of these were the long-established State Employment Service (known in California as the Employment Development Department, or EDD) and the new, competitive, community-based agencies that had emerged from the War on Poverty. Most of the officials interviewed preferred to work with the less experienced community agencies; EDD was criticized for poor screening, sending too many people for each opening, and overabsorption in paperwork.

From the point of view of the Employment Committee, it was what the corporations did to improve the upward mobility of the "underqualified" that counted. Yet, according to the personnel officials, their employers were willing to train and hire only small numbers of "underqualified," poor workers, and these for overwhelmingly clerical "secondary jobs." Since 1971, for example, PTT used a figure of 1 percent of its entire work force to determine approximate yearly training-hiring quotas for "underqualified" poor. Even with company turnover reduced due to inflation, this came to less than 10 percent of hires during 1972-1973, or 150 to 170 employees in the San Francisco-Oakland area. Beginning in 1968, Wells Fargo filled a quota of eighty underqualified poor per year. In the same period, Crocker engaged about half that number. Virtually all the bank jobs were low-level clerical positions. Before the advent of the Employment Committee, Safeway and Standard Oil simply did not hire the "underqualified." Even the three companies that did conduct "special training" depended heavily on written admission tests to get the "cream of the crop."

This corporate context of rising minority recruitment (especially Latinos), frequent utilization of community-based agencies, but sharply restricted efforts to overhaul the structure of job qualifications help explain the Employment Committee's limited accomplishment. PTT yielded eighty jobs per year to the committee. Less than one-third were in the crafts. The remainder consisted almost entirely of low-level clerical positions. Those committee selections admitted to "special training" generally had to be at eighth-grade reading level as determined by the California Achievement Test; those "directly hired" were permitted to score 286 instead of 296 on the company's regular entrance examination. Safeway furnished eighty grocery-checker jobs per year from its San Francisco Division, which employed about ten thousand persons. Although these sales jobs paid slightly more than clerical placements ($520 per month), the recipients were all laid off for approximately two months because of company economic problems and the unmodified union seniority system. Those selected for training had to be good enough to pass the checker test within four weeks or they were fired. Crocker (twenty jobs) and Wells Fargo (twenty jobs) required satisfactory test scores for admission to their clerk-teller training programs. Standard Oil (twenty clerical and service jobs) kept the same testing and other evaluation measures used for regular employees, although there seems to have been increased flexibility in their administration.

As Model Cities shared the job-development difficulties and secondary labor-market dependence of CEP and other manpower programs, it also, as we have seen, partook of their inclination to "cream" poor people—as in sending only the "cream of the crop"—in order to meet employer standards.[29] This can be further illustrated by a comparison of 2,357 individuals who signed up at the Mission Hiring Hall on the eve of the Model Cities Program and the 206 Mission residents who eventually received negotiated jobs from the program. On the Hiring Hall list, 29 percent were under 22 years of age and 7 percent were over 44; but only 25 percent and 3 percent of the placements were in these less desirable (to employers) categories. Median education for the Hiring Hall population was 11.9, as opposed to 12.5 for Model Cities placements. Employment Committee and Hiring Hall staff agreed that their greatest problem was the lack of jobs for language-handicapped Latino men over thirty-five whose main experience was in unskilled or skilled manual labor. An estimated 50 to 75 percent of those attending committee meetings in early 1973 belonged to this group.

So, it appears that the aforementioned institutional barriers in the urban labor market were hardly breached. But, if general constraints operating through private employers limited manpower program outputs, what accounted for the different results achieved by different programs?

From one perspective, the Employment Committee's edge over the better-financed CEP in numbers and in quality of jobs obtained[30] and in the social level of their recipients (see table 2) was most significant. The data appear to support the hypothesis that community-based service agencies that approach employers through paid job developers will get less benefits than community mobilization groups that rely on mass voluntarism—although the latter will pay a price for their success in having to "cream" more. This hypothesis receives further support and necessary refinement from a historical survey of the experience of Mission-based community groups with the five aforementioned employers.[31] PTT had trained thirty-seven CEP enrollees during 1969-1970, 10 to 15 percent for the more desirable craft positions. With federal Affirmative Action requirements stiffening, and with a militant, long-term campaign by the Employment Committee, PTT began providing eighty jobs per year to Model Cities in 1971, one-third of which were in the crafts. Safeway and Standard Oil of California only became involved in Mission manpower programs after committee pressures, and Wells Fargo and Crocker National banks significantly increased the number of clerical jobs previously available through CEP only when they were challenged by the Employment Committee. These overall gains of community mobilization were larger on the neighborhood level than they were citywide, for employers with existing special training programs and/or quotas for the underqualified often reduced the participation of other minorities (especially Orientals and Filipinos) in order to meet their commitments to the Employment Committee.

Finally, if the rewards of confrontation were accompanied by the need to "cream" more, there is substantial evidence that the Alinsky-type group resisted employer selectivity more than the community-based, service-oriented agencies did. For instance, the CEP programs with PTT, Crocker, and Wells Fargo placed 111 persons in overwhelmingly low-level clerical jobs. Of these, 80 percent were high-school graduates compared to 66 percent of all Model Cities placements, even though the latter included a higher proportion of better-paying clerical and craft positions. The PTT, Crocker, Wells Fargo, and Standard Oil representatives strongly criticized the Employment Committee for forcing them to hire unusually "underqualified" workers. The first three companies, veterans of other community-based manpower programs, agreed that, for a given job, committee trainees and hires were less qualified than were those furnished by service-oriented community agencies. The committee convinced PTT to drop test scores ten points for their direct hires, persuaded Wells Fargo to recruit at the Hiring Hall to create a more supportive atmosphere for test-taking and interviews, and won Crocker's consent to repeated test-taking up to four times per person. Everywhere, the committee exerted influence on the more qualitative aspects of hiring decisions: judgments about applicant's motivation, stability, and potential.

In sum, within the decisive parameters established by the changing urban job structure, the political weakness of the poor, institutional barriers in the labor market, and institutional racism in general, community mobilization was more successful than were community services in opening up additional and better-quality jobs for "underqualified" poor people. Yet, the benefits of the former approach were hardly as dramatic as an Alinskyite might be led to expect, and they entailed a direct cost in creaming. Also, the employment gains achieved by a single community's mobilized poor were often paid for by the displacement of another community's less mobilized poor.

INTERORGANIZATIONAL CONSTRAINTS

Another useful way of analyzing the Mission manpower effort is through the perspective of interorganizational relations. As a result of its interactions with private corporations and other organizations, the Employment Committee itself experienced organizational change; it became less of an activist, Alinsky group, and this development further limited its overall achievement. The following discussion is also instructive with regard to the character and dynamic of the variety of urban agencies currently implementing the new decentralized federal programs.

This analysis makes use of some key ideas in contemporary interorganizational theory. First, an organization's formal source of authority, such as its charter or guidelines, and its "dominant elite" determine its operative goals.[32] How an organization deals with its goals is revealed by its "domain": in the social services, this consists of "the claims an agency stakes out for itself in terms of the problem covered, population served and service rendered."[33] Interaction among agencies and their power relationships are determined by the extent to which they accept each other's domains ("domain consensus"), and the degree to which they depend upon each other for resources.[34] For each organization in the Employment Committee's environment, we shall first posit the source of authority and the domain. Then, we shall show how the extent of domain consensus and degree of resource dependency between it and the committee shaped their relationship, with particular attention to resulting organizational change in the Alinsky group. (Information about the interorganizational system came from interviews with participants, from personal observation, and from available agency documents.)

Private Employers

Creatures of an essentially permissive legal framework in a capitalist society, these actors are directed by large investors and professional managers.[35] While they conceded community organizations a role in the furnishing of minority manpower, they regarded the setting of job qualifications and the hiring decision as inherent employer rights—to be regulated only tangentially by Affirmative Action codes or union pressures. As we have seen, the Employment Committee considered such prerogatives illegitimate because they discriminated against poor people trapped in the secondary labor market. Lacking fundamental domain consensus, the two sides were in recurrent conflict over their respective roles in the Model Cities Program.

Still, they regularly cooperated by exchanging resources. The Employment Committee furnished minority manpower and community legitimacy needed by the corporations in an age of Affirmative Action; the latter provided jobs needed by committee members. However, since the committee could fill only a small part of the companies' minority-personnel needs (that relating to "underqualified" poor from a single neighborhood), and since the companies gave out all of the committee's crucial resources, the dominant position in negotiations was inevitably that of the employer.

Informants in both camps said that the committee's militance declined in the course of the Model Cities Program, and they attributed this, in part, to adaptation to the realities of dependence. What is more, the committee's predominant mobilizing tool, the point system, was undermined strongly by employers' insistence on maintaining overall job and training qualifications. By late 1972, the Hiring Hall was sending people with five to seven points to jobs, ahead of those with thirty points, because the latter were often unacceptable to employers. Therefore, the incentive for steady, increasingly committed, and bold participation by the "underqualified"—that is, a job after all that activism—was diminishing. This opened the way for a situation, to be described below, wherein relatively passive seekers of language-training stipends began to dominate the committee, further thwarting its action agenda.

NAB-JOBS (National Alliance of Businessmen-Jobs), San Francisco

This was a federal training program for "underqualified" poor throughout the city. Designed to enlist employer cooperation, it was largely implemented by local businessmen.[36] The State Employment Service was the leading recruiter of trainees. Community-based organizations also "preselected" a significant number who were then certified for eligibility, under federal poverty criteria, by the Employment Service.

In nearly 40 percent of Model Cities placements, employers obtained NAB-JOBS training contracts to subsidize their commitments to the Employment Committee. There was considerable domain consensus between the training program and the committee. Although both organizations served "underqualified" poor, they did so in different, complementary respects: one dealt with political mobilization and placement; the other, with training. Also, NAB-JOBS was one of the few government training programs that countenanced "preselection" of recruits by community agencies, which was discouraged elsewhere to avoid charges of ethnic discrimination or to protect the predominant recruitment position of the Employment Service.

According to one veteran Employment Committee leader, it was the employer's responsibility to hire poor people and to bring them up to standard. How the employer did this was none of the committee's business. With this vision of divided but complementary domains, the committee was willing to accept substantial financial resources from NAB to finance its training-hiring commitments. In return, NAB received trainees from the committee. However, the exchange of resources was not in balance. The committee furnished only a small portion of NAB's citywide recruitment, and controlled no political resources in

NAB's Washington, D.C., headquarters. Yet, NAB dollars represented almost all the training money available to the Employment Committee. The committee's dependent position meant that it could do little about an employer who failed to honor fully his commitments because NAB contracts had not yet been approved locally or in Washington. This was a frequent occurrence, reducing or delaying jobs pledged by PTT, Crocker, and Safeway. Both employers and Alinskyites agreed that the committee was "understanding" about these NAB difficulties, which was further evidence of external dependence diluting activism.

California Employment Development Department (EDD)

Otherwise known as the Employment Service, this was a federally financed but state-dominated placement and service-referral agency. In the Mission and in other low-income neighborhoods, it served mostly poor and near-poor individuals. Its approach reflected a historic employer influence: job orders received from businessmen were matched to applicants with requested backgrounds and skills. There is widespread agreement that the Federal-State Employment Service as a whole is inefficient. It has inspired a sizable literature on its bureaucratic pathology, including the aforementioned symptoms of poor screening, overreferral, and red tape.[37]

EDD not only served the same universe of need as did the Employment Committee, but it also offered the same fundamental placement service and a contrasting means of obtaining it. This made it more difficult to carve out separate domains than in NAB, and laid the basis for interorganizational conflict. Competition was further encouraged by the underlying scarcity of jobs. Hence, neither EDD nor the committee accepted each other's essential domain. Mission EDD staff had attended early Employment Committee meetings in the belief that the committee could help them get jobs for their clients or improve coordination between training programs they used, but they withdrew when the committee opted for autonomy and the Alinsky strategy. Committee leaders regarded EDD as ineffective, inefficient, and "paternalistic." As the U.S. Department of Housing and Urban Development (HUD) prepared to fund Model Cities, EDD launched a vigorous assault on its competitor.

EDD officials attacked the point system for "extracting"–that is, compelling–the participation of the "client" in job development; they roundly condemned Model Cities Mission planners for "duplicating" existing programs and agencies, including the EDD centers.[38]

From the beginning of the Model Cities Program, the committee found itself dependent upon EDD for crucial resources. Under pressure from EDD, HUD forced the abandonment of the point system for about eight months, substituting a job-distribution mechanism based on the chronological order of application. In NAB-JOBS, the committee had to send its members to EDD for certification of eligibility. More importantly, EDD's "clout" in NAB-JOBS caused the latter to condition the receipt of its training subsidies on turning over to EDD up to a quarter of the committee's training slots. Since the committee did not offer EDD any resources it needed, it was particularly vulnerable to agency pressure. The effect of this pressure was to weaken participation incentives in the Employment Committee: first, through the temporary suspension of the point system; then, by the reservation of some committee jobs for EDD clients.

Community-Based Agencies in the Mission Model Cities Program: Mission Hiring Hall, Mission English Language Center, and Arriba Juntos

These funded agencies illustrate various types of citizen participation. The new Mission Hiring Hall was conceived by the Employment Committee and was totally financed by Model Cities. Its manager was a longtime veteran of the committee. The hall was closely supervised by the committee, which successfully limited its domain to record-keeping and implementation of the job-distribution system. The Hiring Hall had only seven full-time paid staff and depended totally upon the committee for its resources.

The more established Mission English Language Center conducted federally financed language training in CEP and Model Cities programs, and received less assistance from the local school district for adult education. The clientele was basically Latino, including many recent immigrants to the Mission. The school had been started by a caucus of Latinos in the Laborers' Union as a means of enhancing members' job security.

Abel Gonzales, the caucus and Language Center leader, appreciated the importance of political organization, and welded his followers into a potent force in the parent union, in the local Community Action Program, and in the mayoral elections. He rose to be deputy mayor briefly in 1967, and was later known as "the mayor's man in the Mission."[39] Gonzales and Language Center officials were inclined to use the beneficiaries of service programs as a political wedge to improve the agency's position. Thus, when they became convinced that a strong MCO would help bring Model Cities funds to the school, they "encouraged" CEP-subsidized trainees to attend MCO meetings. Unlike the Alinskyites, the Language Center staff acknowledged strict limitations on militant action, fearing that it could antagonize program sponsors and other major patrons: the mayor, the Laborers' Union, and employers.

Under Model Cities, the Language Center was to serve Employment Committee members who needed elementary language training. This attribution of domain resembles that which we have seen in NAB-JOBS, where one agency dealt with job development and the other with training. Even so, because the school's program dealt with very hard-to-place people, and because one had to attend Employment Committee meetings to be enrolled, a subtle intrusion into the committee's domain occurred. An increasing number of people came to the committee just to get enough points to enter a four-month, $80-a-week training program. These recruits had little reason to believe that militant activity could get them jobs, and they were generally politically passive or frightened recent immigrants as well. Committee leaders soon realized that the failure to "buffer" their organization from this "training economy" was making their work more difficult.

A direct conflict over domain occurred when the Language Center attacked the point system for benefiting energetic "outsiders" instead of existing agency clienteles. It proposed, and briefly obtained, a "table system" wherein jobs were given to community-based agencies according to the numbers they mobilized for meetings and actions. The agencies then distributed the jobs according to their own, sometimes political, criteria.

The school continued to seek institutional enhancement through organizing tactics. Some staff members succeeded in being elected to top offices in MCO and its Model Cities board. CEP and Model Cities language trainees were increasingly mobilized to attend weekly committee

meetings, but they were not obliged to participate in militant actions!
A huge majority of dependent, training-oriented, nonmilitant immigrants
entered the committee. According to observers, this was a key factor in
the ebbing of Alinsky activism.

Again, resource dependency helps account for the results of domain
conflict. Superficially, the committee had set out to obtain noncrucial
training resources from the Language Center, which was pleased to get
additional program financing. The exchange did not seem particularly
imbalanced. But in reality, the committee had been forced by the power
relations in MCO to set up a large training program for the school. Later,
the committee's Alinsky core could marshal only an unsalaried, inexperi-
enced chairperson and volunteer members, while the school relied on
several paid staff members with experience in community politics and a
clientele of almost seven hundred students, two hundred and fifty of
whom received stipends directly from the agency. There was no contest,
and the committee was transformed significantly by early 1973.

Arriba Juntos received its funds from Catholic Charities, United Bay
Area Crusade (a United Fund-type organization), CEP, NAB-JOBS, and
Model Cities. It ran a bilingual information, referral, and orientation
center, and carried on manpower-related programs of counseling, remedial
education, and training design. While its Model Cities clients were predominantly Mission Latinos, its recent CEP trainees were mainly black
and from other parts of the city. Over the years, it had developed a special
role in and commitment to "New Careers"—programs that enabled more
qualified poor to become paraprofessionals in the social services. The
agency's top staff was predominantly Latino, middle class, college-
educated, and either engaged in or imbued with "the Catholic social work
tradition."[40] Perhaps because of their second-generation backgrounds,
they expressed strong interest in fostering upward mobility into the
middle class as in the New Careers program. Unlike the union-inspired,
restlessly organizing Language Center, *Arriba Juntos* relied on its reputation for middle-class professionalism to assure institutional maintenance
and enhancement. Although their officials were less tied to the local
political structure and more liberal in their political attitudes, they also
seemed to prefer hobnobbing with fellow professionals in corporate
personnel departments. Thus, the agency had a reputation for weakness
in holding employers to their job commitments.

Under the Model Cities Program, *Arriba Juntos* was supposed to perform counseling, follow-up, and referral services for committee members as they became eligible for employment or language training. But it joined other agencies in provoking the temporary abolition of the point system, thereby invading the Employment Committee's domain. It was subsequently less intrusive than was the Language Center because of its middle-class style, its geographically varied and less dependent clientele, and the greater diversity of funding sources. Still, it put forth a "softer" line than the committee wished in its contacts with employers. In carrying out its Model Cities functions, it largely redefined them in light of the agency's New Careers commitment. Paraprofessional counselors engaged to follow up on committee placements did not make the requisite number of contacts, did not keep good written records, and spent quite a bit of time doing nothing. Incompetent supervision was certainly one factor in this situation, but the more important reason for it was the top staff's concentration on the design and implementation of career training *for the counselors themselves.* By early 1973, a twelve-hour-per-week course involving writing skills, public speaking, interviewing, and resume-preparation was launched with the supervisors as teachers. According to the person in charge, this training was largely irrelevant to the counselors' present jobs, but it would help make them more employable in the future.

As with the Language Center, the agency's exchange of resources with the Employment Committee was only superficially balanced since the exchange itself reflected *Arriba Juntos'* power in MCO. Although the committee criticized the agency for undermining its negotiating stance toward employers, and came to consider the counseling budget as "fat," it was in no position to call *Arriba Juntos* to account.

A Changing MCO

Other community-based influences on the committee did not stem from the manpower system per se, but they helped push the committee in similar, antiactivist directions. Particularly important were the changing domain and resources of the parent body, MCO. As MCO became more involved in the implementation of its various Model Cities programs, gaining added resources such as jobs and organizational prestige, many of the most dynamic Employment Committee leaders departed to paid positions in either the larger organization or in its subsidized service programs. Furthermore, as MCO embarked on the Model Cities Program, its leaders became increasingly absorbed with the daily administration of social programs, at great cost to their previous activist agenda; little sustained attention was given to the difficulties the committee was experiencing in realizing its objectives, including the absence of trained leadership. Most important, after the diverse forces in MCO had won Model Cities programs for the Mission, they began to divide over the nature and implementation of the new programs. In particular, Alinskyite leaders and newer, more militant agencies were increasingly opposed by the more established service providers. Activist energies were diverted by the growing internecine struggle. By 1974, MCO had suffered a fatal split, and the Employment Committee was moribund. Deprived of both its source of authority (the Employment Committee) and its funding (Model Cities was being phased out), the Mission Hiring Hall gravitated toward the traditional federally-funded manpower system, transforming itself into a relatively conventional community manpower agency.

It is arguable that MCO and similar community organizations might reduce these internal pressures against activism by taking a less direct role in daily program administration, paying more attention to the development of secondary leadership, and encouraging a more altruistic and long-term approach through ideological political education.[41] But, even with such improvements, neighborhood mobilizers would still face the set of powerful organizational obstacles described earlier.

CONCLUSION

This exploratory study supports much of the criticism that has been made of the Alinsky strategy while recognizing its limited accomplishments. In general, neighborhood-based mobilization strategies for social change fail to reckon with the overwhelming constraints imposed by the external urban environment.[42] In the immediate sense, this environment consists essentially of a range of organizations, from private corporations to traditional government social-service bureaucracies to new, community-based agencies. These decisively mold the output of neighborhood mobilization and its organizational character. But they act within a powerful context of urban economic change and the political weaknesses of the poor.

This study does not quarrel with the Employment Committee's assumption that low-income neighborhoods' employment problems cannot be resolved without political action. However, it suggests the need to develop political programs and coalitions on a broader scale than those the neighborhood activist tends to contemplate. Broader, multineighborhood organization could also facilitate the control or exclusion of the community-based agencies that are most hostile to mobilizing tactics. Citywide and statewide poor people's organizations could press for improved wages and a greater share of primary jobs. However, to the extent that such an approach were successful, it might ultimately generate a counterproductive local backlash since it would diminish the economic attractiveness of targeted communities and antagonize white, lower- or middle-class job competitors in nonorganized neighborhoods or in the suburbs. In the view of an increasing number of economists, political analysts, and legislators, the most promising political strategy would be to focus less on particular neighborhood groups affected by subemployment and more on subemployment itself, calling for national policies to upgrade secondary jobs and to create new primary jobs. (With such a program, there would still be a need to monitor discrimination on the local level.) The economic and political mechanics of this strategy are being actively considered.[43]

This research also indicates that manpower and other social programs operate within a complex and powerful interorganizational system. Insofar as widely trumpeted "reforms" do not disturb organizational domains or modify organizational resources, they will fail to produce meaningful change, thereby discrediting the reform impulse. This seems to have been the fate of CEP and other Great Society programs of the 1960s, and the outlook for such "New Federalism" ventures as CETA is equally ominous.[44]

NOTES

1. James L. Sundquist, *Politics and Policy: The Eisenhower, Kennedy and Johnson Years* (Washington, D.C.: Brookings Institution, 1968), ch. 4; Frances Fox Piven and Richard A. Cloward, *Regulating the Poor: The Functions of Public Welfare* (New York: Vintage, 1971), ch. 9; Steven A. and Judith Lynch Waldhorn, "Model Cities: Liberal Myths and Federal

Intervention Programs," in *Urban Law Annual 1971* (Beverly Hills, Calif.: Sage Publishing, 1972), pp. 45-55; Steven Arthur Waldhorn, "Legal Intervention and Citizens Participation," in *Blacks and Bureaucracy: Readings in the Problems and Politics of Change*, ed. Virginia B. Ermer and John H. Strange (New York: Thomas Y. Crowell, 1972), pp. 289-301.

2. See the discussion in Joseph Sneed and Steven Waldhorn, *Restructuring the Federal System: Approaches to Accountability in Special Revenue Sharing and Block Grant Programs* (New York: Crane, Russak, 1975).

3. U.S. House of Representatives, *Conference Report: Comprehensive Employment and Training Act of 1973*, Committee Print, 93rd Cong., 1st sess., December 18, 1973.

4. *Congressional Quarterly*, August 24, 1974, pp. 2319-2320.

5. On Alinsky groups, see, especially, Charles Silberman, "Up from Apathy: The Woodlawn Experiment," *Commentary* 37 (May 1964): 51-58; and John Hall Fish, *Black Power-White Control* (Princeton: Princeton University Press, 1973). On the Ford experiments, see Peter Marris and Martin Rein, *Dilemmas of Social Reform* (New York: Atherton Press, 1967); and Marilyn Gittell, "Decentralization and Citizen Participation in Education," *Public Administration Review* 33 (October 1972), special issue, pp. 669-86. Baraka's efforts are described briefly in the *New York Times*, December 27, 1974, p. 35.

6. John H. Strange, "The Impact of Citizen Participation on Public Administration," *Public Administration Review* 32 (September 1972), special issue, p. 465.

7. David Austin, "Resident Participation: Political Mobilization or Organizational Co-optation?" *Public Administration Review* 32 (September 1972), special issue, pp. 409-20; Kenneth Clark and Jeanette Hopkins, *A Relevant War Against Poverty* (New York: Harper Torchbooks, 1970); Ralph Kramer, *Participation of the Poor: Comparative Case Studies in the War on Poverty* (Englewood Cliffs, N.J.: Prentice-Hall, 1969); Judith May, "Two Model Cities: Negotiations in Oakland," in *The Politics and Society Reader*, ed. Ira Katznelson, Gordon Adams, Philip Brenner, Alan Wolfe (New York: David McKay, 1974), pp. 68-100; Paul Peterson, "Forms of Representation: Participation of the Poor in the Community Action Program," *American Political Science Review* 64 (June 1970): 491-507; Kenneth J. and Annette C. Pollinger, *Community Action and the Poor: Influence vs. Social Control in a New York City Community* (New York: Praeger Special Studies, 1972); Roland L. Warren, "The Sociology of Knowledge and the Problems of Inner Cities," draft manuscript, October 23-November 8, 1970.

8. Strange, "The Impact of Citizen Participation," p. 465.

9. Bennett Harrison, "The Participation of Ghetto Residents in the Model Cities Program," *Journal of the American Institute of Planners* 39 (January 1973): 43-55.

10. Dale Rogers Marshall, *The Politics of Participation in Poverty* (Berkeley, Calif.: University of California Press, 1971); Louis A. Zurcher, Jr., *Poverty Warriors* (Austin: University of Texas Press, 1970); Pollinger and Pollinger, *Community Action and the Poor;* Daniel P. Moynihan, *Maximum Feasible Misunderstanding: Community Action in the War on Poverty* (New York: Free Press, 1970).

11. James L. Sundquist and David W. Davis, *Making Federalism Work* (Washington, D.C.: Brookings Institution, 1969); May, "Two Model Cities"; Rufus Browning and Dale Rogers Marshall, "Implementation of Model Cities and Revenue Sharing in 10 Bay Area Cities: Design and First Findings," paper presented at the 1974 Annual Meeting of the American Political Science Association, Chicago, Ill., August 29-September 2, 1974.

12. A sophisticated analysis of the impact of Model Cities on city employment of minorities is in preparation. For first findings, see Browning and Marshall, "Implementation of Model Cities." An interesting, but sometimes vague and unsystematic, comparison of the results of neighborhood mobilization in four cities is found in Jon H. Mollenkopf, "On the Causes and Consequences of Neighborhood Mobilization," paper presented at the 1973 Annual Meeting of the American Political Science Association, New Orleans, La., September 4-8, 1971, pp. 10-14.

13. For a discussion in relation to manpower programs, see Subcommittee on Fiscal Policy of the Joint Economic Committee of the Congress of the United States, *Studies in Public Welfare, Paper No. 3: The Effectiveness of Manpower Training Programs. A Review of Research on the Impact on the Poor* (by John H. Goldstein), Committee Print, 92nd Cong., 2d sess., November 20, 1972; and Jeremy A. Lifsey, "Politics, Evaluations and Manpower Programs," paper presented at the 1973 Annual Meeting of the American Political Science Association, New Orleans, La., September 4-8, 1973.

14. Clark and Hopkins, *A Relevant War,* pp. 220-21; Kramer, *Participation of the Poor,* pp. 55-68.

15. Clark and Hopkins, *A Relevant War,* pp. 78-88; Fish, *Black Power,* chs. 3, 4; Gittell, "Decentralization and Citizen Participation," pp. 669-86; Daniel P. Moynihan, *Maximum Feasible Misunderstanding* (New York: Free Press, 1970), ch. 6.

16. Gittell, "Decentralization and Citizen Participation," p. 680.

17. Joint Mission Coalition Stanford University Community Development Study (hereinafter referred to as CDS), *Summary of Trends in Housing and Population in the Mission Model Neighborhood 1940-1970* (Stanford, Calif.: Stanford University, 1973); J. Sneed, "Poverty and Underemployment in the Mission District," draft manuscript, n.d. Bennett Harrison, *Education, Training and the Urban Ghetto* (Baltimore: Johns Hopkins Press, 1972), pp. 48-50, effectively criticizes the Social Security Administration poverty index used to determine eligibility for many government programs.

18. Sneed, "Poverty and Underemployment"; Stephen R. Weissman and Lynne G. Zucker, "External Constraints and Organizational Responses in Urban Social Programs: The Case of San Francisco's Concentrated Employment Program," in Sneed and Waldhorn, *Restructuring the Federal System;* Roger Noll, *Metropolitan Employment and Population Distribution and the Conditions of the Urban Poor* (Washington, D.C.: Brookings Institution, 1970).

19. A leading statement of the dualistic thesis is Peter B. Doeringer and Michael Piore, *The Internal Labor Market* (Lexington, Mass.: D. C. Heath, 1971). For a good overview of the theory, see David M. Gordon, ed., *Problems in Political Economy: An Urban Perspective* (Lexington, Mass.: D. C. Heath, 1971), pp. 57-158, 181-90, 208-13; and Harrison, *Education, Training and the Urban Ghetto.* An excellent critique, which still accepts many of the dualists' conclusions, is Michael L. Wachter, "Primary and Secondary Labor Markets: A Critique of the Dual Approach," *Brookings Papers on Economic Activity* 3 (1974): 637-93. Quote is from Piore, "The Dual Labor Market: Theory and Implications," in Gordon, *Problems in Political Economy,* p. 91.

20. Jules Cohn, *The Conscience of the Corporations: Business and Urban Affairs 1967-1970* (Baltimore: Johns Hopkins Press, 1971), pp. 2-3, 31-33, 39-40; Peter Doeringer, ed., *Programs to Employ the Disadvantaged* (Englewood Cliffs, N.J.: Prentice-Hall, 1969), p. 248.

21. On institutional racism, see Louis Knowles and Kenneth Prewitt, eds., *Institutional Racism in America* (Englewood Cliffs, N.J.: Prentice-Hall, 1969); Harrison, *Education, Training and the Urban Ghetto;* Ivar Berg, *Education and Jobs: The Great Training Robbery* (New York: Praeger, 1970); Eliot Liebow, *Tally's Corner* (Boston: Little, Brown, 1967).

22. The following section is partly based on interviews with MCO principals by the author and Robert Rosenbloom of CDS. The following materials were also utilized: Mike Miller, *A History of MCO* (CDS manuscript, n.d.); Saul Alinsky, *Reveille for Radicals* (Chicago: University of

Chicago Press, 1946); Robert Arthur Rosenbloom, "Pressuring Policy-Making from the Grass Roots: The Evolution of an Alinsky-style Orientation" (Ph.D. diss., Stanford University, 1976), chs. 1, 2; *First Action Year Comprehensive Development Plan, Mission Amendment* and *Comprehensive Development Plan for the Second Action Year* (obtained from Mission Model Neighborhood Corporation), sections on "Manpower and Economic Development." Regarding the effectiveness of service programs, see Weissman and Zucker, "External Constraints."

23. David J. O'Brien, *Neighborhood Organization and Interest-Group Processes* (Princeton: Princeton University Press, 1975), chs. 1, 4.

24. Two Model Cities agencies, the Mission Hiring Hall and *Arriba Juntos,* and CEP headquarters provided data on all Mission residents in their programs. Where there were gaps or conflicts in the records, these agencies were cooperative in checking and verifying data. Of 266 Model Cities placements, 35 lived outside of the Model Neighborhood boundaries, and 25 did not list addresses, leaving 206 Inner Mission placements. The author has a high degree of confidence in the overall reliability of the data; however, he has reason to suspect that information on *previous wages* may be understated in both programs.

25. Compare similar pressures in the public sector as reported by Browning and Marshall, "Implementation of Model Cities."

26. This information was confirmed by Lee Soto, a Mission agency leader who was involved in the demonstration and who received some of the first job commitments.

27. This point was amplified by the author's discussion with Robert Gnaizda, attorney in Public Advocates Inc., which represented the plaintiffs.

28. The Supreme Court's decision in *Griggs* v. *Duke Power Co.* (1971), outlawing testing unrelated to actual job skills, was mentioned by some of the businessmen.

29. For a fuller discussion of these aspects of manpower programs, see Weissman and Zucker, "External Constraints."

30. Based on a previous study of CEP (see Weissman and Zucker, "External Constraints"), the author is convinced that the program itself did not limit community agency job development; rather, CEP program plans generally *reflected* demonstrated agency job-development capabilities.

31. The following section is also based on *Arriba Juntos* and Mission Language and Vocational School subcontracts, 1967-1971, and "Final Report of *Arriba Juntos* Employment Support Program (by subcontractor)," October 1971, CEP files.

32. Sol Levine, Paul E. White, and Benjamin D. Paul, "Community Interorganizational Problems in Providing Medical Care and Social

Services," in *Readings in Community Organization Practice*, ed. Ralph M. Kramer and Harry Specht (Englewood Cliffs, N.J.: Prentice-Hall, 1969), pp. 163, 173; Charles B. Perrow, "The Analysis of Goals in Complex Organizations," *American Sociological Review* 66 (March 1961): 854-66; Philip O. Selznick, *TVA and the Grass Roots* (Berkeley: University of California Press, 1949); Grant McConnell, *Private Power and American Democracy* (New York: Alfred A. Knopf, 1966).

33. James D. Thompson, *Organizations in Action* (New York: McGraw-Hill, 1967), pp. 28-29; Levine, White, and Paul, "Community Interorganizational Problems."

34. Levine, White, and Paul, "Community Interorganizational Problems," pp. 165-73; Thompson, *Organizations in Action*, pp. 25-29; William M. Evan, "The Organization-Set: Towards a Theory of Interorganizational Relations," in *Approaches to Organizational Design*, ed. James D. Thompson (Pittsburgh: University of Pittsburgh Press, 1966), pp. 173-91; Thompson, *Organizations in Action*, pp. 30-32.

35. G. William Domhoff, *Who Rules America?* (Englewood Cliffs, N.J.: Prentice-Hall, 1967); John Kenneth Galbraith, *The New Industrial State* (Boston: Houghton Mifflin, 1967).

36. On the national NAB-JOBS program, see Peter Kobrak, *Private Assumption of Public Responsibilities: The Role of American Business in Urban Manpower Programs* (Washington, D.C.: U.S. Department of Labor, May 1971); Harrison, *Education, Training and the Urban Ghetto*, pp. 2, 34-36, 171-75; and Sar A. Levitan, Garth L. Magnum, and Robert Taggart III, *Economic Opportunity in the Ghetto: The Partnership of Government and Business* (Baltimore: Johns Hopkins Press, 1970), pp. 19-42.

37. Stanley H. Ruttenberg and Jocelyn Gutchess, *The Federal-State Employment Service* (Baltimore: Johns Hopkins Press, 1970); Lawyer's Committee for Civil Rights Under Law and National Urban Coalition, *Falling Down on the Job: The United States Employment Service and the Disadvantaged* (Washington, D.C.: 1971); U.S. Department of Labor, *Manpower Report of the President 1973*, p. 48; Peter Bachrach and Morton S. Baratz, *Power and Poverty: Theory and Practice* (New York: Oxford University Press, 1970), p. 158; Peter Blau, *The Dynamics of Bureaucracy* (Chicago: University of Chicago Press, 1963).

38. San Francisco Cooperative Area Manpower System (CAMPS), "Minutes of the Meeting May 13, 1971," "Minutes of the Special Meeting June 17, 1971," "Semi-Annual Review for Period Ending 6/30/71."

39. See also Miller, *A History;* Kramer, *Participation of the Poor*, p. 45 notes the CAP organizing.

40. See also Miller, *A History*. For both community-based agencies,

compare David Rogers, *Interorganizational Relations, and Inner City Manpower Programs* (Washington, D.C.: Office of Policy, Evaluation, and Research of the Department of Labor, 1971), which portrays community-based agencies in four cities' manpower systems.

41. Internal factors are discussed by Rosenbloom, "Pressuring Policy-Making," chs. 5-7.

42. Localism and lack of a wider political program are criticized in Thomas D. Sherrad and Richard C. Murray, "The Church and Neighborhood Community Organization," in Kramer and Specht, *Readings,* pp. 346-459; Marris and Rein, *Dilemmas,* pp. 186-87; Frank Riessman, *Strategies Against Poverty* (New York: Random House, 1969), ch. 1; and Fish, *Black Power.*

43. Harold Z. Shepard, Bennett Harrison, and William J. Spring, eds., *The Political Economy of Public Service Employment* (Lexington, Mass.: D. C. Heath, 1972); Robert Lekachman, *Inflation: The Permanent Problem of Boom and Bust* (New York: Vintage, 1973), esp. pp. 41-43 and 73-76; Andrew Levison, "The Working-Class Majority," *New Yorker,* September 2, 1974, pp. 36-61; Bennett Harrison, "Inflation and Unemployment: Jobs Above All," *Social Policy* 5 (Jan.-Feb. 1975): 36-42. In a more moderate vein, see Lloyd Uhlman, "The Uses and Limits of Manpower Policy," *Public Interest* 34 (Winter 1974): 83-105.

44. Weissman and Zucker, "External Constraints"; William Mirengoff, "Manpower Programs Under CETA: A Preliminary Assessment," paper presented at the National Manpower Policy Task Force Conference, Washington, D.C., June 1975; "Job Aid Meant for Poor Is Often Spent on Others," *New York Times,* September 26, 1975, pp. 1, 21.

Community Organizing in
the 1970s:
Seeds of Democratic Revolt

HARRY C. BOYTE

Looking at the surface of present-day community activism, any character-
ization of it as a "movement"—or even as a coherent phenomenon—seems
implausible. If one neighborhood fights the banks, another plants urban
gardens. The same community group may simultaneously oppose school
busing, make alliances with black homeowners, and patrol against crimi-
nals. While some community activists have formed a major base for a new
generation of urban politicians such as Dennis Kucinich in Cleveland and
Ruth Messinger in New York, many others shy away from political in-
volvements altogether. If neighborhood training centers often teach
strategies for confronting corporate and government authorities, many
also spend much time battling each other, at least rhetorically, about
different organizing methodologies and the definition of what community organizing is and where it should be headed.

Yet, an identifiable community organizing movement has in fact
emerged during the 1970s. (The terms "community organizing" and
"neighborhood organizing" are sometimes used interchangeably, though
"neighborhood" in fact suggests a smaller-scale and more geographically
specific organization. Here, "community organizing" refers to one specific
strand of activism among the range of neighborhood ferment: mass-based,
advocacy organization, along either geographic or constituency lines, that
draws its main, sustaining agenda of issues out of neighborhood concerns
and problems.) The community organizing movement grows from specific

crises and changes in American economic and political life, and it is given a measure of coherence by common motifs present in a range of organizing methods. Finally, community organizing expresses distinctive themes that suggest material for an insurgent political culture in the coming years.

While tools of left-wing—and specifically Marxist—analytic traditions help illuminate the large-scale developments that form a background for the movement, the themes that characterize community organizing itself confound classic political categories of both the Left and the Right. On the one hand, the new forms of protest come directly out of traditional relations and patterns of life that are under assault—ethnic ties, kinship relations, religious bodies, and other institutions of the community— which the Left has tended to see as monochromatically conservative and provincial. The initial animus of neighborhood struggle is to rebuild and cohere the threatened social fabric. In the course of such struggle, groups often incubate a deepened appreciation for particular group identities and traditional institutions, resulting in their revitalization, not in their demise. And even the most militant, confrontational community organizations often seek the transfer of resources and programs away from the state apparatus, in marked contrast with conventional left-wing emphasis.

On the other hand, while community protests grow from and sustain indigenous and traditional community institutions, such protests also frequently result in an internal democratization of a community's life: opening up existing structures to new and wider forms of participation and sources of leadership, and generating a new tolerance for diversity and pluralism. As community organizing evolved throughout the changing political economy of the 1970s, organizers across the range of training centers and networks developed "majoritarian" and alliance-building strategies that seek to unite constituencies torn apart by the 1960s into large coalitions against the rich and powerful, giving a populist cast to the new generation of organizing efforts. Further, the community organizing of recent years has generated a redistributionist ethos that appears even in the most mainstream expressions of the movement, like the report of the National Commission on Neighborhoods released in the spring of 1979. In sum, the community protests of the 1970s potentially form one vital strand of an emerging force for democratic, structural change in American society. And though its full scope, potential, and implications have yet to be grasped, one fascinating consequence of the movement could well be a reworking of the nation's political and social imagination, with untold but enormous consequences for the future.

By the end of the 1970s, an army of journalists, policymakers, social scientists, and politicians had begun to discover that a "neighborhood movement" formed a kind of invisible saga of the decade, less visible than the antics of presidents, rock stars, and football heroes. On the simplest level, spontaneously organized neighborhood groups had exploded in number. In New York City, since mid-decade, several thousand block clubs had been formed, addressing issues that ranged from rents to health care and crime control. The National Commission on Neighborhoods compiled a list of over eight thousand community groups in the nation, most of which were considerably larger geographically than a single block. A *Christian Science Monitor* poll of communities with populations over fifty thousand, concluding a series that labeled neighborhoods "the politics of the 1970s," found one-third claiming to have already taken part in some kind of neighborhood improvement effort or protest, and a majority declaring their willingness to take some sort of direct action in defense of their neighborhoods in the future.

Moreover, a growing number of large, enduring community organizations and coalitions of organizations gave the movement a distinctive cast. The largest of such urban groups—the now defunct Citizens Action Program (CAP) in Chicago, the Communities Organized for Public Service (COPS) in San Antonio, the United Neighborhood Organizations (UNO) in East Los Angeles, or the Oakland Community Organization—at their peak strength were able to turn out thousands of delegates to citywide conventions. Statewide and multistate organizations, such as Massachusetts Fair Share, Citizens Action League in California, Oregon Fair Share, Illinois Public Action Council, Connecticut Citizen Action Group, and the Association of Community Organizations for Reform Now (ACORN), drawing their consistent agenda of issues largely out of community concerns, had formed in more than half the nation's states. Coalitions such as the National People's Action (NPA) and the National Association of Neighborhoods gave the new insurgency noticeable presence on a national level. Even tenants—traditionally the hardest community constituency to organize into ongoing, powerful blocs—had, by 1979, formed coalitions in twenty states, forcing state legislatures to enact

legislation on such issues as leases, terms of rental agreements, reasonable-
ness of landlord rules, and security deposits. More than a dozen organizer-
training centers had formed to service such varied networks. (The major
organizer-training schools include: the Center for Urban Encounter, the
Industrial Areas Foundation, the Mid-American Institute, the Mid-Atlantic
Center for Community Concern, the Midwest Academy, the National
Centers for Urban Ethnic Affairs, the National Training and Information
Center, the New England Training Center for Community Organizers,
Organizers, Inc., the Pacific Institute for Community Organization, and
The Institute.[1])

Finally, an identifiable strand of neighborhood-based politics became
visible as a new phenomenon. Across the country, a large number of
popular, grass-roots political figures began their public careers directly
out of community battles and organizations. And a populist strand of
urban politics surfaced, with the election of mayors like Kucinich in
Cleveland, Byrne of Chicago, and, before his death, Moscone of San
Francisco, based on political alliances of insurgent community and labor-
union constituencies. In short, ferment in the nation's communities had
grown on a very large scale throughout the supposedly self-absorbed
"me decade," with echoes felt around the world. Thus, Neil Peirce reported from Europe that neighborhood and related protest groups,
visible wherever he traveled, "seemed to be taking on the proportions of
a global movement."[2]

Classic left-wing theory of social change and insurgency slighted the
community context almost entirely. Notably, Karl Marx focused his
attention on the large-scale industrial setting as the main locus of class
struggle, and on the economic enterprise producing capital goods (the
"means of production" themselves) as the basic moving force of capital
accumulation. Marx could not anticipate the enormous changes in the
economy, government, and society as a whole that advanced capitalism
would generate. In the United States, for example, the period after
World War II witnessed the tremendous expansion of social services and
government employment; the emergence of huge white-collar bureacra-
cies in government and in industry; the rapid growth of the media and
communications systems, marketing operations, and extensive technical,
scientific, and educational establishments designed to service the modern
economy. Moreover, the maturation of the consumer culture and expand-

ing state activity brought a number of social projects into the public sphere that were formerly left to the home.

Though Marx did not imagine the shape of modern capitalism one hundred years after his death, his critical method proved a penetrating instrument for describing the essential dynamics of contemporary capitalism. At root, Marx held that capitalism could only be understood as a total system. While institutions of law, politics, religious life, and education at first appear far removed from the economy, they are in fact directly affected by economic forces that tend to introduce market-place relations—"the cash nexus"—into every sphere of activity. Contemporary radical critics have given much attention to the ways in which social life is shaped and organized more and more directly by the imperatives of private profit and by the growing activity of the government. In the phrase used by Christopher Lasch and others, there is a "socialization of social production." The experiences through which people replenish and sustain themselves increasingly resemble a kind of "social factory," where they are dominated and exploited as taxpayers and consumers, in ways analogous to exploitation at the workplace itself. And specifically, leftist economists have demonstrated how market pressures cause land speculation, housing shortages, skyrocketing housing costs, and urban sprawl. In turn, the processes of expanding state activity and "wasteful" (what Marx called "nonproductive") investment in the creation of individual and collective state-provided consumables alleviate the short-term economic difficulties of capitalism. But these processes also worsen long-term structural problems: generating a growing fiscal crisis at all levels of government, rising inflation, massive shifts of capital from region to region and across national lines; and leading to corporate takeovers, transfers of capital from small to big business, and increasing monopoly control of the economy.

Such economic and political analyses have given rise to an analogy of community organization as a kind of "trade union in the social factory," the instrument through which people bargain to get the best possible "terms" for the reproduction of their lives off the job, in a fashion analogous to trade-union bargaining at the workplace itself. And, in fact, in many ways, the neighborhood protests, arising around specific issues— from traffic lights and housing to schools and recreation—resemble the defensive battles workers wage about income levels and working conditions. Steve Max, organizer, theorist of the movement, and trainer at the Midwest Academy, expressed the trade-union analogy:

> Traditionally, trade unions addressed the fact that the workplace was where the exploitation of labor took place. Unions lessened exploitation by winning better wages and working conditions. With the development of monopoly corporations closely tied to government, the picture became more complicated. It was one thing for a union to win higher wages and quite another for it to be able to prevent the corporations from taking back the wages through fixed and inflated prices or to prevent the government from taxing away the wages and returning them to the corporations. . . . It is here that community organization has stepped in to fill the vacuum. Community organization is guided by many of the same principles as union organization—self-interest, pragmatism, emphasis on constant small victories with only slight attention paid to the long-term self-interest of the members.[3]

The comparison of the community organization to the trade union helps clarify the objective circumstances of the community protests against corporations and the government. It aids as well in pinpointing some of the differences between workplace and community battles. Thus, for example, the far more fragmented nature of community life, divided along a crazy quilt of class, ethnic, and racial lines; the multiple authorities that neighborhood and citizen activists must confront; the difficulties in developing sustainable financial bases for community groups and in defining clearly the ongoing constituency—all such characteristics make solidarity and organizational maintenance more difficult in the community context. On the other hand, factors such as the much greater freedom in the community from direct manipulation by authorities, the great variety of tactics available, and the greater responsiveness of government to popular pressure are assets that community groups off the job can draw upon in winning victories and building their power.

While radical criticism helps clarify the background for the community organizing movement, the internal structure of the movement itself has a history and character that does not fit into classic left-wing theoretical models nor mainly emerge from the activity of left-wing organizers.[4] To understand the substance of the movement itself requires a look at the specific tradition of community organizing as it has evolved over the last several decades.

Though community organizing began to receive national notice only in the latter years of the 1970s, in fact, its origins are to be found much earlier. From nineteenth-century ethnic associations to Jane Addams and the Settlement House movement, activists had long sought to organize communities in their own behalf. But community organizing as a distinct and developed method of insurgent struggle came into its own with the work of Saul Alinsky, a man whom Midwest Academy director Heather Booth once called the "Sigmund Freud of the community organizing movement."

Alinsky's passion was to organize the people. He first began in the late 1930s, in that legendary Back-of-the-Yards area of Chicago that Upton Sinclair described as "the Jungle." For more than a quarter-century thereafter, Alinsky was adviser, strategist, and organizer for communities across the country. With Fred Ross, Alinsky helped create the Community Service Organization (CSO) in the southwestern United States, the first major political base for Mexican-Americans, and the group in which Cesar Chavez began his career. In Chicago in the late 1950s, he organized the Woodlawn Organization in Chicago's southside black ghetto, an organization that inspired black communities across the nation during the civil rights movement. Throughout the 1960s, Alinsky worked with church-related community organizing efforts and with poor people's welfare-rights projects. By the end of the decade, several "Alinsky" groups existed in his home base, Chicago, and a growing number of groups modeled on the Chicago pattern could be found around the country. (The first four Alinskyite groups in Chicago—after the Back-of-the-Yards organization in the 1930s—included: the Woodlawn Organization, the Organization for a Better Austin [OBA], the Northwest Community Organization [NCO], and the Southwest Community Congress [SCC]. OBA hosted the first national conference of neighborhood groups in 1972, forming NPA.) Reduced to essentials, Alinsky's approach included three principles:

1. Organizing people for power. Above all Alinsky believed in grass-roots organization as the primary means for achieving power. To motivate people, Alinsky thought that the organizer must appeal to their own directly perceived self-interest on concrete issues. He was nonideological, experimental, and pragmatic, voicing little interest in longer-range goals. Moreover,

Alinsky was tactically expedient, willing to work with anyone who would help win the issue, and forming political alliances across a broad range of opinion. In fact, Alinsky gloried in the political and cultural diversity of his constituencies, with language reminiscent of Walt Whitman's celebration of America. Rednecks, blacks, Mexican-Americans, middle-class homeowners, housewives, or college kids, Alinsky would counsel any group to organize if they lacked power and wanted to acquire some.

2. Building indigenous leadership. Alinsky placed great importance on the need to build grass-roots leadership. In fact, he saw as a central goal "organizing himself out of a job" by training people to take charge of the organizations he helped create. To build organization, Alinsky believed it was essential to work from the foundation of what already existed in a community. Thus, his approach stressed the effort to strengthen and unify in a new way the internal networks of churches, clubs, small businesses, union locals, and other institutions that already functioned as the community's informal social structure. In his view, only through such internal strengthening, which redefined institutions' relation to each other and built their collective cohesion, could a community learn to act effectively in its own behalf.

3. Organizing to win. Alinsky was extraordinarily creative in developing tactics and strategies for grass-roots organizations. He believed it was necessary to use tactics within the range of experience of the constituency, but also tactics that were full of surprises, irreverent, dramatic, and rapidly changing. Using military imagery, he preached the need to keep the enemy off balance, use the establishment's rules against itself, split the opposition, appeal to its self-interest, threaten embarrassment and humiliation—in short, to do whatever was necessary to win. Winning was the lifeblood of successful organizing, in Alinsky's view, the only way in which those accustomed to defeat and disunity could be welded into collective actors in their own behalf. To such an end, Alinsky sought to systematize organizing principles into a rational body of knowledge that actually achieved results. In his view, the major youth protests of the

1960s were mystical and romantic, relying on moral exhortation and rhetoric, not on concrete skills and careful planning.[5]

Despite Alinsky's personal iconoclasm, flamboyant style, and uncompromising sympathy for the dispossessed, Alinskyism in its "classic form" was a method that could be adapted readily enough to liberal, pluralist assumptions. Alinsky mobilized constituencies without longer-range strategic goals, and such organizations could evolve in ways he had not imagined or desired. Thus, Alinsky was bitterly disappointed when the Back-of-the-Yards organization ended up by organizing to keep black homeowners out. In an analogous irony, the Rochester, New York, FIGHT organization he formed in the 1960s forced Eastman Kodak Company to hire four hundred black workers, and it simultaneously laid off four hundred whites.

The changing political economy of the late 1960s and early 1970s wrought major shifts in Alinskyite approaches while it also quickened the pace of neighborhood-based activism in general. To understand such a development requires further exploration of how the terms of politics themselves began to be transformed throughout the last decade.

In the period of rapid economic expansion after World War II, the inner circles of power in American society tolerated a wide range of alternative and oppositional forms of expression. Above all, it was claimed, in pluralist America, economic change was rendering class divisions and conflict obsolete. Backward elements of business in the National Association of Manufacturers might rail against the growth of government, the liberal menace, or civil rights demonstrators, but the self-described statesmen at the pinnacles of economic power in the United States avowed a social conscience of unparalleled size. "Capitalism seems to be entering upon another evolutionary phase, in which its activities and decision making are being increasingly vested with longer-run public purpose," claimed H. Bruce Palmer, president of the National Industrial Conference Board, at its 1967 symposium on the future of capitalism. "The new generation of business leaders is far more concerned than was its predecessors with the whole broad area of public affairs." In such an environment, corporate executives sometimes backed liberal politicians; indeed, many chose Lyndon Johnson in 1964 over that ardent advocate of free enterprise, Barry Goldwater. Similarly, their counterparts on local and state levels could often be found in alliance with labor leaders and with other advocates of expanding local government. As John Mollenkopf and others have documented, such "growth coalitions" formed the characteristic basis for urban politics in many areas of the country during the decade. And demonstration projects such as Sears' inner-city program and the Life Insurance Association of America's "billion dollar investment in the slums" were touted as the most dramatic examples of the new corporate conscience.[6]

From the point of view of community organization (such as other reform constituencies), the rhetoric of corporate responsibility—like that of the Great Society in general—seldom matched the real gains they could expect. And, in fact, fights against key features of 1960s-style urban politics—most notably, urban-renewal programs and highway construction—provided the initial impetus for the formation of hundreds of community groups around the country. For example, by 1970, there were in progress four hundred community battles against different highway plans. Through such struggles, neighborhoods developed a kind of internal cadre of skilled leadership with political acumen, organizational know-how, and public talents that would prove a foundation for subsequent organizing. But throughout the 1960s, community organizing's primary focus remained narrow, fitting into the interest-group form of American politics in which different groups accepted the "givens" of income distribution and of governmental and corporate structures, and competed for scarce but expanding resources through the use of whatever tactics they could devise. The simple fact was that resources—in the form of social services, jobs, federally financed programs, and other benefits—did indeed expand dramatically at local levels. Over the twenty-year-period from 1954 to 1974, the state and local share of total GNP rose far more rapidly than did any other economic sector—from 7.4 percent to 11.6 percent. Poor and minority groups won jobs from new federally funded programs such as Model Cities, Manpower training, and community mental health. And the number of local government jobs mushroomed, from 6.1 million in 1960 to 11.6 million in 1971. Against such a background, a well-organized community group could expect to win many benefits from city halls eager to co-opt discontent before it got out of hand.[7]

Yet, the worsening economic problems of the 1970s evaporated the rhetoric of corporate responsibility; brought to the surface long-developing

urban fiscal crises, caused by sources of revenue growing much more
slowly than expenditures; and precipitated a rapid decay in 1960s-style
politics. From businesses' viewpoint, the new economic environment—
fierce foreign competition, chronic inflation, and an enormous burden of
public and private debt—necessitated a radical change in political strategy.
The entire array of corporate-connected institutions took up a cry
against "excessive public expectations," calling for a transformation of
relations between business, government, and other groups that would
favor business. And cities, in the new corporate perspective, must be the
first to learn "the new realism." An editorial in *Business Week* vividly expressed the new corporate mood:

> Some people will obviously have to do with less—cities and states, the
> home mortgage market, small businesses and the consumer will all get
> less than they want. It will be a hard pill for many Americans to
> swallow—the idea of doing with less so that big business can have more.[8]

The hardening line of corporate America in the 1970s found expression
in a variety of ways: organizations such as the Business Roundtable gave
big business new clout at a national level, employing lobbying, pressure,
and public-relations tactics to get its way. Threats of layoffs and plant
relocations proved especially effective in pressuring cities and states to
grant new tax breaks, to ease regulations, and generally to provide more
favorable treatment for businesses. And within progressive and reform
constituencies, the new facts of corporate politics began to work major
changes. In the labor movement, leaders used the rhetoric of "class
struggle" that was not heard for decades. Thus, for example, United Auto
Workers president Douglas Fraser warned that a new corporate right-wing
offensive had opened "class warfare" against poor, working, and middle-
income Americans, and he called for alliances between labor, community
groups, and others. Ralph Nader and other public-interest advocates
moved from criticizing corporate abuse to criticizing the system of
corporate power itself. Major new funding sources for community and
citizen activism emerged—the Catholic Campaign for Human Development and the Youth Project—with a markedly anticorporate cast to
their funding interests. Thus, new bases of support and alliances for community organizing began to come together throughout the 1970s. And
long before—as the Nixon administration first gave expression to the

rhetoric of "new realism"—the changing environment had begun to impact dramatically on communities and on the field of community organization.[9]

In the first years of the decade, worsening conditions quickened the pace of organizing and activism. In 1973 and 1974, community organizations around the country began documenting widespread and widening patterns of red-lining—refusal by lending institutions to extend credit for property in certain areas, or to offer it on extraordinarily high terms. Frank Ceitel, manager of Chase Manhattan Bank, candidly explained: "We admit that investing in New York is important. But we can give a mortgage rate at 8½ percent or buy bonds from GM at 10 percent. From GM we make more." New York City Council president Percy Sutton charged that "even luxury apartment house owners are having great difficulty getting mortgage money from New York lending institutions." And New York was simply a microcosm of a nationwide pattern. By mid-decade, dozens of battles against bank-lending practices—and soon, also, against insurance company red-lining—had appeared. And in the midst of the general fiscal crisis, as neighborhoods experienced declining services, shifts in the tax burden from businesses to residential homeowners, and escalating costs of housing, spontaneous forms of activism spread in every major city. National People's Action chairperson Gale Cincotta said, "The base was there, and people reached the point where they had to do something."[10]

Moreover, while new protests stirred urban neighborhoods, community organizing methods simultaneously had begun to adjust to the new situation. The results included: broadening the definition of appropriate constituency, a new search for organizational longevity, and an increased self-consciousness about the importance of continuing autonomy from dominant political and economic powers.

TOWARD A BROADENED CONSTITUENCY: FOUNDATION FOR A NEW POPULISM

By the end of the 1960s, signs of change in the classic Alinskyite strategy had begun to multiply, resulting in a kind of populism that sought to ally diverse groups of the powerless against the centers of power. In Alinsky's second book on organizing, *Rules for Radicals,* published in 1972, he directed much of his attention to the middle class, whom he called the "have-some, want-mores." He argued that they, like the poor, the students, and almost everyone in the society, were oppressed by corporations; that corporations must become the ultimate target if significant changes were to be won; and that new coalitions between the "have-nots" and the "have-some, want-mores" were essential. Even before publication of his book, he had begun to put broader coalition-building perspectives into practice in a new Chicago-based organization, the Citizens Action Program (CAP), which organizers, under Alinsky's direction, had turned into a citywide group of diverse neighborhoods. "We began across the board," explained Ed Chambers, director of Alinsky's Industrial Areas Foundation training center. "We worked with upper middle class and middle class whites, blacks, Chicanos. We began looking at community of interest."[11]

Similarly, parallel changes were at work in a distinct but related tradition of organizing pioneered by Fred Ross, Alinsky's associate in the CSO days of the early 1950s. Ross, disagreeing with Alinsky, had argued that a regional organization like the CSO could only be built through organizing on the basis of issues, not the institutions of a community. Instead of pulling together the indigenous community institutions, he developed a method of holding house meetings based on problems of concern to the Mexican-American population as a constituency. Subsequently, Ross and Chavez applied the house-meeting technique to the farmworker support network. Ross also helped shape the approach of the National Welfare Rights Organization (NWRO). And, by the beginning of the 1970s, while Alinsky's own training program was experimenting with broader coalitional approaches, the organizers within the NWRO also reconsidered their definition of constituency. NWRO head George Wiley argued for a new "majority approach" in the aftermath of the welfare lobby's failure to win passage of guaranteed-income legislation. "It was very simple," explained Bert Deleeuw, a co-worker of Wiley's. "Welfare recipients were getting clobbered because they were isolated. So we went out to organize this whole new constituency as allies."

From the perspective of the majority strategy, most Americans— blacks and whites, poor and middle income, welfare recipients and blue- and white-collar workers—were victimized by powerful corporations and their friends in government, and were potential allies in the common struggle against such forces. Welfare-rights organizer Wade Rathke, moving from Boston welfare rights to community organizing in Little Rock, Arkansas, began to apply such perspectives. And the Association of Community Organizations for Reform Now (ACORN) resulted, with its first chapter in Arkansas. ACORN's community-based chapters, organized around issues, specifically sought "power for the majority." As the ACORN organizing manual put it, "Behind the organization's concern with these issues is a basic understanding which says that all these issues are mere manifestations of a much more fundamental issue: the distribution of power in this country."[12]

CAP and ACORN became models for a generation of large-scale community organizations across the nation. At times, such groups defined themselves, in part, directly in response to the changing political economy. Thus, for example, Massachusetts Fair Share, the nation's largest, statewide citizen organization, came into being with the overt purpose of responding to the new corporate agenda: "Without resistance, a massive drive on the part of the business community in Massachusetts will end up severely reducing the standard of living for a majority of the state's low and middle income families," explained one of Fair Share's funding proposals. "Fair Share will need to build a countervailing power to offset and resist this mobilization." The Ohio Public Interest Campaign (OPIC), a hybrid of both Alinskyite and Rossian methods, which coalesced existing community groups with labor unions, senior-citizen organizations, and others around such issues as plant relocation and tax structure, formed specifically, according to staff director Ira Arlook, "to attack the roots of the problems" posed by the 1970s—"the structure and behavior of the giant corporations, national and global."

Even in the organizations and training centers that do not target the corporate power structure in such an explicit fashion, the 1970s produced far greater attention to the creation of alliances among groups of the powerless—alliances made increasingly *possible* by the parallel changes within labor unions, churches, public-interest groups, and other reform constituencies. In turn, larger-scale definition of constituency and its allies greatly expanded the scale of issues that community groups could address. Statewide and multistate organizations such as Fair Share, ACORN, and OPIC have been able to take on issues of statewide nature—from industrial exodus or regressive taxes to insurance rates and utility structures. And by banding together into national coalitions such as the Citizen-Labor Energy Coalition and the National People's Action, community organizations have been able to begin addressing questions of national policy. Along with the search for larger-scale organization across lines of previous group division, moreover, has come a new emphasis on organizational survival over time.[13]

BUILDING ORGANIZATIONS TO LAST

The diverse community organizing networks vary enormously in a number of dimensions: extent and nature of involvement of local community institutions; structure; nature and size of staff; constituency definition; kind and range of issues addressed; funding approaches. Yet, throughout the field of organizing, activists have been consistent in their effort to build organizations that last beyond five or six years, the average for older-style, Alinskyite groups. Even among those constituencies hardest to organize on an ongoing basis, the focus is on durability. According to John Atlas, an editor of the national tenants' newspaper *Shelterforce* and a leader in the New Jersey Tenants' Organization, such a development had occurred in the last half of the 1970s. "What traditionally happened in tenant organizing was that people organized themselves in a building to stop a rent increase or to deal with deteriorating conditions. Then because of the transient nature of the tenant population, the protests soon died, whether they won or lost." But major changes had begun to take place, Atlas continued, "Especially in the last four years or so there's been a tendency toward more permanent forms of organization and a new recognition among tenant leaders that they have to unite with other tenant groups and also with groups like the NPA, which are mostly homeowners."[14]

In ongoing organizations with sizable staffs, pressures toward staff domination often exist, which truncates the process of leadership development, especially on a collective basis. Paul Wellstone, surveying a number of different groups around the country, discerned some of the pressures that exacerbate the problem:

The problem is that organizers are under a strong pressure to ignore this development process. In part, the pressure may be ego-related. The organizer feels a real need to have something she or he can point to as a concrete victory. Unrelated to ego problems, there is a compelling need to keep the morale of the people up by having early successes. Finally, organizers are responsible to other people besides the people they organize. There are the outside funders—church groups, foundations, liberal contributors, and the canvassing operation.[15]

Canvassing, especially door-to-door solicitation of funds from the general public to support the group's efforts on specific issues, is a controversial fund-raising mechanism, a business operation in an otherwise largely voluntary organization. Tim Sampson, a leader in the Citizens Action League of California, explained the ways in which such a funding mechanism contributed to staff domination. "For members to run the organization requires ownership of the organization. People who contribute at the door, you could only nominally call members. They don't participate. And for the active members the fact that the money is still coming from outside of them is a problem." Yet, such funding also aided enormously in the effort to sustain large organizations throughout the 1970s. And, as such organizations have grown and developed, other fund-raising techniques have emerged as well. ACORN, the Illinois Public Action Council, and many local community groups have service components such as tax consultation or discounts for members through which they help fund themselves. And for groups that achieve considerable membership involvement, internal fund-raising has developed into highly successful projects. COPS, for example, raises over $100,000 each year through its annual fair.

Moreover, at their best, the new generation of community groups have developed novel and extensive mechanisms for membership training that create a deep sense of "ownership" and very skilled leaders who are able to achieve extraordinary group democracy. Thus, Ernie Cortes, chief organizer of Communities Organized for Public Service (COPS) and United Neighborhood Organizations (UNO) in East Los Angeles, originated training programs for indigenous community leadership, drawn from churches and other institutions, that taught such leaders the skills of organizing *themselves:* how to interview community residents about problems, do research, break problems down into manageable issue parts, hold house meetings, find allies, plan winning campaigns, and school a whole neighborhood in what must be done to win. Moreover, training centers such as the Midwest Academy hold regular leadership training sessions in a variety of organizational and political subjects around the country. Through such training experiences—and most important, the actual experiences of struggle—a new generation of poor and working-class leadership began to emerge out of 1970s community groups, determined to build power for ordinary Americans. In turn, such power building is facilitated by a third concern of contemporary organizing methodology: the maintenance of autonomy from dominant centers of power.[16]

MAINTAINING AUTONOMY

The course of any social protest depends, in the final analysis, on its political power, which, in turn, is shaped by all the constituent elements of organization and insurgency: program and vision; size; skills; alliances; and, crucially, autonomy from dominant centers of political and economic power. In the development of independent action, difficult problems exist that have plagued radical and social change movements throughout the history of industrial society: how to sustain internal democracy in groups and also be effective in the broader environment; how to enter or influence the political process without becoming bogged down in administrative trivia or being co-opted; how to get money from large institutions and not be fatally compromised. But here again, 1970s-vintage organizers have posed such questions with a new degree of self-consciousness. Mike Miller's much-used piece on the relationship between organizing and broader structural change outlined the dilemma clearly: "The trick is to be able to make [broader social] institutions change . . . without becoming responsible for their day-to-day operations. To do this, [peoples'] organizations must retain organizational and financial independence from government, corporation and most foundation programs."

Community organizations have tried a number of techniques to guarantee such autonomy, from barring public officeholders as members or leaders to declining government grants or VISTA workers. Yet, in the end, the only final guarantee of independence is the subordination of every other form of activity to the priorities of grass-roots organizing. ACORN organizers recently made the point, especially in relation to service-provision:

> The major question for ACORN is not whether we can adequately deliver services but how we can build the power of ordinary people

> to decide what services should be provided and how they should be delivered. We do not reject the service delivery model out of hand . . . but our primary concern is neither to define our clients as potential members nor, worse, our members as potential clients [but to] organize people around issues which will point to the structural foundation of society from which unequal distribution of goods and services derives. . . . It is the wielding of . . . power which will ultimately bring about the change.[17]

Throughout the range of community organizing networks, there is frequently voiced this kind of insurgent, democratic vision of change, stressing community organizations (sometimes in alliance with others, particularly unions) as foundations for structural transformation of the society from the bottom up. The National Association of Neighborhoods articulates a vision of what it calls "Jeffersonian democracy." Father Geno Baroni, who worked with hundreds of ethnic neighborhood groups throughout the decade, expressed their animus to Congress: "We are building democracy, you know." Richard Harmon of the Industrial Areas Foundation also voiced the "faith that a continually multiplying group of trained radical leaders and organizers will create and develop mass organizations capable of transforming the Watergate institutions." And the presidentially appointed National Commission on the Neighborhoods, in its report to Congress in the spring of 1979, demonstrated how such perspectives have penetrated the most mainstream and cautious expressions of the community organizing movement when it called its readers to

> join the residents of urban neighborhoods in a united effort to re-organize our society—away from the stranglehold of a relative few with a near monopoly of power and money in political, social and economic institutions to a new democratic system of grass roots involvement that allows individuals to have control over their own lives.[18]

While community organizing in the 1970s incubated a kind of radical democratic sensibility, such a spirit—and the actual organizations sustaining it—also represented raw material for reworking dominant political categories of both the Left and the Right. Seeking a transfer of power to actual human communities themselves in all their cultural, ethnic, and ideological diversity, it suggested a fundamental alternative to a future dominated by mega-institutions of either corporatist or statist design. Infused with a kind of democratic social conservationism, the ethos of community organizing in the 1970s expressed a deepened understanding of the richness, creativity, and vitality to be found in traditions, particular institutions, and group heritages, even while it often sought the opening up of parochial patterns as well. Such an ethos constituted a direct challenge to what Gale Cincotta called "the insidious throwaway mentality afflicting America which classifies older people, older homes and old neighborhoods as expendable—like pop bottles and Kleenex."

How community organizing might evolve in the coming years was uncertain; it is dependent, not only on community organizing itself, but also on developments in the broader society. But the 1970s-vintage efforts had opened a kind of free democratic space in the neighborhoods of American society through which formerly silent citizens learned that they could fight (and sometimes take over) city hall; that the world is not simply dog-eat-dog; that ordinary people can learn the public skills necessary for exercising some control over their lives and institutions. As Cincotta summarized: "There aren't many vehicles for blue-collar and marginal people to feel that they can do anything. That's what organization does: it gives a sense of control and dignity." Through the free space in American communities—and elsewhere in the society—belief in the rights of citizenship and popular sovereignty had experienced a rebirth. Such conviction held potential for reshaping the future.[19]

NOTES

1. Training centers listed in Janice Perlman, "Grass Roots Empowerment and Government Response," *Social Policy* 10, no. 2 (1979): 17.

2. Figures from the National Commission Report cited in Perlman, "Grass Roots Empowerment," p. 16; *Christian Science Monitor* poll, December 23, 1977; figures on tenant coalitions from John Atlas and Peter Dreier, "The Housing Crisis and Popular Revolt: A Tenant Strategy for the 1980s," unpublished paper, 1979, in author's possession, p. 6; Neil Peirce, "West German Citizens Groups," *Minneapolis Tribune,* August 21, 1977.

3. A great wealth of neo-Marxist analysis of changes in contemporary society is available. For a sampling, see Richard Edwards et al., eds.,

The Capitalist System (Englewood Cliffs, N.J.: Prentice-Hall, 1972). The phrase "socialization of social production," used by Christopher Lasch in *Haven in a Heartless World* (New York: Basic Books, 1977), has been used by others as well. See, for example, Eli Zaretsky, *Capitalism, The Family and Personal Life* (San Francisco: Agenda Publishing, 1973), and Sara Evans, "The Origins of the Women's Liberation Movement," *Radical America* 9, no. 2 (1975). James O'Connor, *Fiscal Crisis of the State* (New York: St. Martin's Press, 1973), has given a pathbreaking Marxist description of the growing range of state activities and certain of the economic crises that flow from them. Jeff Faux and Robert Lightfoot, *Capital and Community: Notes on Financing a New Economy* (Washington, D.C.: Exploratory Project for Economic Alternatives, 1976), have described in detail the accumulative troubles facing the American economy, through the 1970s specifically. For Marxist and left-wing treatments of the roots of the urban crisis and pressures on neighborhood institutions, see Roger E. Alcaly and David Mermelstein, eds., *Fiscal Crisis of American Cities* (New York: Vintage, 1977); Manuel Castells, *The Urban Question: A Marxist Approach* (Cambridge, Mass.: MIT Press, 1977); Stephen E. Barton, "The Urban Housing Problem: Marxist Theory and Community Organizing," *Review of Radical Political Economy* 9, no. 4 (1977); Kathleen Blee and Glenn Yago, "The Political Economy of Class: A Revision," paper of the University of Wisconsin Center for Research on Politics and Society, 1979; and Steve Max, "Class Consciousness and Community Organization," Midwest Academy mailing to the Committee of Correspondence, fall 1977, pp. 3-4. For an early theoretical treatment of the community organization-trade union analogy, see Harry C. Boyte, "The Populist Challenge," *Socialist Revolution*, no. 32 (1977), pp. 39-91.

4. The ways in which community organization efforts do not fit leftist theories of social protest are described in more detail in my articles "Neighborhood Power," *New York Times*, August 19, 1979, and "A Democratic Awakening," *Social Policy*, September-October 1979, pp. 8-15.

5. Description of Alinsky's history and method is drawn from his two books on organizing, *Reveille for Radicals*, paperback ed. (New York: Random House, 1969), and *Rules for Radicals*, paperback ed. (New York: Random House, 1971); Robert Bailey, Jr., *Radicals in Urban Politics: The Alinsky Approach* (Chicago: University of Chicago Press, 1972); and a number of interviews, including especially Msgn. John Egan, South Bend, Ind., September 14, 1979; Mike Miller, San Francisco,

May 11, 1977; Ed Chambers, April 29, 1977; and Heather Booth, Chapel Hill, N.C., February 14, 1976.

6. H. Bruce Palmer, Preface, in National Industrial Conference Board, *The Future of Capitalism: A Symposium* (New York: Macmillan Co., 1967), p. xx; John H. Mollenkopf, "The Crisis of the Public Sector in American Cities," in Alcaly, *Fiscal Crisis,* pp. 113-31; for a description of the Insurance Association's program and its dubious benefits, see Karen Orren, *Corporate Power and Social Change* (Baltimore: John Hopkins University Press, 1974).

7. Figure on highway controversies are from Richard O. Davies, *The Age of Asphalt: The Automobile, the Freeway and the Condition of Metropolitan America* (New York: J. B. Lippincott, 1975), p. 32. On percent of GNP from local and state spending, see Roger E. Alcaly and Helen Bodian, "New York's Fiscal Crisis and the Economy," in Alcaly, *Fiscal Crisis,* p. 40. On figures for employment, see Mollenkopf, "Crisis," p. 124.

8. *Business Week* editorial, October 12, 1974; New York furnished a splendid example for corporate strategists to use in bringing home the point. As *Business Week*'s special issue on the capital crisis put it, "Cities and states must either cut spending and services or go the way of New York City," September 22, 1975, p. 84; Faux and Lightfoot, *Capital and Community,* give an excellent background analysis of the corporate shift. Its first explicit, public expression could be seen in a revealing interview with John Connally in the *Wall Street Journal,* April 24, 1972, about the needs for a "transformation" in American political relations through the 1970s.

9. The political implications of the shifts in corporate strategy are discussed in my pieces, "Coping with Corporate Power—Prospectus for a New Party," *The Progressive,* July 1974; "The New Corporate Agenda," *Viewpoint* 1, no. 2 (1977); "Quiet Knights, The Business Roundtable Behind the Scenes," *In These Times,* September 14, 1977, among others; Fraser quoted from United Auto Workers press release, Detroit, Mich., July 19, 1978.

10. Ceitel and Sutton quoted in Ellen Spitz, "Redlining Politics," *Our Town,* December 12, 1976; the widening patterns of red-lining were extensively documented in the national newspapers *Shelterforce* and *Disclosure* during 1974 and 1975, and also in Arthur J. Naparstek and Gale Cincotta, "Urban Disinvestment: New Implications for Community Organization, Research and Public Policy," a publication of the National Center for Urban Ethnic Affairs and the National Training

and Information Center, entered as testimony before the Subcommittee
on Housing and Commercial Development of the Committee on Banking, Currency and Housing, Hearings on the National Commission on the
Neighborhoods, HR 14756, 14361, 15388, September 9, 1976, pp. 136-
53; Cincotta interview, Chicago, April 29, 1977.

11. Chambers interview.

12. Miller's interview proved especially useful in helping to understand
the roots of the different organizing methodologies in the 1950s; on
NWRO, interview with Bert DeLeeuw, Washington, D.C., May 3, 1977;
on ACORN, interview with Wade Rathke, December 20, 1977; quote
from "ACORN: An Overview," *Community Organizing Handbook # 2*
(Little Rock, Ark.: Arkansas Institute for Social Justice, 1977), p. 3.

13. Fair Share funding proposal from 1977, in author's possession,
p. 2; Arlook interview, Washington, D.C., November 12, 1977; an in-
depth description of the generation of citizen groups can be found in
Harry C. Boyte, "Citizen Activists in the Public Interest," *Social Policy*
10, no. 3 (November-December, 1979), pp. 3-15.

14. Interview with John Atlas, Washington, D.C., November 13, 1977.

15. Paul Wellstone, *How the Rural Poor Got Power* (Amherst, Mass.:
University of Massachusetts Press, 1978), p. 211.

16. Interview with Tim Sampson, May 11, 1977; on COPS fund-
raising, Milton Kotler, "A Public Policy for Neighborhoods and Community Organizations," *Social Policy* 10, no. 2 (1979): 40; Kotler's
piece describes a number of fund-raising activities by different community organizations, drawn from the research of the Commission on
Neighborhoods; the description of training programs of COPS and UNO
drawn from interviews with Ernie Cortes and activists in UNO, Los
Angeles, May 17 and 18, 1977.

17. Mike Miller, "Notes on Institutional Change," *Social Policy*
(November-December 1972, January-February 1973), p. 38; the quote
on ACORN's perspective on services from Wade Rathke, Seth Borgos,
and Gary Delgado, "Taking Advantage of the Fiscal Crisis," *Social
Policy* 10, no. 2 (1979): 35.

18. Geno Baroni, testimony, National Commission on the Neighbor-
hoods hearings, p. 72; Richard Harmon, "Making an Offer We Can't
Refuse," Industrial Areas Foundation, Chicago, June 1973; National
Commission on Neighborhoods, *People, Building Neighborhoods: Final
Report to the President and the Congress of The United States* (Wash-
ington, D.C.: Government Printing Office, 1979), p. 29.

19. Cincotta, testimony, National Commission on the Neighborhoods
hearings, p. 185; interview with Cincotta.

Bibliographic Essay

Popular interest in community organizing has resulted in a large number of analyses and case studies of recent organizing efforts. There is, however, surprisingly little published secondary literature on the history of neighborhood organizing efforts. The best materials on the history of neighborhood organizations remain, at this point, in the unpublished primary materials in archives, in libraries, and in the basements of organizations and participants. Leaflets, letters, annual reports, memos, photographs, interviews with participants, and newspaper and magazine articles are the basic sources for research in the history of community organizing. But most people are not interested in doing primary historical research. What follows, then, is a suggested reading list of the more accessible published materials on the history of urban community organization. The list focuses primarily on published books and only occasionally mentions articles or unpublished dissertations.

HISTORICAL OVERVIEWS

As noted before, most of the materials with a historical perspective are written by social work academics. The only book-length survey of the history of neighborhood organization is Sidney Dillick, *Community Organization for Neighborhood Development: Past and Present* (New York: William Morrow, 1953), which traces the history of community organization for social welfare from the late-nineteenth century through the early 1950s. Monna Heath and Arthur Dunham, *Trends in Community Organization: A Study of Papers on Community Organization Published by the National Conference on Social Welfare, 1874-1960* (Chicago: University of Chicago Social Service Monographs, 1963), is an excellent overview and analysis of articles written by community workers and academics, and it includes a fine bibliography. For a most helpful article appraising changes in community organization theory since the early twentieth century, see Meyer Schwartz, "Community Organization," in the *Encyclopedia of Social Work* (New York: National Association of Social Workers, 1965), pp. 179-89. Schwartz's piece very nicely chronicles how the social-welfare community has struggled since the 1920s with defining the term "community organization" and with establishing it as a legitimate subfield of social work. Howard W. Hallman, "The Neighborhood as an Organizational Unit: A Historical Perspective," in *Neighborhood Control in the 1970s,* ed. George Frederickson (New York: Chandler Publishing Co., 1973), pp. 7-16; Fred Cox and Charles Garvin, "Community Organization Practice: 1865-1973," in *Strategies of Community Organization,* ed. Fred Cox et al. (Itasca, Ill.: F. E. Peacock, 1974), pp. 39-58; and Arthur Dunham, *The New Community Organization* (New York: Thomas Y. Crowell, 1970), chapter 4, all provide good, brief surveys of the history of community organization. Dunham's book, which includes an excellent bibliography, demonstrates his close association with the materials and personalities during the period 1940 to 1960. Milton Kotler, *Neighborhood Government: The Local Foundations of Political Life* (New York: Bobbs-Merrill, 1969), is a polemic on the need for decentralized political structures, which provides some materials on the historical origins of neighborhoods and on different approaches to neighborhood organizing. Jeffrey H. Galper, *The Politics of Social Services* (Englewood Cliffs, N.J.: Prentice-Hall, 1975), is a leftist critique that includes some interesting criticisms about community organization as practiced by members of the social work profession. Surprisingly little has been written on community organization by historians interested in the history of social welfare. Even the overviews of social-welfare history, most recently James Leiby, *The History of Social Welfare and Social Work in the United States* (New York: Columbia University Press, 1978), devote but a few pages to the subject.

COMMUNITY ORGANIZATION BEFORE 1920

The period from about 1890 to 1920 was the first phase and, until
the 1960s, the heyday of neighborhood organizing. A vast quantity of
literature came forth during those years, proclaiming the need to meet
the challenge of industrialization with progressive social reform. One of
the methods often suggested was to organize urban neighborhoods into
efficient, democratic, and, of course, enlightened units within the
metropolis in order to counteract problems of "bigness" and urban disorganization. These liberal reformers were as prolific as they were
optimistic. Influenced deeply by the social settlement movement in
England, they churned out theoretical statements on the importance of
neighborhood work and countless first-hand accounts of their work in
the immigrant ghettos of the nation's largest cities. The first account
in this genre was Stanton Coit, *Neighborhood Guilds: An Instrument of
Social Reform* (London: Sonnenshein, 1891). Other excellent examples,
describing organizing activities in Chicago, New York, and Boston, respectively, include Jane Addams, *Twenty Years at Hull House with
Autobiographical Notes* (New York: Macmillan, 1910); Lillian D. Wald,
The House on Henry Street (New York: Henry Holt and Co., 1915); and
Robert A. Woods, ed., *The City Wilderness: A Settlement Study by
Residents and Associates of the South End House* (Boston: Houghton
Mifflin, 1898). Just after World War I, some even stronger statements
were written on the need for community organizing, the best examples
of which are Mary Parker Follett, *The New State: Group Organization
the Solution of Popular Government* (New York: Longmans, Green,
1918), and John Daniels, *America Via the Neighborhood* (New York:
Harper and Bros., 1920).

American historians have written widely about the activities of settlement workers, but rarely from the perspective of reformers as community organizers. Thomas Lee Philpott, *The Slum and the Ghetto:
Neighborhood Deterioration and Middle-Class Reform, Chicago 1880-1930*
(New York: Oxford University Press, 1978), however, assesses the role of
social settlements in Chicago, with an eye to the process of community
organization. Other works by historians that address the issue of neighborhood organization include Zane L. Miller, *Boss Cox's Cincinnati:
Urban Politics in the Progressive Era* (New York: Oxford University
Press, 1968), and, more recently, Joseph Arnold, "The Neighborhood

and City Hall: The Origin of Neighborhood Associations in Baltimore, 1880-1911," *Journal of Urban History* 6 (November 1979): 3-30. Arnold's piece focuses on middle-class protective and improvement associations rather than on the working-class and low-income social-change organizations emphasized in this volume.

COMMUNITY ORGANIZATION, 1920-1940

The 1920s witnessed the professionalization of community organization as a subdiscipline within the field of social work and the continued advocacy of the neighborhood unit. The first texts on community organization were written by Eduard C. Lindeman, *The Community* (New York: Association Press, 1921), and Jessie Steiner, *Community Organization: A Study of Its Theory and Current Practice* (Chicago: University of Chicago Press, 1925 and 1930). Steiner, Lindeman, Leroy Bowman, and Clarence A. Perry were the leading proponents of community and neighborhood organizing in this period, and their work is widely apparent in such contemporary materials as *Social Work Year Book, Journal of Social Forces, American Journal of Sociology*, and in various publications of the Russell Sage Foundation. The *Proceedings of the National Conference of Social Work* are especially valuable for the 1920s, as social workers became increasingly interested in evaluating this new aspect of their work. One of the best community studies of the period, with a focus on the role of neighborhood organizing efforts, is Harvey W. Zorbaugh, *The Gold Coast and the Slum: A Sociological Study of Chicago's Near North Side* (Chicago: University of Chicago Press, 1929). Walter W. Pettit, *Case Studies in Community Organization* (New York: Century Co., 1928), is one of the first to use a case study approach and the work describes efforts in suburban and rural communities as well as in urban neighborhoods. Wilbur Phillips, *Adventuring for Democracy* (New York: Social Unit Press, 1940), is the autobiography of the founder of the block organizing Social Unit Plan used in Milwaukee, Cincinnati, and other cities in the first decades of the twentieth century. For secondary sources, Roy Lubove, *The Professional Altruist: The Emergence of Social Work as a Career, 1880-1930* (New York: Atheneum, 1965), is an excellent and often-quoted work that contains some information about the origins and professionalization of the field of community organization. For an analysis of the ideology of community organization in the 1920s and 1930s, see Michael J. Austin and Neil Betten, "Intellectual Origins of Community Organization, 1920-1939," *Social Service Review* 51 (March 1977): 155-70.

Surprisingly little has been written about decentralized, neighborhood organizing efforts during the Great Depression. While the period abounded with organizing efforts on both the Right and the Left, most organizations, especially after 1933, had a national basis or orientation; economic problems that the nation faced did not seem to lend themselves as readily to solutions at the neighborhood level. The best example of community organizing in this period is the Unemployed Councils. In addition to the work of Mark Naison, two other secondary sources skillfully address the work of these councils: Roy Rosenzweig, "Organizing the Unemployed: The Early Years of the Great Depression, 1929-1933," *Radical America* 10 (July-August 1976): 37-60; and Frances Fox Piven and Richard A. Cloward, *Poor People's Movements: Why They Succeed, How They Fail* (New York: Pantheon, 1977). Studies need to be done on the relation between the community work of such organizations as the Communist party, the Socialist party, and the Musteites, and the organizing efforts of the Congress of Industrial Organizations within local factories. An impressive film, *Union Maids* (1975), makes some connections between CIO organizing work in Chicago and the efforts of the Unemployed Councils to stop evictions.

COMMUNITY ORGANIZATION, 1940-1960

The years during and directly after World War II witnessed a reemergence of interest in the neighborhood as an organizing unit, and in the possibilities of community organizing. In the social work profession, a number of now-classic monographs on community organizing were published in the decade or so after the war. Most notable are H. Wayne McMillen, *Community Organization for Social Welfare* (Chicago: University of Chicago Press, 1945); Clarence King, *Organizing for Community Action* (New York: Harper, 1948); James Dahir, *The Neighborhood Unit Plan: Its Spread and Acceptance* (New York: Russell Sage Foundation, 1947); Arthur Hillman, *Community Organization and Planning* (New York: Macmillan, 1950); Murray G. Ross, *Community Organization:*

Theory and Principles (New York: Harper and Bros., 1955), and *Case Histories in Community Organization* (New York: Harper and Bros., 1958); and Ernest B. Harper and Arthur Dunham, eds., *Community Organization in Action: Basic Literature and Critical Comments* (New York: Association Press, 1959), a book of readings on the state of the art up to that time. For examples of how the cold war affected the practice of community organization, see Elmore M. McKee, *The People Act: Stories of How Americans Are Coming Together to Deal with Their Community Problems* (New York: Harper and Bros., 1955), and Marvin A. Palecek, *Battle of the Bureaucracies* (New York: Vantage Press, 1972), which includes a chapter on the community organizing efforts of the United Community Defense Services during the Korean War. On the work of Saul Alinsky, see Saul D. Alinsky, *Reveille for Radicals* (Chicago: University of Chicago Press, 1946), and *Rules for Radicals: A Pragmatic Primer for Realistic Radicals* (New York: Random House, 1971). Also worthwhile are Robert Pruger and Harry Specht, "Assessing Theoretical Models of Community Organization Practice: Alinsky as a Case in Point," *Social Service Review* 43 (June 1969): 123-35; Michael P. Connolly, "An Historical Study of Change in Saul D. Alinsky's Community Organization Practice and Theory, 1939-1972" (Ph.D. diss., University of Minnesota School of Social Work, 1976); and Marion K. Sanders, *The Professional Radical: Conversations with Saul Alinsky* (Evanston, Ill.: Harper and Row, 1965).

COMMUNITY ORGANIZATION, 1960-1980

The literature on the "neighborhood organizing revolution" of the past two decades is abundant. The best place to start is the numerous anthologies published by social workers, sociologists, urban planners, and community workers surveying recent theory and practice. See, for example, Fred Cox et al., eds., *Strategies of Community Organization: A Book of Readings* (Itasca, Ill.: F. E. Peacock, 1974); Ralph M. Kramer and Harry Specht, eds., *Readings in Community Organization Practice* (Englewood Cliffs, N.J.: Prentice-Hall, 1969); George Frederickson, ed., *Neighborhood Control in the 1970s: Politics, Administration, and Citizen Participation* (New York: Chandler Publishing Co., 1973); Hans B. C. Spiegel, ed., *Citizen Participation in Urban Development,* 2 vols. (Washington, D.C.: National Training Laboratories for Applied Behavioral Science, 1968 and 1969). Many of these anthologies, and other books on community organization written in the past two decades, are still available in paperback, and they often contain excellent bibliographies. For an invaluable codification of the social science literature related to community organizing and to other areas of social action during the years 1964-1970, see Jack Rothman, *Planning and Organizing for Social Change: Action Principles from Social Science Research* (New York: Columbia University Press, 1974).

On the origins and practice of the antipoverty, community action programs of the late 1950s and early 1960s, the best analysis I have read thus far is Ann Neel's as yet unpublished Ph.D. dissertation entitled "Experimenting with the Black Community: A Case Study in the Sociology of Applied Sociology" (University of California, Berkeley, 1978). It is an excellent sociopolitical case study of the Richmond Youth Project in Oakland, California, and the work includes a nicely formulated historical analysis linking the origins of antipoverty efforts with the cold war. Peter Marris and Martin Rein, *Dilemmas of Social Reform: Poverty and Community Action in the United States* (New York: Atherton, 1967), and Ralph Kramer, ed., *Participation of the Poor: Comparative Case Studies in the War on Poverty* (Englewood Cliffs, N.J.: Prentice-Hall, 1969), are valuable as well. Other studies on community organizing in the 1960s and 1970s include George Brager and Harry Specht, *Community Organizing* (New York: Columbia University Press, 1973); Lyle Schaller, *Community Organization: Conflict and Reconciliation* (Nashville, Tenn.: Abingdon Press, 1966); James B. Cunningham, *The Resurgent Neighborhood* (Notre Dame, Ind.: Fides Publishers, 1965); Douglas Yates, *Neighborhood Democracy: The Politics and Impacts of Decentralization* (Lexington, Mass.: Lexington Books, 1973); Alan Altshuler, *Community Control: The Black Demand for Participation in Large American Cities* (New York: Pegasus, 1970); Frances Fox Piven and Richard A. Cloward, *The Politics of Turmoil: Poverty, Race, and the Urban Crisis* (New York: Random House, 1965), and *Poor People's Movements: Why They Succeed, How They Fail* (New York: Pantheon, 1977); Curt Lamb, *Political Power in Poor Neighborhoods* (New York: John Wiley, 1975); Robert Bailey, Jr., *Radicals in Urban Politics: The Alinsky Approach* (Chicago: University of Chicago Press, 1974); and Sara Evans, *Personal Politics: The Roots of Women's Liberation in the Civil Rights Movement and the New Left*

(New York: Random House, 1979), which very nicely, if briefly, gives an insider's view of the process of community organizing in the 1960s and 1970s. Also see *South Atlantic Urban Studies* 4 (1979). This issue, which was guest edited by Bernard Ross and Milton Kotler, focuses on "The Role of Neighborhood in Urban Policy." For a view from the perspective of the social settlements, see National Federation of Settlements and Neighborhood Centers, *Making Democracy Work: A Study of Neighborhood Organization* (New York: National Federation of Settlements and Neighborhood Centers, 1968). For criticisms of community organizing in these years, see Katherine Coit, "Local Action, Not Citizen Participation," in *Marxism and the Metropolis: New Perspectives in Urban Political Economy,* ed. William K. Tabb and Larry Sawers (New York: Oxford University Press, 1978); the debate between Frank Ackerman and Harry Boyte printed in *Socialist Revolution* 7 (September-October 1977): 113-28; John Cowley et al., *Community or Class Struggle* (New York: Stage 1 Publishers, 1977); and Charles F. Grosser, *New Directions in Community Organization: From Enabling to Advocacy* (New York, Frederich Praeger, 1972).

Quite a few "how to" books and pamphlets were published in these years. The most notable are David Morris and Karl Hess, *Neighborhood Power: The New Localism* (Boston: Beacon Press, 1975), and The O. M. Collective, *The Organizer's Manual* (New York: Bantam Books, 1971), the latter having an interesting bibliography-directory of publications and agencies associated with the myriad organizing efforts of the late 1960s.

Index

About the Editors and Contributors

ROBERT FISHER is Assistant Professor of History at the University of Houston Downtown College. He is the author of articles on urban and social history in *Social Service Review, Teaching History,* and the *Journal of Popular Film,* and has been active as a community organizer, especially in Cambridge, Mass., where he has worked on a wide variety of progressive neighborhood issues.

PETER ROMANOFSKY was Associate Professor of History at Jersey City State College in New Jersey. Specializing in the history of social and child welfare, he published *Social Service Organizations* (a two-volume encyclopedia of the history of social-welfare institutions) and articles in such journals as *Missouri Historical Review, New York Historical Society Quarterly,* and *Jewish Social Studies.*

HARRY C. BOYTE served as field secretary for the Southern Christian Leadership Conference during the civil rights movement; he organized trade unions and poor white communities in the Deep South, helped found the New American movement, and is currently director of the Citizen Heritage Center. Boyte's writings on citizen action and political theory have appeared in the *New York Times, Progressive, Social Policy, Dissent, In These Times, Socialist Review,* and a number of other publications, and he has recently authored *The Backyard Revolution: Understanding the New Citizen Movement.*

NEIL R. McMILLEN is Professor of History at the University of Southern Mississippi. A specialist in twentieth-century race relations, his publications include *The Citizens' Council: Organized Resistance to the Second Reconstruction.* He is presently at work on a history of blacks in Mississippi, 1890-1942. In 1978, he led a "have-not" coalition against a Mississippi community's political, business, and professional elite in a losing effort to prevent the relocation of a downtown hospital to a lily-white suburb.

PATRICIA MOONEY MELVIN is Assistant Professor of History at the University of Arkansas at Little Rock. She has published articles on the development of neighborhood health centers in the *Journal of the West* and in the *Cincinnati Historical Society Bulletin.* Her research interests include urban history and women's history, as well as the history of public health. Melvin has also been active in various inner-city community projects in Cincinnati.

ZANE L. MILLER is Professor of History in the Department of History, McMicken College of Arts and Sciences, at the University of Cincinnati. He is an urban historian whose work includes *Boss Cox's Cincinnati, The Urbanization of Modern America,* and *Neighborhood and Community in a Suburban Setting: Forest Park, Ohio, 1935-1976.* Miller has been active in Cincinnati-area political and civic affairs, serving as a member of the Hamilton County Democratic Party's Steering Committee, the City of Cincinnati Charter Review Commission, the Cincinnati Architectural Board of Review, the Cincinnati Urban Conservation Task Force, and as a board member of the Miami Purchase Association for Historic Preservation.

MARK NAISON is Associate Professor of Afro-American Studies at Fordham University and is director of the school's Urban Studies Program. He is the author of numerous articles on Afro-American history, the history of American radicalism, and sports in American life, and of the forthcoming *A Dream Deferred: The Communist Party in Harlem,* to be published by University of Illinois Press. Since his undergraduate days, he has done community organizing in East Harlem, the Upper West Side, and the Bronx, and is currently chairman of the board of Sports for the People, a sports advocacy organization with headquarters in the South Bronx.

JOSEPH A. SPENCER is a program and policy analyst for the New York City Mayor's Office. He has taught at LaGuardia Community College,

Brooklyn College, and New York University. His article is part of a dissertation, "New York City Tenant Organizations and the Formation of Urban Housing Policy, 1915-1943," which he is presently completing at the Graduate School of the City University of New York.

STEPHEN R. WEISSMAN, formerly Associate Professor of Political Science at the University of Texas at Dallas, is currently Staff Associate with the Subcommittee on Africa of the House Foreign Affairs Committee. He is the author of articles and chapters on urban politics and social policy in *Polity, Western Political Quarterly, Impact,* and in J. Sneed and S. Waldhorn, eds., *Restructuring the Federal System: Approaches to Accountability in Post-Categorical Programs.* He has been a consultant to various community organizations, including the Marion Gardens Tenant Association in Jersey City, New Jersey, and the Mission Coalition Organization in San Francisco, California. He has authored policy reports on elderly, youth, and environmental services for local and national, public and voluntary government agencies.